S0-AIB-639

301.5
Sch5a

88206

DATE DUE			

WITHDRAWN

AUTOKIND VS. MANKIND

By Kenneth R. Schneider

DESTINY OF CHANGE
HOW RELEVANT IS MAN IN THE AGE OF DEVELOPMENT?

AUTOKIND VS. MANKIND
AN ANALYSIS OF TYRANNY, A PROPOSAL FOR REBELLION,
A PLAN FOR RECONSTRUCTION

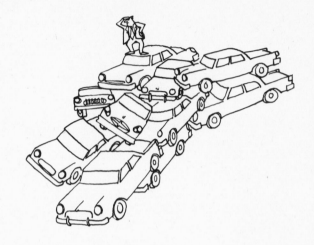

Illustrated by Richard D. Hedman

AUTOKIND VS.

AN ANALYSIS OF TYRANNY

A PROPOSAL FOR REBELLION

A PLAN FOR RECONSTRUCTION

MANKIND

KENNETH R. SCHNEIDER

W · W · NORTON & COMPANY · INC · NEW YORK

301.5
Sch5a
88206
april 1974

First Edition

Library of Congress Catalog Card No. 79–139388
SBN 393 08638 0
1 2 3 4 5 6 7 8 9 0

CONTENTS

FOREWORD

To BUILD A SHELTER for himself and his family, to put shelters together to build towns and cities: this is one of the oldest and probably one of the most important activities of man. But the human settlement through history has been the simultaneous result of both creative and destructive forces.

Man, the creator of cities, is also the enemy of cities. He attacks them in war, bombs and destroys them with more advanced technologies than he uses in creating them. Nature also attacks cities. Earthquakes, floods, and hurricanes smash many towns, and kill millions of people. But the elements have never been so brutal and precise in their destructive action against the human settlement as man himself.

Man's destruction of cities in war is selective, focused on the most valuable elements. Nature, selective as well, strikes mostly at the weakest elements. Man is most interested in liquidating the vital components of the settlement—including its inhabitants—when nature gives men a generous chance to escape.

It happens that planning for the reconstruction of cities and towns has occupied the best part of my life—for Warsaw and other cities smashed in the Second World War; for towns destroyed in "local wars" in other parts of the world; for Skopje, Yugoslavia, destroyed by earthquake; and for other human settlements torn by natural devastation.

Although man-made and natural disasters differ, people always suffer. They always look to the builder to rebuild their town, to protect them against future disaster, to make a better, safer environment for the children.

Today man has come to a paradox. A third kind of destruction of cities has now been added to nature and men at war. The builders of the city are now simultaneously the destroyers of the city. Man does not require a war any longer to destroy the settlements of his fellow men. He virtually destroys the towns directly in the process of construction. That process, although creative and progressive in principle, is disastrous to the well-being of the people and to the reasonable function of the town. Herein is the theme and the importance of Kenneth Schneider's book.

Schneider describes how simple the steps of destruction really are. Man builds the automobile, then he builds or rebuilds the town for the automobile. He forgets that the town or metropolis is a delicate physical and social organism, tuned to perform necessary human functions and to elevate human enjoyment.

The automobile itself is one of the wonderful inventions of humanity, offering, in theory, more freedom and more choice. It speeded contact between urban and rural life, expanded production and circulation of goods, promoted travel between countries. But in restructuring the city, the automobile broke apart the orderly ecology of urban living, burdened movement, congested the most valuable places, wasted resources, and killed people. It pushed people from the desirable central areas and hardened the conditions of social behaviour. Although the automobile was invented as a good, sympathetic creation to help and assist man, it has become, it seems, a dangerous tool in human hands which is able not only to advance development but to destroy or deny life to its creator.

In visiting many of the major cities of the world it is evident that the shape of life of those cities is now being reorganized to meet the demands of the automobile, hardly to serve the people who are supposed to command this creation. If transportation in the city is similar to the blood vessels in the body, the automobile explosion occurring throughout many parts of the world today is now creating the same problems for the health of the city as blood clots create for the body.

Modern development creates many illnesses in the environment, such as pollution of air, water, soil, and sound. These are consequences of the intensity with which man and machines interact in the cities. However, we should fight not with the cities but with their illnesses. The automobile is today one such illness.

We need the doctor. We need him, however, not only to negotiate the present illness but to recreate the human settlement in the process. Everyone needs to understand the functional and aesthetic problems of the man-made environment, and we need to plan for the development of cities. Development and preventive measures must be applied together, directly in the course of creating the town.

The hypertrophy of the town represents a deadly sign for the settlement. As useful as automobiles are, they destroy the town when they are overemphasized, when they receive the unjustified status of the ruler of the town. The only valid goal in building the city is to create good living conditions for its inhabitants. The people have to understand the town too. They have to understand what the role of automobiles in the human environment means, how to make the best use of it, and what dangers automobiles create for the whole course of their lives.

Mr. Schneider's book will be highly useful in developing such an understanding by both the builders and occupants of the human settlement. I hope that it will help all of us to protect our environment against this new kind of man-made disaster.

ADOLF CIBOROWSKI

Mr. Ciborowski was chief architect of Warsaw, responsible for the reconstruction following its destruction in World War II. In 1964 he was nominated United Nations Development Programme project manager for planning the reconstruction of Skopje, Yugoslavia, devastated by earthquake in 1963. At present he is deputy director, Centre for Housing, Building and Planning, United Nations.

rebellion, harder if one has not yet started on this path of enlightenment.

The automobile is one of those brutal facts of society that must be faced frontally and with complete honesty. When something is manifestly wrong in its use and incorrigible by society's normal due processes it sets the foundations for general rebellion. Then no other course is worthy of being human.

Autokind vs. Mankind is therefore a tract for an overdue rebellion, a rebellion against the fraudulent claims of technology and enterprise that everything they do underwrites the good life, a rebellion for a civic trust which is at the heart of any civilization. The automobile is, beyond destruction of the human environment, a heavy weight in that all-embracing burden on modern man, the establishment. By any measure, it is more critical for life and liberty than peace in Vietnam. As a tract, the book is provocative rather than definitive. It aims at both thought and action, since time is short.

However, America is still democratic in form, and the establishment liberally supplied me with reports and information about the automobile. I am particularly indebted to the Eno Foundation for Transportation for a large selection of articles from the *Traffic Quarterly* covering nearly twenty-five years. I also received assistance from hundreds of individuals, far too many to be named. However, a few must be singled out for special thanks: Peter S. Craig, John and Linda Eddington, Ernst Hacker, Abraam Krushkhov, Joseph Leiper, Robert Lenz, Melvin Selzer, and to Edith Karottke and Betty Campbell, who prepared the manuscript. I wish to express my gratitude to Star Lawrence of W. W. Norton & Company, Inc., for his determination to achieve clarity of that illusive phenomenon: meaning. Finally, once again, gratitude is an inadequate tribute for my family, which knows each page by a different meaning: my mood and my absence.

AUTOKIND VS. MANKIND

INTRODUCTION:
TYRANNUS MOBILITIS

MAN HAS ALWAYS HAD HIS TRAGEDIES. Today he has the automobile, a tragedy of love.

Of course, the automobile is different. A plague, a famine, or an old-fashioned war were always disapproved, at least in public.

But the car? Well, this is a tragedy man invented and builds. Unblushingly he founded a mechanical harem of immense numbers. He tries to love and support them all. He claims he can't do without any of them.

Love and necessity! What steps toward disaster could be more irresistible?

As always, love and necessity are connected. Man first took his love into his urban habitat. Then he rooted about to make the habitat commodious for her. In time the human environment is shaken apart for her. She demands pavement voraciously. She commands entrance to man's most exclusive courts and plazas, parks and promenades. She takes her private space in homes and office buildings, as well as in those edifices her special make-up requires for her very own.

The amazons of the harem eagerly help remake the whole city to suit their own special scale and behavior. The result is an uprooting of man's civic and social heritage. He is soon rudely disenchanted about his harem. But it is too late. Automobiles are in control. They are now a necessity.

Without doubt the automobile is a marvelous thing. It could not have succeeded otherwise. But whenever we find anything so attractive to man as the automobile, we must always beware of tyranny. Autos are a serious affliction, one of those peculiar to modern man's touch of Midas: television, nuclear fission, rich foods, California. The wealth and power behind these tyrannies of progress grow.

The social malignancy underlying automobility, *tyrannus mobilitis,* draws men into inescapable dependence. Dependence arises from a vicious circle in which the charm of the car and the remaking of the environment reinforce each other. Automobility gradually permeates the daily behavior of people, the purpose of institutions, and the structure of the cities and countryside. This tyranny has been promoted under the cunning popular myth of expanding freedom and affluence.

The current reality of auto tyranny is cultural power, social blackmail, physical deprivation, injury, and death. We must not mistake the brutal grip. The automobile is defended by a tradition of three generations, by a popular belief which finds expression in prayers for parking and by a disciplined establishment spanning the highest and lowest levels of industry, government, and science. When the automobile is challenged, Detroit and its allies brandish the specter of economic decline as an open threat to our whole society.

And automobilism still grows amidst us. The city is becoming ever more deranged by freeway divisions and parking wastelands. The auto's claims on iron and petroleum resources are accelerating. What's more, the tyrannous forces brag about it and claim that more and more resources are required. They are able to construe the acceleration of consumptiveness and systematic waste as ideals.

There can be only one meaning: a new will of immense power and wily ego steadily saps the very sovereignty of Mankind. History and language present neither examples for comparison nor terms to describe such a phenomenon. Tyranny it is. But more, it is a new social purpose defined by the new sovereignty. That sovereignty is the possession of what we will call *Autokind*.

The lines of the coming conflict, therefore, are clearly set: Autokind vs. Mankind. The goal for man in the struggle is simple: to recapture his sovereignty. Understandably the struggle between man and motor will be revolutionary, for the aggressive tyranny now enjoys a Quisling's support from the conservative tradition of Mankind itself.

Imagine clean air, fifty thousand fewer dead, and the end of congestion. Imagine the city renewed man-size. Imagine converting the tense journey to work into a stroll, possibly with a brief, comfortable, and direct ride by aerial tramway.

The city designed for man will assure the diverse and intense interests of urbanity: the many shops, plazas, and places for easy congregation; the large open areas of serene urban beauty, all within minutes of every door. But today both urbanity and openness are lost experiences in the vast Lakewoods and Levittowns. The automobile disperses and isolates the homes and places of interest that together constitute urbanity, while it simultaneously divides and therefore destroys natural openness.

In liberating the city from the car we will make the city efficient, ironically, just as Henry Ford made his auto factory efficient with the assembly line. But our efficiency will be organized for people—their behavior, their bodies, their senses, their associations, and even their casual inclinations. It will not accelerate the incestuous cycle of runaway production and compulsive consumption. The environment will be made free for men, not wild machines.

For our rebellion to succeed, a revolutionary leadership is required to purge the motor myths, rebuild the human ideals and social goals, formulate the grand strategy, recruit and organize the cadres, and lead the uprisings. And through the struggle and victory we will discover new wellsprings of the human spirit, as we have in other struggles against tyranny.

Before man can be freed from servitude, the machines must be totally subordinated. Ideally they should be as obedient, silent, and unobstrusive as the city's sewer system. For the first time in the modern era it will be possible for society to be organized of, by, and (without question) *for* people. Yet to exercise their renewed franchise the people require considerable rehabilitation. Their will has been reduced to buying habits and route planning.

The tasks for this volume are to describe how the human defeat took place, analyze the nature of the auto tyranny, report how autokind continues to advance against us, prepare the general strategy for reconquest, and, lastly, to plan for the new *free* society.

1

AUTOS, AUTOMOBILITY, AND
THE RISE OF AUTOCRACY

History Is Bunk

IN THE BEGINNING there was steam. In 1769 a French major, Nicholas Cugnot, ran his artillery tractor around a corner and into a ditch at three miles per hour. That was that for a generation. In 1805 Oliver Evans' *Orukter Amphibolos* ran through Philadelphia, but it had no permanent influence on the town, as it was intended to dredge the harbor.

Proper steam wagons had a heyday, however, in the 1830's, when puffing Russell carriages regularly plied English roads. But the public recognized the growing menace of these Vehicles of Satan and gradually forced the enterprise to abandon its runs. The *coup de grâce* occurred in 1840, when the Court of Sessions completely banned the Russell carriages, prophetically named *Infant, Automaton,* and *Autopsy.* That slowed development of self-propelling road machines for two more generations.

It was near Detroit in 1875 that a steam road engine meant

to power threshing machines and sawmills stopped to let a team and wagon pass. A young farm boy excitedly jumped down and examined the vehicle. Were it not for that trifling incident we might today identify Ford with watches (his first love) rather than cars. Still, the time was not quite ripe. Another ten years passed before Daimler and Benz in Germany successfully put internal combustion on wheels.

The people themselves were well pleased with the bicycle, having taken it up after a fling with roller skates. A self-propelled highway vehicle had been an old dream, though hardly as inspiring as flying. Yet most people were skeptical at first, thinking it would pass on like roller skates.

In 1895 Thomas Edison saw events in true proportion: "Ten years from now," he said, "you will be able to buy a horseless vehicle for what you would pay today for a wagon and a pair of horses." But Edison's prophecy about the effects of the horseless vehicle were less accurate, for he concluded that the "money spent in the keep of the horses will be saved and the danger to life will be much reduced." The same year a new magazine, *Horseless Age,* surveyed the realm and made its estimate of the future: "Those who have taken the pains to search below the surface know what a giant industry is struggling into being. . . ."

Before long the Devil Wagons of '96 began their rush into society, first as the "instrument of the adventurous," then as the "toy of the rich," then as the "ambition of the poor," and in time as the "servant of everyone." That was the story up to 1911.

Dusty, greasy, virtually incapable of negotiating mud and snow, impractical, and derided; how could this frail and undependable carriage carry the seeds of civic tyranny? Yet, those seeds were there: they sprouted when Henry Ford pulled that first chassis by rope down the assembly aisle and soon multiplied by tenfold the number of cars he could crank out in a day. They blossomed when the astounding five dollars a day Ford's men earned for assembly work also gave them all enough money to buy the machines they toiled on. Mass output and high wages made it possible for this machine to embed itself on farms and in cities, for work and for pleasure, and to become, in effect, the

basis for membership in society.

Nor was the will to conquer lacking. When Ford said, "History is bunk," he really meant that *people* are bunk. And he set out to make it so. He saw life "not as a location, but as a journey. . . . Everything is a flux, and was meant to be." This was matched by his opinion of society: "Our civilization—such as it is—rests on cheap and convenient power." And the automobile? That was, he said, "just a way of using power."

His underlying dislike for society shows up best in his view of cities: "City conditions of work and living are so artificial that instincts sometimes rebel against their unnaturalness." Still, Ford found them ideally suited for the advance of automobility. Given the historic facts of the city's defeat, the Autocrat of Dearborn seemed to indict himself when he exclaimed that "tomorrow it will cease to be."

Horse of the Future and Future of the Horse

The motor age dawned rapidly in America. By surprise, it seems, doctors found the car superb on missions of mercy. San Francisco discovered in 1906 that, unlike the horse, the automobile never tired during the emergency of the Great Fire. Men then began to realize that it could *work* for them. After 1910 the farmer was awed to find he could get to town in fifteen minutes instead of an hour and a half. But when the city man concluded that the Colt Runabout he used for Sunday outings was wasting away when it might just as well carry him to the office, the automobile was in.

In that earliest era—when love could be true—affection, discovery, and boundless expectation made spring eternal. A piece in *Harper's Weekly* of 1902 swells with romance: ". . . the road comes moving towards me like a bride waving palms, rhythmically keeping time to some melody of gladness." And, in joyous rhapsody, it continued, "now the entire road is one long succession of arrivals."

Good tidings of the automobile were everywhere. "It has brought God's green fields and pure air seemingly nearer to our lives of industry," reported *Country Life* in 1911. To many, the automobile had a mission, as if ordained. Had it not proved its mission, asked Herbert Ladd Towle in a 1913 *Scribner's Magazine*. "Greater liberty, greater fruitfulness of time and effort, brighter glimpses of the wide and beautiful world, more health and happiness—these are the lasting benefits of the motor car. . . . We shall thank God that we live in the Motor-Car Era."

But what did the automobile really mean, asked Winthrop Scarrett in "The Horse of the Future and the Future of the Horse," in a 1907 *Harper's Weekly*. "In the last analysis the automobile means that man has finally segregated a little bit of the giant forces of nature and hitched it to his individual chariot. What human mind can measure the meaning of this mighty fact?" And so "the automobile," assured Scarrett, "is to become the ready, tireless and faithful servant of man throughout the world where civilization has a home or freedom a banner. Yesterday it was the plaything of the few, to-day it is the servant of many, to-morrow it will be the necessity of humanity."

Essayists not only surveyed their emotions to laud motoring but taxed their scientific and social insight as well. Wondrous benefits seemed to extend to all branches of life. Health and serene living were decidedly among them. In 1914 a White House assistant to Woodrow Wilson reported obtaining "real rest and relaxation from an hour's ride through the parks in and around Washington." In the same *Country Life* mailbag was a letter from a Madame Chang at the Chinese Legation, who saw "a royal road to health and contentment" in the automobile. "I do not know," she said, "of a surer antidote for the nervousness and unrest with which so many modern men are afflicted than the new interest, the enthusiasm, and the hours in the open which are the experience of every automobile owner."

Towle, impressed by the auto's lordly mission, knew "men who date their first real grip on business from the time they began building up their physical energies by motoring." And the doctors? One, at least, was wildly enthusiastic: "For genuine pleasure, health and excitement an auto is better than medicine, vacation or religion. It makes one forget he is living. It makes him feel that if he must die the auto route is the best."

"The Automobile as a Rest Cure" (*Atlantic Monthly,* 1906) even seemed to apply to the revival of machines that had played out, as one garage scene was biblically described: "The oil-soaked asphalt floor, the white beams overhead, the silent machines in rows against the walls, made a picture of peace and tranquility. The listless movements of the picturesque workmen as they talked their strange jargon in subdued undertones . . . seemed in tune with the place and time. For three long hours [we] sat and rested amid these ideal surroundings."

The wondrous benefits of motoring seemed to extend to all branches of life. One author noted that "the reawakening interest in a normal and well-balanced life . . . is slowly but steadily gaining ground." Another saw that the automobile "has actually rejuvenated the holiday spirit in America and has brought into popularity once more the family picnic. . . ." A correspondent writing to the *Scientific American* described how "the compulsory mechanical education" which the car had put upon men was a "notable benefit to society."

In a 1910 *Outlook* it was reckoned how the automobile "helps to promote social relations . . . to increase knowledge of the local geography, and to make village and farm life livelier and more attractive." Winthrop Scarrett, the seer of the "tireless horse of the future," proclaimed that it will also "break down class distinctions, because one touch of automobilism makes the whole world kin."

And character? Shouldn't it be strengthened by motoring? "Automobilists are almost without exception enthusiasts," said a frontiersman of '03. "They are apt to be impatient with those who have not passed through the exhilarating experience which comes with the successful handling of a steering-wheel for the first time."

And one needed character. In the memory of one nostalgic romanticist "there was the charm of novelty, the tang of danger, the irresistible attraction of uncertainty, the tempting call of the open road, and, if you got there and back—the supreme reward of accomplishment; yes, and perhaps a little boasting."

"Well, good friend, that is just the way the fever starts," sighed an old master in '09.

Romance and character aside, events were converging to bring the automobile into the real world of business and public affairs. This forced everyone to take a new look at Old Dobbin. At first, to consider replacing him by the car after many millennia of service to man "marked one as an imbecile." But by 1913, when there were still 140,000 horses in Manhattan, even *Country Life* conceded that "considerations of hygiene and sanitation are conspiring with those of speed and economy toward his complete elimination."

Initially there was hesitation and ambivalence about automobiling in the real world. In 1899 the War Department purchased its first three machines. But the department kept one foot solidly in the nineteenth century, stating in its news release that "each is equipped so that a mule may be hitched to it, should it refuse to run."

What ambivalence there was faded remarkably during the era of romance. Cities did not yet have traffic engineers to tackle "over congestion." All enlightened opinion was certain that the automobile would solve "that embarrassing problem of cities— because the car occupies less space than horse machines, carries double or treble their loads, and moves at a pace twice as fast."

Such immovable logic was reinforced by observations more peculiar to modern man. It was, for instance, increasingly apparent that "the old nag is too sluggish in resuming his march after the traffic officer has signaled to go ahead. Therefore he clutters up the arteries of commerce. He will have to clear the track."

Another argument also bore down on Old Dobbin. He was wasteful.* His stables were considered economically lost space to business. An estimated 1,750,000 people were required to care for all these "equine parasites." Leather and iron (for horseshoes) were considered to be a drain on our resources. Finally, Dobbin

---

* It should be noted that this was before we reversed our logic, that is, before we began to figure that consumptive waste generates production.

had to be fed whether he worked or not. That's the way *Outlook* analyzed it, as of March 22, 1913.

Seedling Years

It is a mystery why the French rather than the Americans should believe that "transportation is civilization." Wasn't the New World the place to prove it? Didn't the clipper ships and Conestoga wagons, the Cumberland Road and the Union Pacific lay the promising foundations? In any case, after Ford presented his humble Tin Lizzy to the world, Americans sought civilization with such speed and in such numbers that man has not quite figured out what happened to the older heritage.

In its earliest days the automotive civilization was far from assured, despite the growing enthusiasm. "Autoneers" tried hard to be confident about the future when, as in a 1901 *Outing,* one stated that "there is hardly room for the assumption that automobilism may be a huge fallacy, and that the thousands of motor vehicles may disappear completely . . . as did the steam roadwagons which . . . appeared and reappeared on the scene at intervals of about thirty years."

In those days the services for a first-line civilization were meager. The only place fuel could be purchased was a drugstore. "Mechanicians" were few; blacksmiths had to be relied upon. And the attitude of the people toward automobiles was simply unprogressive—until they got one.

Often cities were unfair obstructionists, as when San Rafael, California, enacted a law requiring a driver to stop dead within 300 feet of every passing horse. Speed limits of eight miles an hour were enforced by brutal fines of twenty-five dollars. One 1907 protestor in Fresno complained: "They go so fast you can't tell the color and you can't tell the number and you can't tell who the driver is . . . when an auto runs over a man it disappears and there is no way to find it."

The worst prejudice was embedded in England's "red flag law," dating from earlier steam carriage days, which required a man to precede each motor vehicle on foot waving a red flag.

This suppression with insult was abandoned in 1896. Now a London-Brighton rally of antique autos each year regales that "first day of motoring freedom."

Early in America the progressives formed automobile clubs, knowing that "for many years an organization will be necessary to defend the automobile from unjust and oppressive legislation resulting from prejudices of the public during its introductory period." Such were the foundations of the AAA in 1902, with nine clubs and less than 1,000 members. Membership grew to 10,000 in 1910, 1 million in 1940, and over 11 million in 1969, suggesting that much prejudice has yet to be overcome during the remaining period of introduction.

Initially, defense of the auto was highly experimental. In 1902 the California Club offered to station one or more automobiles at convenient locations throughout San Francisco to inform timid and frightened horses about the true nature of automobiles. The results: one response, no show.

Other difficulties beset automobilists. Such as it was, the Good Roads movement had come in on the wheels of the bicycle. And in those days it was just not politic to admit being an automobilist when pleading for new road projects. The new "fairy horse" then had none of its latter-day establishment, no patronage, no ponderous surveys, no intimations of economic decline, and no threats of municipal strangulation. In 1903 it was sheer madness to ask legislators to back a measure having for its object the comfort or convenience of automobilists, who had to demand to be treated as ordinary citizens, subject to the same laws in traveling as the man in a buggy or the pedestrian on the sidewalk.

But Americans then still had their own get up and go. Club members not only got out and got under, with wrench and hammer, but also got out and pitched in, with pick and shovel. That they did in the toddling years of roadbuilding until auto strength was powerful enough to attack the general tax resources.

Even the railroads participated at an early date with "Good Roads" trains. Somehow they assumed that road improvements would end at the railheads. Industry rapidly recognized its stake after 1910 and tried to draw government into action. Thus the Lincoln Highway Association was created in 1913, the year automobiles first outproduced buggies and wagons, to promote a highway between New York and San Francisco. U.S. Rubber gladly contributed $130,000; General Motors, $100,000; Goodyear, $75,000. Carefully selected "seedling miles" were built along the entire route to create merciless contrasts between good and bad roads, demonstrating what automobility should be like.

The drama was successful. Other highway associations appeared. In 1916 the first major national roadbuilding law was enacted. That set the stage for two decades of roadbuilding that dwarfed the seven decades of railroad construction of the nineteenth century.

Rapid improvement throughout those two decades made almost every project over five years old out of date. According to one historian, "the interplay of better roads and better cars set up an endless competition. . . . Every year produced a new definition of what constituted an adequate highway. From stone surface it advanced to concrete strip. From single concrete lane, it spread to two or three or many. . . . And the interplay had no end. . . ."

No end to the interplay of automobiles and roads! And what about the interplay of automobiles and industry, automobiles and farming, automobiles and cities? Years earlier, in 1902, a lighthearted and admiring question was asked about the automobile. "We burn to discover," it asked, "what it is in itself, what it grants and what it withholds, what obedience it will offer its strange master, and what new lesson the new horizon may teach us. . . ." Well, it was in the 1920's and 1930's that the first real hints of what "the new horizon would teach us" appeared.

Of course, the interplay of action requires a counterpart in the interplay of belief. Automobility evolved its own logic, starting with such simple questions as, "Does the automobile earn its keep?" In 1920 the National Automobile Chamber of Commerce did a scientific investigation, reported the next year in *Outlook*, which showed that "the average passenger automobile has increased the working capacity of its owner by 56.7 percent," meaning, as they said, a "56.7 percent larger earning capacity . . . worth 56.7 percent more in economic value to the community."

Once this research could be transposed into the common sense of popular belief—and it didn't appear to hit any snags— the logic gained strength. One pioneering road study in the Midwest proved the value of good roads was $2,432 per annum per section of farmland, the calculated benefit of saving fuel, time, wear, and tear. The better roads would also increase the value of the land and thereby raise the tax valuation to help pay for the improvements.

The logic is plain. Cars increase the working capacity of men. Good roads increase the working capacity of cars. The next step for auto rationality was the traffic census. Proposed as early as 1903 to set up road priorities, the counts did much more for the endless interplay of automotive logic. Every additional car tallied would increase the savings attributable to the next construction project. From the time when *Scientific American* reported the daily average of 199 vehicles on the Ames–Des Moines road in 1917, the multiplication of road benefits could be proven, endlessly. The more cars there were the more important it was to surface the road, widen it, relocate it, and finally construct a freeway.

Quite wonderfully, the process was endless. The logic was sound in 1907, when $2,432 was good enough "to construct several miles of good highways" in the country. It would be better in 1967, when $2,432,000 was good enough to construct a quarter-mile of good highway in the city.

Once the logic got firmly implanted, there could be no question about "The Assured Future of the Automobile"—as *Scientific American* headlined its 1920 review of the Chamber of Commerce research. Ford knew it, too, when he pointed to "another big reason . . . why automobiles will be used in ever increasing numbers. For every good road built, more automobiles will be used, and with the use of every automobile the demand for more good roads increases." But even Ford didn't know how endless the interplay could be, and how sophisticated the auto rationality could become. A great civilization was assured.

180, 100-Percent Growth

No age is more glorious than the time after a certain maturity has arrived but before youth has entirely escaped. That was the motor car in 1910. Commentators could still impress their readers with the novelty, even the existence, of cars. Adventure and surprise were yet decidedly a part of the experience.

About 1910, however, commentators became preoccupied with a new realization: Automobiles were a big industry, important in the real world, already changing society. Despite the failure of the industrial census to honor the automobile with its own manufacturing classification in 1909, production that year surpassed 100,000 for the first time.

In 1908 Ford had offered his Model T to the farmer and the common man. The rough shakedown period was largely past. Then, too, 1910 was the eve of the great leap forward into mass production. The hand of every worker would then be rationalized and disciplined, just as the hand of every driver would eventually be. So writers stumbled over each other to chronicle the changes of machines, men, and organizations, to estimate the endless ramifications and count the wonderful benefits. What could be more glorious than to multiply output twenty-five times in nine years between 1908 and 1916, to roll out 1,167,000 vehicles in one year!

Well, it was hard to believe. In 1911 "the automobile manufacturers of the United States produced 209,000 cars. But how could we possibly show a picture of this vast number of automobiles in the *Scientific American* and have room for anything else in the same issue?" Growth was "meteoric" indeed. A few years earlier a manufacturer's investment to produce 5,000 cars annually "seemed madness." Nevertheless, the manufacturer continued to invest and soon produced 42,955 in one year. Beamed the *Scientific American:* "A most wonderful spectacle."

That journal saw fit in 1912 to say that "the automobile industry may now be said to have passed its period of infancy and adolescence, and attained an age of maturity." What they meant was that automobiles were now solidly embedded in economics. And economics was shifting into high gear.

The worm began to turn. Words changed. Facts changed. Ever so subtly Americans ceased to judge the motor car and the motor car began to judge America. *The Outlook* marked the change in a 1913 series called "The Motor Conquest," saying "the United States is the most wonderful automobile market in the world—a market which will take care of perhaps 200,000 cars a year for a great many years to come." From then on this theme would have endless variations. Subject and object had switched, not only in grammar. So had means and ends. By 1920 it was common to use such phrases as "the faith of motor-car makers in the future buying power of the Nation."

Naturally, then, the 1913 *Outlook* series could assert confidently that "no one talks nowadays about the motor car as a passing fad or darkly hints that the automobile craze is doomed to repeat the bicycle fiasco." The motor conquest, they could say, was "all but complete." A half-century later *Fortune* could add that "it is as if America were made for the automobile."

The new look of the automobile after 1910 was not merely that of millions of cars or that "the automobile has made life . . . one grand sweet song" in Hutchinson, Kansas. It was the growing power and steady penetration of a new monolith. It was not only the power of the automakers, but steel, petroleum, and rubber as well. And it was auto dealers, gasoline dealers, and garagemen. Soon it would be the highwaymen. It was not only how many cars *were* sold but ownership ratios, future consumer demand, and economic equations.

Already it was noted that the poor were spending their last savings and mortgaging homes to buy cars. After 1915 direct automobile financing progressed swiftly. The used-car market was ready to develop via a new selling device, the trade-in. Even scrappage was beginning to be watched closely.

The automobile then became important for the country's

dinner pail. Auto employment leaped into the millions. Automobiles had their initial influence on real estate, as the first shift away from the streetcar helped establish the motorcar suburbs. Trucking and farm tractors made immense gains during and after the World War I. And, as the Lincoln Highway Association revealed, the forces necessary to improve the roads were gathering. That was almost as important as the automobile's own development.

Discovery and triumph, romance and auto clubs; these were still the prevalent stories of the automobile in 1908. But in ten years both the reality and the meaning had changed. The brief renaissance of persons taking up the sweet challenges of motoring had given way to the statistical progress of institutions competing for markets, money, power.

A half-century later Walt Rostow characterized the automobile's growth with a scientist's penchant for precision. Auto output between 1899 and 1937, he quoted, increased by 180,100 percent. The heart of that growth appeared in the decade before World War I. That in turn set the stage for the great commercial transformation of the 1920's—with styling and annual models—which permitted the automobile to fully penetrate the power center of society.

Creating the New Necessity

Bleak is the outlook for a new product requiring an entirely new industrial system, nearly a fifth of all economic resources, a disciplined citizenry, the degenerative possession of the city, and a reworking of the countryside. But America was able. And the automobile led the way.

Yet, for all its growing numbers, the automobile in 1918 was still a superficial addition to society. Injected into society it was. But it was not yet fully a part, still a gigantic social toy. Hardly the first symptomatic changes of courting or commuting had appeared. Little of suburbia and no shopping centers had emerged. These were longer, slower steps toward an automotive civilization. Only a second generation of drivers, good roads, and a new round of urban development could restructure society to make the car a public necessity. That was the accomplishment of the twenties and thirties.

American roads were pathetic. But by 1918 the lobbies and Lincoln Highway associations were beginning to have their effect. The federal government that year made its first grants for highway construction. All states had highway departments by then. A heavy flow of money was not long in coming. Oregon led the parade with fuel taxes in 1919.

From a mere $139 million the states spent in 1918 the annual bonanza built up to $1,296 million in 1930 and $1,780 million in 1940. Minor retrenchment occurred during two years in the Depression and four years during World War II. The strained $75 million spent in 1914 would surpass $10 billion in half a century—a tidy 13,300-percent growth.

By 1940 the continental highway network was complete. America had created the most extensive system of highways the world had then seen. It had pioneered new methods of construction and enjoyed most of the superb roadways on earth. The forces behind highway improvement had been strong enough to initiate the national system at the brink of the first war and complete it through the Great Depression. "Depression or not," said an historian, "the public demanded roads, and the cars continued to roll over them. The United States was motorized." More than that, the motor car had by then become a necessity, as wartime fuel rationing soon would have to recognize.

The paradox and irony of those first "great" highways—and of automotive civilization—was that they were always judged to be more inadequate after they were improved. For whatever reasons (congestion, accidents, or new demands for convenience and speed) the inadequacy that raced past every improvement was the new reality. The greater the improvements, the more urgent the inadequacy became.

Meanwhile the infrastructure for car culture made rapid headway. By the end of the twenties gas pumps were in front of most general stores, and fillin' stations had spread along Main Street. Blacksmiths turned to internal combustion as quickly as the horse was put out to pasture. Auto agencies multiplied to 43,000 by 1924. School buses made a rapid entry, numbering 63,000 in 1932. Thousands of little red schoolhouses closed their doors as a consequence of school-bus mobility.

Even the early successes were not without repercussions. As early as 1925 alarms were being heard about the effects on the railroads of autos and the new buses. That year the Boston and Maine asked to abandon 1,000 miles of track because of the auto inroads. Railroads suffered but one of the many declines that accompanied and reinforced the auto's success.

The auto began to force-feed urban growth. In the rural areas, mobility sped the consolidation of more activities into fewer large towns farther from each farm. Thousands of small villages and rural service centers shrank, or died, from the impact. Then, too, workers flooded Detroit, Akron. Cleveland, Oakland, and many other cities, not only to construct chassis or tires, but to produce steel and machine tools, and to finance and service the output. Just as the village gave way to the town, the town gave way to the city, the city to the metropolis.

The auto-accelerated growth led naturally to auto-controlled urban form. Since 1900 there had been simple infiltration of traffic and curb parking, and a multiplication of filling stations and service agencies. This was followed by the auto suburbs. The spilling out, eventually to outer suburbia, was accompanied by wider streets and boulevards, the isolationist pattern of zoning and the Great American Strip of commerce along the major streets.

With the expansion of *urban* highways, the infiltration turned into a frontal assault. Each accommodation of the automobile but strengthened motordom's offensive power. Auto authority increased with every measure that broke up the traditional urban form to suit the gargantuan scale and the stampeding character of auto movement.

The auto's impact on the city was degenerative possession. The very nature of cities made the city use of automobiles less beneficial and the liabilities more profound. But full automotive possession would be slow. Complete motorization of the city would require far more than twenty years. The city's concentrated form gave it natural defenses that could be overturned only in a longer span of time.

Nevertheless the automobile's steady conquest of the city was somehow construed as an ideal. Automobility seemed to be the foundation for renaissance. Early automobilists believed that cars would relieve both the overstuffed life in cities and the understimulated life on farms by bringing the best of one to the other. Specifically, they believed, the city man could move into the country, perhaps in motor colonies, and drive to town for work and services.

The lingering image of the ideal rural-urban life was followed by the notion that the automobile was essential to accommodate the explosive urban growth. Predictably, it was a Chamber of Commerce report in 1925 that idealized "the ability to live in pleasant and healthful surroundings yet depend on transportation facilities that permit work in the urban centers. . . ." The report then invoked the new rationality—automotive necessity —saying that the problem of a growing urban population "would perhaps be incapable of solution except for the development of motor transportation."

These are the steps by which urban life and urban form were made dependent on the automobile. First, the urban centers became "congested" and required parking. Bit by bit parking lots and then garages appeared, decomposing the area immediately around the town center. Second, driving to work promoted the Great American Strip with its nondescript markets, used car lots, lumber yards, drive-ins, and dog kennels. Third, the new low-density urban conditions deprived transit of a basis to serve efficiently. and therefore to grow and improve. These events armed automotive progress and elevated it to its first stage of control over the whole urban existence.

Little wonder, then, that *Fortune* in the late 1950's could say that Americans still appeared "willing, in this sweet land of plenty, to go on spending a growing percentage of their income on the passenger automobile." Given the forces that had been shaping the urban environment for three decades, the result was understandable. But in the end the "willingness" revealed more necessity than a measure of freedom.

Indeed, by 1940, *Autokind* was a reality on earth, for it claimed sovereignty; pursued an inner progress of its own, independent of men; commanded huge realms in economics and politics; and had maneuvered close to civic reign.

Escalating the Point of Saturation

People were important, of course. The auto industry had always wondered how many automobiles they could take.

At the beginning predictions were often bleak. "It's a fad that will soon die out, like the bicycle," they said in 1903. That talk died hard. Rather, it changed into speculation of "overproduction" by 1906, a year in which 34,000 cars were turned out. In 1910, when output was 187,000, the "pessimists began calling for a halt," fearing that the market could not long absorb such numbers.

In 1913 some 485,000 motor vehicles were produced. Would it "be possible to keep up motor car merchandising on such a scale much longer?" asked Reginald McIntosh Cleveland in *The World's Work* early in 1914. "It does not require an especially sensitive finger on the pulse of things to inform you that it will not. The market is pretty well saturated." Recent years had been a sort of gold rush, and the best ore had been mined, Cleveland observed. Now that the automobile was practically standardized, production would be limited to replacements and a small arithmetic growth of ownership, then already at more than one car per hundred people.

Well, production jumped to 1,617,000 in 1916, exceeding human births for the first time. The automen (who had always been optimistic) then reported their views: "The rate of increase in production is going to keep up for a good long time." What about saturation? Pure conjecture, they said.

The pessimists had a comeback, however, in 1921 when production dropped from a 1920 high of 2,227,000 back to the 1916 level. Was the slump a sign of saturation? Yes, they reasoned.

"Very nearly all the Americans who can afford to buy automobiles have them already."

This time the spoilsports were also armed with new arguments: street congestion and lack of parking space. "Everybody who drives [and] . . . who is daily obliged to dodge automobiles . . . must have asked himself: 'How many automobiles are there going to be in this country, anyhow? Where are we going to put them all?' "

Between limited buying power and congestion, it looked as though saturation was approaching in 1921. That was, "even by a liberal estimate," less than 20 million cars. But registration reached 20 million in 1925. Yet the pessimists continued. "This vanishing saturation-point has been flitting just over the horizon," wheezed the *Literary Digest* in 1926.

"Thirty million cars is our maximum capacity," reported a University of Michigan professor in 1927. By elaborate tables he demonstrated that saturation would be reached about 1933. Lo, we find an estimate that was too ambitious! But we can blame the Depression. Thirty million were not registered until 1937.

More than one car per family had not been considered a practical possibility in earlier speculations. But by 1929, when almost anything seemed possible, the idea of the two-car family began to be broached in industrial circles. By the mid-1960's, a few land developers began putting demands for three and four garage spaces per family.

Nor was the question of saturation limited to numbers. Ever since the new Chevrolet six helped kill Ford's Model T in 1927, the phenomena of selling "more car per car" has been growing: the enclosed body; more weight, power, and chrome; annual models and style variations; the automatic transmission; power brakes, steering, and windows; air conditioning. These created the second dimension of saturation—that of stretching cars beyond "basic transportation."

The meaning? *Fortune* was led to say in 1959 that "familiar as it is, the American people's affection for passenger cars . . . must give pause to even the most sophisticated observer. American consumers today, for example, spend eleven times as much on buying and operating cars as they do on all forms of public transportation, local and long distance. . . ."

We now see that there is no saturation point for automobility, only the various stages of dependence to which society falls. *Fortune* in 1967 put it in the language of growth: "The auto population curve has begun to bump against the human population curve and level off. There is, of course, no demographic law that says the vehicle curve cannot push right through the human curve." Confidently, *Fortune* concluded that saturation "cannot now be considered a serious threat to the auto market."

The hurdles of saturation have been few: (1) everyone who can afford one, (2) everyone who wants one, (3) everyone who needs one, (4) everyone.

Unlike sandpaper or shaving cream, which are mere utilities of civilization, the automobile has elevated its position to an independent goal of civilization. Can one have too much culture? Hence, the changing views of saturation over the years merely represented the specific *vision* of attainment at any given moment. Every attainment set the foundation for a new vision. From a toy the automobile became convenient, then practical. First, one car became necessary. Now two are becoming so. Three or four are in prospect.

The most critical single factor escalating saturation was revealed in a statement of Alvan Macauley, then president of Packard: "We did not talk about saturation so much" in the early days, he said, "as we do today, but my market study had made me give it serious consideration. To me it seemed, as it does now, that the volume of automobile output is only limited by the city planning, which has never given it proper consideration." But even then the automobile was being given more attention than Macauley knew.

Earthly Art

As everyone now knows, highway development is a highly advanced art. A town and country art. It evolved in two broad stages: The first, according to George Romney, when he was still an automan in 1949, was getting "out of the mud." The second, he suggested, was getting out of the "muddle."

In 1900 the art of getting out of the mud mostly meant a fifteen-foot width of gravel. The country claimed about 150,000 miles of such humble improvements, which covered only a twentieth of the total road mileage. But America's best were ages inferior to the old Roman roads, which boasted a foundation of large stones planted upright, covered with rammed gravel, and sometimes overlayed with large, carefully cambered stone slabs.

Nevertheless, stones placed side by side offered little to modern roadbuilding. So the road agents started virtually from scratch to develop new materials and methods. Although Bellefontaine, Ohio, had laid the first concrete street in America in 1891, twenty years passed before cross-country highways could afford such extravagance. Today most of the Interstate system is concrete.

But the magic highway material for the age of internal combustion turned out to be merely a black petroleum waste, asphalt. While petroleum fueled the automobile it also paved the highway. Asphalt thus reveals another example of diversity and reinforcement that contributed so much to the auto conquest. Its applications ranged from dust inhibition to the best interstate highway standard. It would be good in the early years, when there was little knowledge or money. It would be equally good later, when standards were rigid and money plentiful.

The reinforcement between fuel and paving was but part of the reinforcement. Francis Turner, the Federal Highway Administrator, wrote in a 1967 *Petroleum Today* that the automobile and highway "developed like Siamese twins, each utterly dependent on the other."

Hence, the principal cutlery required to build the highway, the crawler tractor, carryall, dump truck, and motor grader, are as much a part of the automobile as asphalt is of petroleum. They are of the same parentage, serve in the same campaigns of conquest, and are of each "utterly dependent on the other."

The crawler tractor was especially useful in getting out of the mud. It was conceived for this role in 1904 by Benjamin

Holt, father of the Caterpillar, when he put a "treadmill" on a tractor which laid "its own roadbed before itself—like a portable railroad." The following year a journal observed that "in a tract [near Stockton, California] where a man could not walk without sinking to his knees . . . the new traction engine was operated without a perceptible impression on the ground."

With the blade that made it a bulldozer, the tractor could penetrate new terrain, brush aside small trees and large boulders, level pioneer roads. As the full lineup of machines acquired brute muscle, the pick, shovel, and sledge were pitched aside. Roads could then grow up and go anywhere. From simple grading for surface and drainage the roads graduated to true "high-ways," first with the filling of gullies, then the straightening of mountain curves. Cuts could be made hundreds of feet deep, fills to millions of cubic yards. In California single cuts now sometimes involve 10 million yards of earth.

The underlying sciences advanced along with the technology behind the highwayman's art. Basic research flowed from the Highway Research Board of the prestigious National Academy of Sciences. Each year since the 1920's dozens of treatises have been completed, varying from "Nuclear Principles" and "Night Visibility" to "Soil Freezing" and "Sign Supports." Their work is supplemented by a number of special university institutes and the proprietary research centers of the Asphalt Institute at College Park, Maryland, and the Portland Cement Association at Skokie, Illinois.

The power of highway research is illustrated in one of the famous road tests, that in Illinois in 1958–60, sponsored by the American Association of State Highway Officials. After ten years of planning and two of construction, U.S. Army soldiers drove 126 vehicles 17 million miles over 716 concrete and asphalt sections of 169 different pavement designs in five loops going from nowhere to nowhere. The affair cost $27,114,220—all in the name of perfecting better pavement for a better American civilization.

Looking forward to another half-century of highway research and development, we may be assured of a nationwide stoneware one hundred times longer than the roads of the Roman Empire. That legacy to the future will be the world's weightiest, and probably the most durable. For future man, it may appear as a continental Rosetta Stone telling of our time and our accomplishments, perhaps of our fate.

Unearthly Art

Science and technology proved what could be done with mud. However, society was soon faced with the booming muddle of the automobile itself. The muddle is immobility arising precisely from overmobility of the society. For forty years now the establishment has attempted to rectify the problem by constantly expanding automobility.

As we know, unless the environment is thoroughly remade, the automobile is prodigiously awkward, barely usable, and unsafe. What the muddle shows is that after the environment is radically reconstructed for the automobile, as it has been in Los Angeles, the automobile remains prodigiously awkward, barely usable, and unsafe.

Traces of the muddle reach back to World War I, but it didn't show up in earnest until after World War II. As soon as simple paving gave the automobile the foundations to mass its movements, each city had to increase roadway capacity. First, existing streets had to be widened, then short extensions and connections made, then thoroughfares built, and finally full freeways constructed.

Nevertheless it was necessary to squeeze ever greater use out of old street systems. Those old democratic passages didn't easily submit to the automotive conquest. Largely for that reason it was necessary to create a new profession: traffic engineering.

The traffic engineer is strategic. Ostensibly he coordinates the automobile, the highway, and the driver for smooth traffic movement. More accurately, he is Detroit's man in the council chamber, fulfilling two missions. First, he forestalls breakdown from congestion. That would be disastrous for Detroit because it would force cities to make sensible city plans. Second, he is an expert who can best advance the auto rationale in the crucial domain of public decision. His data proves the auto necessity and his plans set the stage for its growth.

The traffic engineer could not have been successful without a growing popular consciousness of the automobile's requirements. That, of course, was strongest in California. In 1946 Governor Earl Warren called a special session of the legislature to expand highway construction, pleading that, after all, 'it was human nature for all of us to want good highways."

However, the important sign of things to come appeared in 1947, when Thomas MacDonald, Federal Commissioner of Public Roads, made the case for *urban* freeways. City freeways, he said, were to *save* "cities from stagnation and decay." The question cities were asking themselves, he observed, was: "Shall we build highways which will enable traffic to move into and through the city quickly and safely, or shall we try to get along with things as they are?"

The steady convergence on the city is illustrated in the shifts of federal road programs. The first grants to states after the 1916 highway act were solely for rural mail routes. Then, in 1921, attention centered on 200,000 miles of the U.S. sign highways. This first national system linked the cities and towns, but federal money could not be used within them. After 1944, when the urban muddle could be felt, federal aid for urban highways was initiated on a small scale. The same act created the Interstate system.

Envisioned first in 1922, the Interstate idea was slow to take hold, since it was at least two decades ahead of auto necessity. In the 1930's Roosevelt took an interest in it, believing that three east-west and three north-south routes would be sufficient, about 15,000 miles. In 1939 the Bureau of Public Roads completed the first nationwide study to underpin the Interstate proposal. All the facts, it said, suggest that urban sections of the system are the "most important" and the "least adequate." Hence, when routes comprising 37,700 miles were designated in 1947, 4,400 miles were in urban areas. Three-quarters of the next designation of 3,300 miles was urban. Of the principal system of 41,000 miles, 6,800 miles and 45 percent of the money were devoted to the "urban connections" of the *Interstate* system.

By 1956 the pressure of automotive necessity for good highways was so great that the bill to finance the Interstate highways was voted in both houses with but one dissent. "That," said the *Saturday Evening Post* at the time, "should answer any questions . . . as who runs this country." Indeed, it did, with a $101-billion-dollar package for the Interstate and other highways.

The early automobile had faced the problem of rural mud. That problem was solved. The automobile created the problem of the urban muddle. That problem could not be solved. It could only grow. As the former problem waned after World War II the latter took up the slack, continued to accelerate highway construction, and shifted it towards the cities. The cities today suffer from the problem, which grows directly in proportion to the efforts to solve it.

Sovereignty, Integrity, Freeway

Ever since Hitler built the first *autobahn* the freeway has commandeered the integrity of both town and country for the automobile. It builds an organic integrity of *movement* while bulldozing the traditional integrity of *place* into fractured disarray.

Historically, cities gave integrity to place rather than movement. City walls, narrow streets, and enclosed courtyards, which were really access controls, put a premium on locality and its human functions, not on mobility. The nineteenth-century American city changed this with its endlessly open grid of streets and blocks. Both blocks and streets could be entered at any point. That is, free access exchange between land (or place) and street (or movement) was virtually universal.

But between 1920 and 1950 the ascending auto completely annihilated the free exchange. A new doctrine, purified in the freeway, brought armored force into civic affairs. That doctrine today honors and protects automotive integrity while rigorously disrupting the functions and integrity of places within the city.

There is no recourse against splitting neighborhoods, not even against disrupting the peace.

Three general conditions underlay the "uninterrupted flow" necessary for integrity of the freeway: (1) multiple lanes separated for those who go east and those who go west; (2) control of access to screen off all activities which flock to a roadway and interrupt the flow; and (3) separation of grade to bridge over and eliminate all intersections (since, as the experts knew in 1929, "a highway is no swifter than its intersections"). The benefits, they say, are safety, capacity, and speed. And these, they thought, were permanent—until freeway congestion itself would again raise the stakes of highway expansion to a new magnitude.

Paradoxically, the freeway principles were not created by the highway experts. Nor were they created for safety, capacity, or speed. Flowered *center strips* had long adorned boulevards for proper promenades by coach and horse. They were, in fact, an essential sign of urbanity. The flowers on New York's Park Avenue today are a vestige of that day. *Bridges* of one road over another were first planned for Central Park in 1858 by the

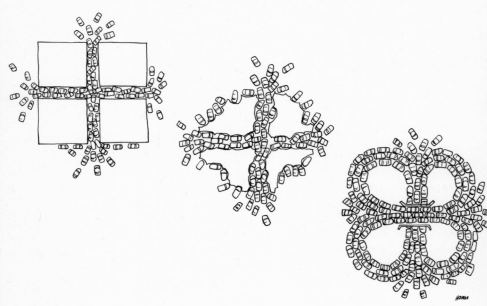

great park planner Frederick Olmstead. *Control of access* was introduced in the plan for the Bronx River Parkway in 1906 so that the driver could concentrate on the scenery rather than the traffic. (Ironically, in 1970 the Bronx River Parkway was being reconstructed as a "freeway," thereby sacrificing the trees and amenities of the parkway to safety, capacity, and speed.)

Even the first highway claiming completely uninterrupted flow, the Avus in Berlin, did so for sport. Planned in 1913 and opened in 1919 by a club, Avus was an experimental speedway of six straight miles. Today it is West Berlin's main artery to the west, and probably the world's only freeway with a grandstand.

Though all freeway principles were known by 1920, the traffic muddle had not yet taken precedence over mud. So bridges, center strips, and limited access continued to be used mainly in parkways in the vicinity of New York until the middle thirties. True, the Italians built their first-generation *autostrade* in the late 1920's, but they violated more principles than they followed. Then, between 1933 and 1941 the Germans built an incredible 1,326 miles of *autobahnen* at full standard. Hitler could impose a national system of highway access controls with impunity. He also stayed out of the cities.

But democracy in America could not be defeated this way. Only when faced with threats of civic strangulation were Americans deceived into accepting infringements on their environmental rights. They retreated piecemeal, where congestion and accidents were worst. But that also meant freeways would be thrust like cold steel into the heart of every city, where the automotive muddle was always worst.

In 1930 America was still very complacent, confident that the widened boulevards then called "superhighways" would solve congestion. Little attention was paid to planners who pleaded for the "townless highway," and less to its counterpart, the highwayless town.

But, as the highwaymen knew all along, the superhighway would one day mean the freeway. In 1930 Edward Bassett proposed the name "freeway," saying that freeway "connotes freedom from grade intersections and from private entranceways, stores, and factories. It will have no sidewalks and will be free from pedestrians." This was a declaration of freedom for motoring, whatever it might be for cities and human beings. That doctrine demanded a single-minded and precise control of the environment. Highways built to freeway standards would strive to fulfill Walter Chrysler's prophecy that the automobile "knew no limits except a right of way."

The precedents were accumulating. In 1928 New Jersey built the world's first cloverleaf interchange at Woodbridge. Never one to be outdone, Robert Moses actually opened a freeway to Jones Beach on Long Island in 1934, a full seven months before Hitler opened the first *autobahn*. The Pennsylvania Turnpike was opened in 1940, built partly on an old, unfinished railroad bed. The same year California opened the Arroyo Seco in Los Angeles, aligned in a riverbed. From then on only the war delayed America's turning to freeways with increasing desperation.

There were a few legal skirmishes. Some states balked at legislating the subtle and oblique repression of environmental rights required for freeways. But these were only brief hesitations. The issue hardly became public at all. Officials were pleased to find in the freeway what they thought was relief from stupefying congestion. And by 1950 most states were building them out of the new necessity. So today even the coyotes out in Nevada have had to learn to cross the desert freeways through underpasses, though they prefer the greater security of culverts.

Miles, Money, and Rational Mayhem

If "the Road moves and controls all history," as one historian has said, then Americans are seeking their place in history by a tour de force. The campaign began as a gigantic contest between the building of cars and the building of highways. It became a professional power struggle between those who make national problems and those who solve them. Now it has sunk to a communal gladiatorial contest. All society has been barricaded into the arena to play the grizzly sport.

The sport is framed by rules which we may describe as interest-group rationalism. Human purpose and social responsibility become bound to the promotion of mobility. Rational mayhem is created in society by dispassionate and purposeful systems of finance and administration. The rationality is growth. The growth is infinite.

The promotion has been highly successful. From 1944 to 1968 auto travel increased each year nearly as much as all auto travel in 1920. During the same twenty-four years street and highway expenditures increased each year nearly twice as much as all street and highway expenditures in 1920.

To *Motor Age* magazine, 1968 was "The Year of the Magic Numbers." "Now automotive statistical numbers are entering a new realm," gloated the editors, "the trillion—or thousand million." That was how many miles Americans traveled by motor vehicle in 1968.

Could we now be approaching the saturation we have heard so much about? Hardly, according to Resources for the Future, Inc. With a statistical sobriety befitting its rationalism, RfF predicts that America will register between 199 and 372 million passenger cars in the year 2000. Add about 20 percent for trucks and we may expect between 240 and 440 million vehicles to inhabit America in 2000.

Impossible? Not quite, for we don't know the limits to which automotive necessity may carry us. We don't know the limits of our toleration, or whether our toleration is relevant any longer. We don't know about the continued evolution of special cars for special uses, such as those already used in huge parking lots, industrial plants, campuses, or golf courses. We don't know the extent to which the continued development of freeways will require a kind of vehicle not permissible or practical on the streets. We don't know whether the auto-makers might succeed in further differentiating cars, for example, by creating special models comparable to skirts and trousers for each sex. Then too, there are signs of major improvements to come in parking, comparable to freeway development principles, and this could open central cities to many, many more cars.

Now, if we reflect back upon Governor Warren's and Commissioner MacDonald's words we see a rising chorus of runaway pragmatism which can argue that a multiplication of destructive traffic is the best case to build more and more roadways to serve that traffic. President Eisenhower used it in his message supporting the interstate highway act in 1955. The system itself was designed on the same reasoning: The original forty-one thousand miles cost about fifty billion dollars over a twenty-year period. Those highways will serve 20 percent of all traffic when complete. But while they are being built traffic will nearly triple. What could one expect in the end, then, but an immensity made senseless by its utter insufficiency.

Based on the RfF projections, America will require between three and six additional Interstate highway systems in 2000.

Well, California is taking the Resources for the Future projections seriously. In 1967 the state Division of Highways and the state Chamber of Commerce published estimates in identical lengthy articles in their two magazines, stating that "if spending continues at the present level [about $1 billion annually] until 1975 an additional $23 billion will be required to meet the needs in the 1975–1985 period." Those are high stakes, and the late Herbert Hoover, Jr., then head of the chamber's Freeway Support Committee, knew it. That is why he was on the committee. Twenty-three billion dollars in one state in one decade is equal to all expenditures for all streets and highways for all states from 1900 to 1939. It is twenty-three times what the San Francisco Bay Area is spending for a transit system to save itself from complete transportation breakdown.

"Oh, highway . . . you express me better than I can express myself," said Walt Whitman. We wonder what his reflections might be today, or whether he would be able to express himself at all.

Third Bastion: Immobility

When massive numbers of machines are set in motion a problem of equal magnitude is created: that of bringing them to a stop.

Parking experts will tell you that Rome provided parking to get the chariots off the roads, and that English common law decreed that drivers couldn't stable horses on the King's Highway. This is their way of saying that things don't really change. Rome suffered from congestion. Why do we complain?

We have seen that there are two ways to face a problem: eliminate it at its source or expand it. Once America took the course of highway expansion, there was no alternative but also to expand the realm of parking.

With the rise of the parking problem, the experts can speak of the relationship between highways and parking as the "balance" in the transport system. Once the automotive necessity is established, it may be claimed that "adequate parking is important for the continued prosperity" of the central business district. This is another way of saying that parking is the new frontier of automobility.

Parking is the third and latest bastion in the triumvirate of automotive necessity. As the highway was slower to take hold than the car, so parking is slower to take hold than the highway. As the car compelled the development of the highway, so the highway (especially the freeway) forces the development of parking. However, the triumvirate cannot lick the urban transportation crisis. It is the condition of that crisis.

A theoretical note is pertinent here: When a type of mobility requires a complete system of immobility, such as parking, and together they cover more area than they were designed to serve, severe practical problems are bound to arise. Already one-third of many downtowns are occupied by auto-moving spaces, one-third by auto-parking spaces. Only one-third remains for local activity spaces. Yet civic occupation by the automobile is far from complete. History has indicated that the thesis of automobility is growth. Paradoxically, it is now apparent that the antithesis of automobility is also growth.

Pioneering in parking goes back to the 1920's, the first years of modern congestion, when complaints began to grow across the nation about the lack of hitching posts for cars. The *Literary*

Digest got worried in 1924 because it rightly feared that Americans were thinking more about a place to park than about the League of Nations.

There were the parking visionaries. New York's special deputy police commissioner, Dr. John A. Harriss, proposed to store 30,000 vehicles under Central Park and another 4,000 under Bryant Park, near the public library. Grant Park in Chicago was proposed as the site for 7,000 beneath its trees and turf. Its bowels were eventually carved out, but for only 2,359 vehicles. Central and Bryant parks have so far been spared.

The builders of the 1920's were at first nearly as active as the visionaries. In Los Angeles, the Pacific Mutual Building was built to hold 140 cars in its two lower floors. Exclusive parking garages were also appearing. Pittsburgh had one for 450 vehicles. Washington, D.C., planned an automobile "hotel" for 800 cars.

Nevertheless, parking was then far less pressing than highways. Public transit was still effective and inexpensive. The automotive necessity was not pressing. So after a false start in the 1920's the momentum of parking flagged.

To overcome the loss of initiative the automobile made an asset of its mobility and took an end run around the old city center in the 1930's by creating the suburban shopping center. Naturally, highways and parking were the major planning components. At first the centers were merely a quarter-acre at a busy intersection, consisting of shops in an L shape with ten or twenty parking spaces. In twenty years they would grow into 150-acre giants, like Detroit's Northland Center, with 10,000 spaces.

By the 1950's shopping centers gave solid competition to downtown. Then, combined with the precipitous decline of transit, the growing automotive necessity could bring new economic power and urgency to downtown parking. The threat was real, particularly for retailing. Parking was clearly "important for the continued prosperity" of the downtown, as the new parking experts argued.

In self-defense the large downtown department stores acted to protect their investment. While some lots and garages had been built, these became antiquated, like 1920 roads serving where freeways were demanded. So the big merchants—Sears, May's, Macy's, Rich's, Kaufman's—brought murderously high-priced adjoining land and built their own garages, ranging up to 2,000 billets.

Congestion and shopping center competition brought many cities to astonishing acts of self-sacrifice to appease the conquerors. Rather than face the future of the downtown squarely, cities began to *require* parking with all new buildings. West Palm Beach, Florida, appears to have been a pioneer, passing a parking requirement in its zoning ordinance in 1926. Seventy cities are known to have had such provisions by 1946. The requirement became common in the 1950's.

Such sacrifice of urban land, efficiency, and amenity in the downtown areas was largely avoided in New York, which *restricts* the amount of parking in new buildings in the most valuable areas. This is done on the elementary consideration that if all 3.5 million commuters to Manhattan drove to work they would require five levels of parking on all usable building land from Fifty-second Street to the Battery.

But in most cities the threat of decline put both merchants and city fathers at the mercy of the generals of automotive expansion, who warned that auto "terminals have been perhaps the most neglected part of the transportation system components." Of course, the expert advice was solidly pragmatic, once automotive necessity had set in. It seemed like good heat-of-battle responses. But it always set the stage for bigger battles at less merciful odds. The parking programs merely contributed to the flood of automobility while forestalling more basic decisions and creating deeper dilemmas for the downtown. Such is the lesson for all cities, a lesson the experts prefer to ignore.

Dead Center in the City

Clearly, parking programs today are the automotive frontal assault force. They are aimed dead center at the city. Each parking place in the center represents the impact of the highway and the staying power of the automobile.

A parking map or aerial photo of any American city center reveals devastation as obvious as that resulting from a London Blitz. Saturation bombing is the only adequate comparison. Hundreds of buildings around the immediate center have been wiped out. In the photo the rubble seems to have been cleared by vast bands of glistening .beetles who wait disciplined and ready in the empty blocks to clear the debris of unbombed sections. Others are already on the move in the streets.

A closer inspection reveals that even many new buildings which we might think defendable are really armored stalls for the beetles. Sweeping open tiers reveal rows of headlights plaintively peering into the street. In some a monstrous elevator moves constantly, tending the cells of these better-housed beetles.

The effects of saturation bombing are analogous to the effects of parking, with one exception, for there is always a small central area without parking facilities. It is as if the bombing runs had a calm "eye" like that of a hurricane, wherein serious damage is avoided. That is necessary in parking, the experts say, because the high land values are out of reach of the parking industry. But that's just professional modesty. The "eye" exists because the area of highest land values can be served conveniently by parking on all four sides. If parking penetrated the eye it would eliminate the reason for parking, i.e., the buildings people go to. That would eliminate trip generation, as the traffic engineers say.

The sheer ability of parking to pay was attested to by a visionary writing for *Atlantic* in 1953. "We feel that it is perfectly sound financially to use land with high assessment value . . . for parking facilities. The economics of a garage that we now have on the drafting board—it is a 35-story affair—indicate that if the streets can take care of the traffic, this garage can compete with the highest productive improvement for the most expensive downtown land, and will justify paying the full price for it, without tax subsidy or any boondoggling or anything else." The point isn't changed because William Zeckendorf went bankrupt years later—without constructing the 35-story affair. What he spoke about, though a vision, is precisely the direction of civic affairs.

The bright future for parking is concretely illustrated at Century City in Los Angeles, an old film lot of Twentieth Century Fox turned into a fantasy for the twenty-first century. The architect of this multipurpose urban development, Welton Becket, tells us that "although the site is 173 acres, well over 200 acres of parking have been provided" in the design.

And now parking is moving onto the legislative priority list. For the first time, under the Highway Act of 1968, federal highway money can be used to construct parking as a part of any federally aided highway. Only seed money is provided thus far. But it points the way, just as the 1944 Highway Act first allocated seed money for urban highways.

Earlier, in 1966, the U.S. Senate held lengthy hearings on the parking problem in Washington, D.C. The record ran to 745 pages, worthy of a complete reappraisal of foreign policy. The issue was not the future livability of the nation's capitol, which happened to be at stake, but whether public or private means could best expand acutely needed parking in the capital.

At one point, tucked away on page 542, was a proposal from the Committee of One Hundred on the Federal City to further study the problem. The committee chairman, former Senator Joseph Tydings, took particular plans to refute the proposal, apparently because it was bold, arguing that there is "too much parking for too many cars in the wrong places for the wrong purposes, and at the wrong time. Existing legislative proposals would not solve these problems; they would compound them." Tydings kindly pointed out that this proposal did not coincide with the views of the expert witnesses. Nor will it, as long as the experts seek to "balance" parking with highway expansion and auto production.

Iron Law of Automotive Expansion

What Mankind has experienced in the past seventy years is a new natural law of society: the *Iron Law of Automotive*

Expansion. Sooner or later automobility will affect all societies, but its development in America has taken place in an unusually fertile environment. Operation of the Law is as precise as the genetic code, revealing an organic, really super-organic, force that rises above men. A new citizenship has been claimed by the car. The voting power of that citizenship is the lobby. Its broader social power is expressed through interest groups.

However, there is a power of the automobile in society which is fully its own, beyond normal social decision. This is what justifies the term *super-organic.* That power arises through varied conditions and developments (like mechanical improvements and highway expansion, or parking facilities and annual style changes) which coalesce for automotive expansion, and then ramify and radiate into a new set of conditions and developments (like highway congestion, parking shortages, and the decline of transit) leading to a new round of automotive expansion.

Cycles follow cycles. Each is progressive, not repetitive. Each carries automobility to a new frontier. Nor does it matter very much whether the specific developments are beneficial or socially destructive. For as the automobile makes itself a more absolute necessity it thrives on the problems it creates just as smoothly as upon the benefits it brings. Both the problems created by the automobile and society's responses to them have the same general effect of alienating man from his environment, from his society, even from his body and his social sensibilities.

The Iron Law is fundamental in city planning. It is very simple: *The scale and form of the city expand to serve the city's predominant citizens.*

Today this law means that the automobile is master of the metropolis, having clearly governed urban growth and change for a half-century. Encirclement by freeways and penetration by parking are not the only direct influences. These are abetted by the disjointed suburbs, endless commercial boulevards, and scattered industries. Auto requirements were wrought into all urban existence. The auto created the motel, the trailer camp, and the drive-in. It multiplied the demand for virgin land outside the city and prompted people to want to escape from the old inner city, strengthening class and race divisions along the way. Stop-and-go commuting, courtship and sex, and the long weekend reveal how the car profoundly affected economics, family life and recreation. The consequence is that the urban anatomy is designed for wheeled citizenship.

What are the operating principles of the Iron Law of Automotive Expansion? There are essentially three: The demand requirements, the command capacities, and the catalytic feedback.

1. *Demand Requirements.* Every new urban car requires urban space. Each car typically commands one residential parking space and two others at work, shopping, school, airport, hospital, theater, club, stadium, church, restaurant, drive-in, etc. Then each requires moving spaces. The total, approaching 4,000 square feet, is half or two-thirds of a good-sized urban lot. But cars enjoy far more space, like long driveways, highway center strips, roadside spaces, and freeway cloverleaves (which now range up to the size of university campuses).

The auto's space requirements go much farther, of course. Gas stations, garages, and used-car lots each now verge upon that fine figure, the acre. New-car dealers and junkyards passed that long ago. Together these are the urban spaces devoted to delivering newborn cars, feeding and nursing them, holding them for readoption, and burying them. (When the end comes there are not many ceremonies, but a lot of cannibalism, suggesting a rather early stage in the progress of automobilism.)

There are, then, three kinds of spaces required for the car: moving, stopping, and nurturing. Each has its own history, justification, and growth momentum. And the advance of one bolsters the advance of others. They represent the minimum *requirements* of the automobile.

2. *Command Capacities.* The more dynamic elements of the Iron Law begin to reveal themselves through the *capacities* of the automobile. With a clear road, urban distances are nearly insignificant. Before congestion sets in, it hardly matters whether a man commutes two miles or ten. The open road and the open country at the fringes of the city therefore beckon the frustrated

urban motorist to escape from and therefore to spread the city ever farther in the search for openness and congestion-free movement.

At this point the operative secret of the automotive conquest is laid wide open. Initially the automobile makes impossible space demands on old cities. It congests fine old boulevards, encourages non-rational lines of movement, undermines transit, and contributes to decay. Then this very same instrument of civic chaos presents its owners with a solution: escape to the suburbs.

Rarely in history is there a tyrant who creates intolerable social problems and then presents himself as the savior. But that is precisely the nature of the automotive advance. First it congests and disrupts and deteriorates. Then it provides the means to open up the countryside for multiplying the urban expanse.

What, then, is achieved? The best of town and country life? Hardly, for the automobile is master. The city is thinned out to a no-man's land: the natural landscape is utterly destroyed. Qualities of European city life, such as a decent walking environment and active plazas and marketplaces, are denied to men. An anti-urban, anti-social consumptive isolation of total dependence on the automobile is the achievement. Then only the automotive umbilical cord, combined with great personal resources and resourcefulness, makes urban existence minimally workable.

Yet that is America's habit of response. It is the American way of potlatch.

3. *Catalytic Feedback.* At this point the Iron Law begins to reveal the human toll. This is when the automotive growth feeds upon the problems it creates. First, it will be seen that the automobile population increases more rapidly than the people who move to the suburbs. A second, third, and even fourth family car appears. More members of the family must make more auto trips in more directions for more—and sometimes all —of their necessities. Traffic grows enormously, and in a few years jammed highways prevail. New freeways shoot out on Long

Island or down the San Francisco peninsula. But they quickly congest.

Congestion sometimes occurs on roads where no development save billboards is yet visible. Plainly, congestion is a condition of automobiles more than of cities. Compact, even dense, urban development is not congestion, and may sometimes help reduce it. The kind of mobility is what is important, for that determines the kind of urban development.

Development shaped by automobility feeds upon itself. New highways are built. Then everywhere parking must be expanded to many acres, many floors, or under parks, and over stores—always in or near the most desirable parts of town. A motor ideal is expressed at Macy's in Queens, where its multilevel circular store is surrounded by a 2,000-vehicle parking garage. Ever so steadily the new highways and parking facilities separate one activity from another, making the car ever more necessary.

The scale, character, value, and behavior of every part of the city inexorably rises from man to motorcar. In the end, the life-size City of Man becomes the Motor Megalopolis. The environment is recast for two tons, 425 horsepower, and 70 mph. The simple walkway is narrowed, diverted, or blocked. The integrity of the automobile prevails over that of the pedestrian, the neighborhood, the school, the (public) park.

The Iron Law brings about an organic redevelopment of the city, responding in progressive cycles to the automobile and reinforcing the auto's sovereignty. Nevertheless, the Law could not operate in its later, more oppressive cycles without the active political and propagandistic support of the powerful organizations the automobile has brought into being. For example, the Asphalt Institute can openly promote what it calls the "Magic Circle" in its effort to propel autocracy to greater triumphs. The Magic Circle reads thus: "More tax $$ Build → More Roads Encourage → More Travel Sells → More Gas Yields → More Tax $$ Build → . . ." And so the wheel turns.

Automobility—particularly in cities—entrenches itself in concrete, monopolizes movement, then congeals it, makes every roadway a barricade, reduces choice, hogs resources, increases costs, ravages the landscape, endangers and oppresses the pedestrian, boxes and deforms the body, contaminates the breath of life, enrages the ears, insults the eyes, makes an automaton of the nervous system, puts every citizen nearer the clutches of the law, denies casual association, rigorizes organization, distorts public purpose, and dulls the human sensibilities. Oh, yes, and it kills half a million people each decade and maims millions more.

Known by its effects, the automobile is tyrannous. Its power has become autocratic.

Autocracy Takes Over

Country Life magazine was not merely prophetic in 1913 when it observed that "civilization is adapting itself to the motor car, not the motor car to civilization." It was witness to a blind willingness to let the automobile take society wherever it would. We have seen its rise to power. From the earliest days the power grew on a perverse interplay between willingness and necessity, benefit and destruction.

Someday we will wonder why society ever permitted the coup. Up until 1910, even 1920, the American city was reasonably unified, compact, and vigorous. Rapid transit was healthy, expanding, and advancing in technology.

Then, about World War I, profound changes began to take place. By insidious advantages and a short circuit in public reasoning the automobile cornered the popular concept of progress. In 1920 the National Automobile Chamber of Commerce was already gloating that 34 percent of all auto usage was in substitution for the streetcar or railroad. Transit services faded and its influence on urban form dropped precipitously, when it might have held the city together.

All along, the auto interests have pointed to the car's speed, door-to-door flexibility, and versatility as the reasons for its overwhelming "choice" over all other forms of transportation. Powerful evidence, but it is superficial and loaded. Even the auto apologist *Fortune* admitted in 1961 that the American "has for years been presented with a market heavily rigged in favor of using his own car in city traffic."

The heavily rigged market and the short-circuited public reasoning involve—besides interest-group maneuvers—a pragmatic trap. The first is the famous out-of-pocket rationale: Here the car owner figures only his out-of-pocket expense, not the total costs, when deciding whether to drive or take a bus or train to work. The car is a little more expensive, but the convenience of driving seems to outweigh the added expense. So he abandons public transit in favor of auto commuting.

The trap is not immediately apparent. It is based on private decisions, which multiply rapidly. Then, when congestion sets in, the public problem has its built-in special interest group. The problem demands response and the interest groups see that it dominates public policy. Each city seeks to relieve the mushrooming pressure. But the relief then merely opens the floodgates.

The effect is as if each commuter suddenly required the scarce transport space of twenty-five men to get to work, forgetting parking space. Already by 1925, a writer in *Atlantic* reported that "this tremendous demand for more street room has compelled numerous and expensive street widenings—imposing a heavy burden on the general taxpayer, of which the railroads and trolley companies are among the very largest." Public policy is forced in the long run to make a regular subsidy to chaos, directly in transportation, indirectly in all civic life.

And the trap is progressive, with endless ramifications. Once habituated to car commuting the driver may decide to move to the suburbs after calculating that the time and cost do not increase nearly as much as the additional commuting distance. But this time the private decision also has a private bite. The family is far more isolated. They soon find it *necessary* to buy a second automobile. Dependence upon the automobile thus becomes more absolute.

Family specialization is magnified. Mother becomes chauffeur for pre-drivers. Driving age then becomes the "birth of freedom." Trips and distances expand in proportion. A 1950's study in Detroit revealed that families living within three miles of downtown made 3.6 auto trips daily, while those beyond twelve miles made 8.0 trips daily.

Within a few years congestion envelopes suburbia as well. Instead of traffic relief costing $100,000 per mile for widening a boulevard, the public is forced to pay from $5 million to $50 million per mile for urban freeways. Then it becomes necessary for every department store to increase prices to build a massive garage. Factories must double their parking. At home, the longer sewer, water, gas, and electric lines cost more—and these are usually subsidized by the inner-city residents. Milk delivery has its hidden subsidy. The post office must use more vehicles and assign more manpower to deliver every suburban letter.

The scheme is self-defeating. Victor Gruen has reported that in Milwaukee the automobile has shifted to a new level of destruction. As elsewhere, it first replaced other means of entering downtown for large numbers of people. But in recent years auto congestion and parking demands have so weakened the center that the number of people entering downtown by auto has begun to drop off as well. *Fortune* itself noted the self-defeating nature of automobiles in the city, saying that "it would never be possible to provide parking space in the largest cities for all the motorists who want them. There wouldn't be anything left worth coming to."

For every person and every city the trap is like that described in a story by Jack London, a baited, sharp-pointed knife protruding from a depression in a log. When a hungry mountain lion bites at the meat he cuts his mouth. He licks at his own blood and slashes his tongue. Lapping up the rising flow of blood he slashes it again and again. The faster he works the more blood he loses. Soon his energy is sapped and he falls, still trying to drink his own blood.

Any authority without bonds to automobility will tell you that the only artery capable of sustaining a metropolis is rapid transit. Wilfred Owen, the Brookings expert—after noting that from 1955 to 1965 motor cars increased by twenty-four million while transit patronage dropped by 25 percent—has asked "whether it is possible to be urbanized and motorized and at the same time civilized."

"*But transit? Impossible! Never in your life*" (Notice how our reactions are compulsively conditioned to the bloodletting automobile.)

The subway-gray reputation of transit has its reasons, of course. For over a half-century it has remained undeveloped, underfed, and shackled. The fact that it returned to carry an unprecedented burden in World War II, despite severe handicaps, only contributes to its bad memories. And the bad memories reinforce equally bad logic.

Capacities illustrate the addictive unreality. An ordinary street lane can serve about 300 cars per hours, but auto passengers are never likely to exceed 600. A freeway lane may serve 1,500 cars in a peak hour, but commuters there are not likely to rise above 2,500. Even a humble streetcar track could carry five times as many. Express subway trains are rated at 60,000 persons per hour per track—twenty-four times the freeway lane. (The Japanese estimate that one of their tracks can carry 120,000 persons, and say that 40 lanes of freeway would be required to serve as many people—not to speak of parking—but we will not press this case against autocracy.)

Americans spent $1.8 billion for local public transport in both 1941 and 1963, while motorcar expenditures nearly tripled, rising from $13.2 to $38.3 billion. Nor is a change in sight. In 1967 *Fortune* was confident about motordom: "As the U.S. prospers, Americans consume more space and therefore require more transport. Transportation needs in general are expanding, but the auto market is not simply growing along with other types of surface transportation—it is growing faster."

Of all the forces of autocratic conquest working against transit, the explosion of urban space and dispersion of people throughout whole regions is most basic. The car came on the scene when the American city was growing most rapidly, and quickly took command over the form of that growth. When everything is built for cars, everyone must drive cars. Even buses, the conqueror's compromise, must operate over longer routes and drive as many miles for fewer riders, while suffering extreme inefficiency necessitated by heavy burdens at peak hours and emptiness at all others.

The power of auto conquest is on every side. While the federal government spent seventy-three cents of its transportation dollar on highways in 1967, only three cents served public transit.

Decline and Disorder

A free market supposedly balances the needs and desires of people with the means of providing for them. In 1910 a Mr. Edward Martin was concerned about "The Motor Craze," and put his thoughts in *The Outlook:* "People who have autos that they cannot afford soon find it out. This is a sort of miscalculation," Martin said confidently, "that is certain to set itself right."

There is a belief that the sum of private decisions equals the public good. Martin was confident that the free-market principle would set things right with the Motor Craze then ablaze in society. It has taken six decades for the automobile to demonstrate the dangerous flaw in a society where there is hard industrial promotion and easy civic leadership. One is unrelenting, the other passive. Thus, says Robert Heilbroner, "however dangerous, foolish, expensive, troublesome and inconvenient the car may be, all these demerits are far overshadowed by one consideration: The automobile has become indispensable."

Since the automobile is indispensable, it is a fallacy to talk about "choice" in mobility. There is no longer an option. And yet Federal Highway Administrator Francis Turner uses choice to justify an infinite extension of hard pavement: "People have chosen to live in suburbia and exurbia," observes Turner dispassionately, "and whether this is good or bad is not a matter for highway and traffic engineers to decide. However, we do have an obligation to fashion a transportation system that will accommodate the choice which the people have made."

A law has been observed to operate in urban transportation which makes certain that oppressive congestion occurs. Presented in a 1962 *Traffic Quarterly* by Dr. Anthony Downs, an economist, the law states: *"On urban commuter expressways, peak-hour traffic congestion rises to meet maximum capacity."* It reflects both the accumulation of conqueror's advantages in every part of the metropolis and the destructive incompatibility between automobiles and cities.

The best illustration occurs when a new freeway is built parallel to transit tracks. It first attracts substantial traffic from congested local streets. But its remaining capacity provides the alternative for transit commuters—many of whom must already drive to the station—of driving all the way downtown. Within a short time the freeway draws transit patrons up to its point of saturation. Because the city and the automobile have been rebuilding for each other for some time, transit loses its flexibility, service, and convenience. Transit therefore loses patronage as fast as the massive road subsidies add new freeway lanes.

The effect is highlighted between rush hours, when the freeway is relatively free of congestion. In those hours it attracts a larger percentage of the transit patrons, mainly shoppers and visitors. For example, the number of peak-hour inbound transit passengers entering Manhattan between 1948 and 1956 dropped by 11.7 percent. But in the other twenty-one hours the number of inbound passengers dropped 20.8 percent. Transit service thus becomes more sharply concentrated at the peak hours, when freeway capacity is most congested. Consequently the fewer riders reduce the total income of transit and its ability to operate efficiently. Transit's bread and water diet loses more of its bread.

This peak-hour relationship between the automobile and transit illuminates two fundamental conditions of American urban transportation. First, the automobile is directly responsible for transit's starvation diet and its half-century of technological non-advancement and non-expansion. We may specifically charge the automobile with the crowded transit in the morning and evening, as well as the mediocre service. With a fifty-year deficit of expansion and improvement resulting from auto diversion, what can one expect? But to someone suffering the consternation at being herded like cattle at peak hours, the crowding and rising fares seem to point only to bad transit management.

The second fundamental condition is that peak-hour loads carried by metropolitan transit protect auto movement by keeping traffic volumes always within a narrow range of "tolerable" congestion. The transit system has subtly changed its role; it has become a pressure valve that relieves the streets and highways and prevents a final breakdown from congestion. Otherwise Downs' Law is avoidable only with a system of freeways having such an enormous capacity that all commuters could use them at optimum speeds. Few highwaymen claim this is even possible.

Downs' Law has now been tacitly recognized by the highway establishment. This is seen by a moderation of attitude that sounds like objectivity, if not statesmanship. The highwaymen have actually begun to accept the fact that transit cannot be completely killed off. They know it will save them.

Observe the statesmanship of Mr. Turner, writing for *Petroleum Today* in 1967. "Enlightened opinion on both sides [of the highway-transit debate] holds that it is not an 'either/or question.'" It's a matter of balance, or modal split, between them. And what is Turner's "rule of thumb" for public policy? ". . . for small cities, highways and cars; for medium-sized cities, highways and cars plus buses; and in a relatively few cases, rail rapid transit"—namely those already existing.

Evidently, according to Turner, the present system, based 95 percent on the auto, is not really far out of balance. The people, then, can go on freely making a lemming's choice of the automobile and the highway. That's the way freedom of choice has been routed since the Motor Craze got underway.

"Yet," continues the highway administrator, "some groups are still proposing to install [new] rail rapid transit, which is the least flexible of all systems, in cities lacking the population densities required for economic feasibility." The reasoning is simple. Having rebuilt the city to its inhuman scale the automobile now requires its inhuman raceways to span the distances.

Despite Turner's advice, some metropolitan areas like San Francisco and Washington, D.C., are constructing new rapid transit systems with a technology surpassing 1920. But having to span the automobile's urban sprawl, the routing is far less than desirable. And Turner may be pleased in the end, for the transit lines in both cases are double rather than four-track systems. They compromise between local and express service, and *cannot* provide either to full satisfaction. Freedom of choice is not greatly enlarged: very few persons in either metropolis will be relieved of the *necessity* of car ownership (though some may be able to avoid a second car). Yet these basically modern, fast, and efficient systems will accommodate very large peak loads, thereby protecting the highways from collapsing of their own monstrosity.

What the new systems are likely to do is demonstrate Downs' Law with a new twist. Whereas freeways have been constructed as the vanguard of assaults on public transport—and civic sanity —the new transit lines will enlarge the fail safe mechanism for autocracy. They could become a new special domain, a fourth automotive bastion, protecting autocracy at its most vulnerable point, the peak-hour loads. (Chicago's Congress Street Rapid Transit line symbolizes the captive role of transit, imprisoned as it is in the center strip of the Congress Street freeway.)

Nevertheless, transit systems may yet break loose from automotive captivity to become the vanguard of a new revolution to which society must dedicate itself for survival. The supreme test of transit, especially new and expanded systems, will be whether they can significantly influence the future form of urban growth. Can they stem the formless onrush desecrating cities? If they are able to start to do this—to give distinctiveness, centrality, efficiency and social form to urban existence—there may well be a surprising discovery: that transit has become flexible, versatile, convenient, and inexpensive for nearly all people for most urban travel.

Invertebrate Menace

To the extent that our civilization becomes dependent upon the automobile we reduce ourselves and our character of mind to a new species of being, a society of invertebrates as clumsy as a convention of turtles. The way we honor our new shells makes one wonder whether we have an atavistic urge to junk our whole mammalian inheritance.

Men daily lock themselves into their padded isolation shells of steel and subject themselves to rigid and lonely queue discipline. The piston of traffic daily takes them by implosions and explosions to and from the city center. Neither man nor city is any longer organic. They are a mechanism united and separated by force. While the movement follows an old routine of earth and sun the effect is that of a forge and its stampings, not a rhythm of life.

The forge crushes down upon men: It draws the law-abiding into conflict with the law. It regiments the nervous system. It is a tyranny of examination and licensing, registration and insurance. It presents experts with their most varied and regular grip upon men. It dominates many family budgets, often surpassing food or lodging, or a child. The car raises the American's deepest fears of violent death. The morbid death predictions, death counts, and skull-and-crossbone cartoons flowing from the newspapers convert every holiday into an omen of highway catastrophe.

The sheer penetration of vehicles into the minutia of life demands a flattening conformity. A congestion and pressure of daily routine arises from the interminable urban scattering the auto has created. Behavior is reduced to functions organized by trips. Casual and purposeful activities intermingle less freely. Friendship must be forced into existence, and is therefore spasmodic and brittle. Feelings of friendship are guarded, formal, shallow, and suspected of either compulsion or ulterior interest. And the more men become dependent upon the auto for their linkages, the more these tendencies are accented.

Together the burdens, restrictions, and penalties make conditions ripe for social inflammations: inexplicable delinquency, neuroticism, protest, and riot. Of course the automobile does not work alone. It is but a part of a more fundamental exploitiveness of resources, regions, cities, neighborhoods, and people. How many thousands of neighborhoods have been divided and bulldozed in the name of automobility? How much easier is it to spend $10 million for one mile of freeway through vital living areas than to raise $10,000 (one-tenth of 1 percent) for a first project of neighborhood improvement?

Plans, improvements, integrity, and power all flow to the highway. As every city on the interstate system knows, there "is no local option. It's you do it—or else. . . ." But when the mayors go to Washington for help in the urban crisis, observed a prominent redevelopment official, "they are characterized as wild-eyed spenders, grubbing for a handout and evading their own responsibilities."

These are the taproots of the inflammations. Grudgingly we recognize a slum problem, then apply limited means for limited and mediocre results. Simultaneously, and on a scale dwarfing the renewal, we promote bad housing and bad neighborhoods in isolation wards of the auto-spread city with massive highway subsidies. Nothing compares with the motorcar in the harm it does to every cell of urban living or in the depression it imposes on the qualities of life.

A doctor might diagnose the urban condition as an inflammation of circulation. A psychiatrist might hypothesize that man had found a way to act out his alienation wish—the death wish held in suspension. But the politician instinctively knows the condition is simply a result of the new citizenship of the motorcar. Political power has responded to it with particular sensitivity for two generations.

The motor citizen soon will be able to travel cross-country without stopping for a red light. The man afoot will not do as well walking one mile across his own town. Giant shopping centers are made accessible only by car; they brag of a half-acre pedestrian mall, although forty out of fifty acres are a desolation of blacktop. Downtown there are massive mechanized parking garages but rarely a public plaza, fountain, seat, or restroom.

The growth of motorized citizenship and autocratic power is revealed in the transitional role of the Great American Strip. First, downtown enterprises began to relocate, to line up along major streets for easier access by motorcars, rather than for pedestrian convenience, as formerly. This was the stage of democratic disintegration. It was necessary, for the auto obviously needed to break up the old human scale of urban living before it could command proper attention to its own requirements, or develop its own pattern of integration.

Of course, the old strip-commercial boulevards were inefficient and dangerous, especially when attempting to fulfill all kinds of movement and shopping functions. That threatened the full psychic commitment required for autocracy. However, once the boulevard had accomplished its basic task of disintegrating the democratic scale of the city, the unprecedented wealth and space required to achieve full automotive control and integrity became a comparatively minor hurdle. After that the autocratic reintegration could take place in the shopping center, the industrial district, and, naturally, the freeway. Then the elimination of the old democratic right of universal access to highways, with which there could be no freeways, was also a minor effort. Reintegration in the freeway would respect what Lewis Mumford calls America's "worship for speed and empty spaces."

Yet, despite the reintegration, the Great American Strip today remains a vigorous symbol of the city's transmutation to a medium of mobility. The Strips remain vigorous because the freeway was unable to give necessary access and the shopping center proved incapable of accommodating the full range of commerce. So the Strip continued to provide the access to land and the variety in shopping. In the end the automobile not only got the freeways for moving and the shopping centers for parking, but permanently retained the eclectic commercial Strips —the flesh wounds where the civic bloodletting began and still continues.

Both the boulevard and the freeway demonstrate again the ingenious and deceptive trap sequence always posed by automobility. First, there is the deep attraction of the automobile, with its immediate benefits and unquenchable prestige. Then pressures arise, and the automobile itself seems to answer its own demands. In the end the price is fierce, though each step always seems to be within reason.

With its ability to create pressures and to apparently relieve them, automobility establishes and maintains a vision of autopia in the public mind, whatever the reality of events. It is this interplay between heaven and hell that sets society's course toward autocracy. It is this rhythm of enclosure and release that make men grateful to their jailers, serfs loyal to their lords.

Civic Liability

It is now plainly apparent that the motor vehicle is not a system of transportation at all. What is really closer to the truth is that the car has effectively compelled society to establish a system of transportation to carry vehicles instead of men or goods. The whole burden of mobility has been reconstructed and multiplied. This is to be expected from the car's emergence as society's leading citizen.

The interesting feature of the transformation is that the handicap of the automobile is so fearsomely bad that it has had to be suppressed in economic circles. While experts press home the argument that freeways are three to five times more efficient per lane for moving vehicles than ordinary thoroughfares, they rarely point out that rapid transit can be twenty to thirty times more efficient than a freeway for moving persons. Automobiles are thus terribly extravagant brokers between man and free mobility.

Why is such an abysmal civic liability tolerated? It is simply because our superior economic system requires major economic handicaps such as the automobile to function properly. The problem arises because for over a century the marriage of competitive industrial organization and science has created a phenomenal productivity. Society simply must find a way to resolve enormous competitive productivity with full employment.

Society resolves the dilemma like this: Any single organization in the economy must be efficient, or at least appear so to its board of directors or stockholders. But for the society as a whole this idea is reversed. Social waste is necessary to overcome organizational efficiency and productivity. We prefer to waste through the operation of the free market and intensive corporate promotion, but we also heavily support organization for waste by government agencies. Social inefficiency and waste are ideals of the establishment, since they contribute to both production and consumption. That is why they can exist comfortably alongside the ideal of efficiency. In fact, there are many companies and public agencies, each operating to their maximum internal efficiency, that exist wholly to perpetuate and amplify this larger social inefficiency.

The system expands corporate profits and boosts statistics of gross national product. Capitalist doctrine is reconciled and the old bugaboo of depressions is avoided. The need for social inefficiency is the reason why economists feel they should suppress information about the economics of automobility. The need for inefficiency also helps explain the rise of automotive citizenship.

Cars are near-perfect means to perpetuate social waste. They have a profound appeal to men, and can be promoted through advertising having nothing to do with transportation. Their numbers are unlimited so long as they can transform the pattern of cities to their own scale and to their wasteful requirements. Finally, since automobiles are not susceptible to a final satisfactory transportation solution, they present increasingly weighty problems for the corporations and the whole society to strive to overcome by ingenious applications of technology.

Hence auto producers are now able to continually improve their internal efficiency and still be assured of growing profits. So can oil companies, highway contractors, and the emerging parking industry. Profits remain high, capitalism secure.

Here, then, is a theoretic basis for autocracy in American life. It may be summarized succinctly in three related propositions: (1) America is a country with a tradition of continental conquest, ritualized daily in successfully completing the journey to work. (2) America is a country where civic action takes place as private action breaks down, that is, where controlled chaos is the limit of the civic ideal. (3) With a large population, vast lands, rich resources, and huge productive capacities, America creates outrageous problems and tackles them with outrageous solutions.

2

AUTOCRATIC FORCES
OF CONQUEST

Detroit's Doctrine of Destruction

PLAINLY, the modern corporation has become addicted to the endlessly rising expectation of success and new profits. The successes are accompanied, of course, by radical social changes, and these spawn sweeping problems for the whole society. Consequently the struggle for social readjustment calls for unprecedented public expenditures generating new rounds of economic expansion—and new levels of profit. The result is prosperity amidst crisis.

No mechanism is more effective in this process of economic expansion than the automobile. The corporation has discovered that the automobile is a much better tool for social and economic engineering than for transportation. Someday society is bound to make the same discovery.

But how did it all come about? First, a huge initial success (1900–1920) made immense demands upon society for highways.

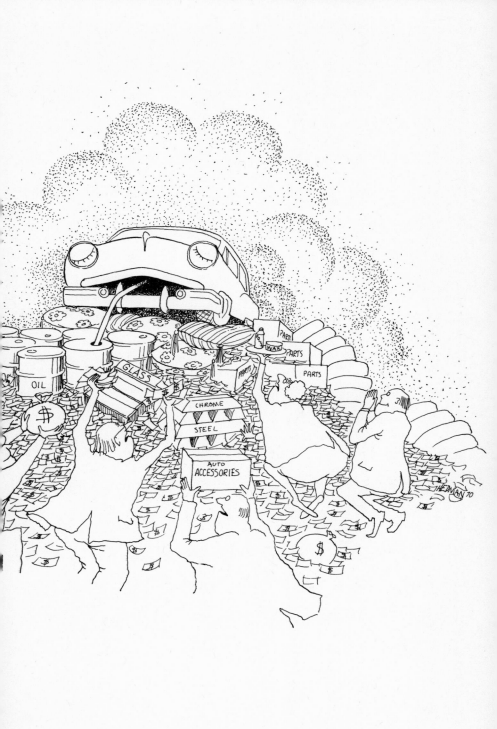

Second, the fulfillment of those demands and a new round of success (1920–1940) created profound problems of congestion and parking. Third, the responses to these problems and another round of success (1945–1970) have in turn created problems of maintaining simple mobility, improving auto safety, reducing air pollution, and facing incredibly complex crises of urban life.

Undeniably the automobile is an historic masterpiece of social engineering; it has taken our whole society for a ride in the rumble seat. Admittedly Detroit was fortunate. At the outset the social and economic environment was just right. Road and parking congestion problems arose by small stages; they didn't mature so rapidly that they might backfire against automobility. Similarly, the automobile was usable in the city even while destroying it for man.

Nonetheless, the engineering was a complex affair and required a fully accommodating rationality. The foundation was simple popularity. According to the *Annals of the American Academy* in 1924, the automobile "contributes to the happiness of the human race far beyond anything that has ever been produced before. . . ." That was the objective conclusion at the very end of the era of youthful exuberance.

A decade later the depression would create an economic rationale. "Last year," said *Collier's* in 1937, "not less than 6,225,-000 Americans had jobs because of the automobile. That is something in any nation's economy." It was something, commanding as it did nearly one job in seven.

Whether in boom or depression the automobile steadily became important to Americans more for the power it added to the economy than for the contribution it made to transportation. Paul Hoffman, president of Studebaker, expressed in 1947 the prevailing logic of automobility: ". . . the motor vehicle, together with the roadway it uses, has become a basic condition of our *future* progress. The United States must have expanding highway transportation if we are to maintain an expanding economy."

This marks the transformation from a new freedom to a binding conformity. The automobile was at first merely a plaything. But men rapidly discovered its marvelous range of utility, its happy get-up-and-go versatility. When utility led to widespread use, the car was then viewed in terms of the prosperity it bestowed on the economy. And when the car became a necessity, belief in automobility shifted, with the blessing of the industrialists, to the economic importance of the new necessity. Thus it was easy to rationalize the deep destructive thrusts of the automobile into all urban life.

What is the special character of this new conformity in social thinking? For some six decades the prevailing belief behind automobility focused upon its contribution to prosperity. If measured by the sheer weight of automotive employment the "contribution" is indeed great. In 1968 nearly 15 million Americans were working directly or indirectly to support the automobile—one-fifth of all wage-earners. And given another thirty years of continued progress the auto establishment could grow and require one-fourth or possibly one-third of all workers in society. Of course, this would also add mightily to the gross national product.

The economic persuasiveness of auto rationality is fully matched by its raw political power. At the top of the ladder, close to the heart of public decision, the automobile accounts for eleven out of the twenty-two largest American manufacturers (seven petroleum, three auto, one rubber). At the bottom of the ladder, close to the grass roots of decision in every city and town, 823,000 enterprises are also automotive—one-sixth of all American businesses. When automobility has its claws both upon the center of power and at the grass roots few economists or politicians are going to question the place (or the gross excesses) of automobiles in society. Political prospects and business prosperity are too dependent upon the motorcar.

Now, given the auto's importance in maintaining and expanding prosperity, it then becomes possible for the auto propagandists to persuade public authorities to construct highways and parking facilities on the basis of *savings* that would result *for the automobile*. That propaganda has risen to an elaborate, analytical science from the simple surveys that could prove that better roads in Iowa were worth $2,432 per section of land.

Once the country was out of the mud the same economics could then be applied to getting out of the muddle. The fact that the muddle originated with the automobile did not matter.

When the role of the automobile is unimpeachable the case for highway investment is watertight, forming a closed system of logic. Thus in 1956 Richard Zettel, California's master highway economist, calculated that $775 million spent on 185 miles of freeway (at $4.2 million per mile) would amortize itself in seven years through savings to motorists and truckers on such items as fuel, brakes, depreciation, etc. By similar calculations others figured that the John F. Kennedy freeway in Chicago would conserve .013 gallons of gasoline per travel mile, for a total annual fuel saving of $478,000.

The closed logic in economics could apply more tellingly in accident prevention. All along the experts claimed that good roads reduced accidents. The California Division of Highways claimed in 1968 that the state's freeways were saving 800 lives and $215 million in accident costs per year because freeways kill people at a lower rate per million vehicle miles. The state chamber of commerce made this boast when the loss of life due to automobility in the state was rising faster than during any period since the 1920's (despite a billion-dollar annual highway budget) and when the national accident industry counted an annual turnover of $15 billion. The reason, of course, is that freeways assure that there will be many more millions of vehicle miles.

Only occasionally does anyone point to one of the many basic flaws in the logic of Detroit, as, for example, in 1952, when *American City* magazine suggested that "in a way, the traffic authorities' absorption in trying to handle happily all the cars spawned from month to month and year after year is faintly like a doctor trying to maintain and expand a fever." Such criticisms, made hesitantly and failing to gain popular appreciation, could be easily ignored.

Detroit and Its GHQ

Weakness of doctrine never deterred the Generals of Detroit from attack. One of their most able and articulate front-line strategists (and yet one of the few to suffer defeat in recent times) was William Zeckendorf. In a 1953 address before the Economic Club of Detroit he put the hard but crucial question of conquest on the line: ". . . we have to make up our minds," said Zeckendorf, "either to redesign the cities to cope with the situation, or to eliminate the use of cars in cities—one or the other. It's just a question of which is the more expensive." Of course, the elimination of cars was not a serious proposition because the living quality of the city was not the question. But economic expansion was at stake. It would be unthinkable to permit the city to exist without making enormous expenditures to derange it for automobility.

For decades most autocrats had merely lamented the fact that "cities and their street layouts were designed for the most part before the requirements of the new vehicle were visualized." Although its field forces were succeeding in undermining the city far better than Detroit knew, here was a clear and decisive plan to attack the last urban defenses and to prepare the cities for complete motor occupation. Yet, Detroit hardly needed the advice. Despite the failure to formulate effective strategies, its field commanders in every state and city continued to fumble ahead with great momentum.

Planning cities solely for the advantage of transportation was not new, of course. Leonardo da Vinci had conceived of towns with buildings whose roofs formed the roadways. In Spain, Arturo Soria y Mata devised a Linear City in the 1880's in which urban development would be stretched along transportation lines until it formed a complete European net. In 1911 Edgard Chambless published *Roadtown,* a da Vinci idea upside down, in which a city would be built in one structure over the complete length of transportation lines.

The theory in each case was to huddle the city close to the advantages of transportation. However, the old concept was completely reversed by the automobile, which dispersed the city all over the countryside. The clearest notion of urban scattering as an ideal was developed in 1932 by Frank Lloyd Wright. His Broadacre City was a systematic working model of Henry Ford's expressed desire to abandon cities. Wright proposed to scatter people on acre sites hither and yon. His debt to wheels is clear, if not grandiloquent: "What greater, nobler agent has Culture or Civilization than the great Open Road made safe and beautiful for continually flowing traffic when it is a harmonious part of the great whole?" Broadacre City, which guaranteed isolation and absolute dependence upon the automobile, thus made credible the anti-city that has been realized in suburban sprawl.

So when the automotive muddle began to be acutely pressing, the automotive establishment was roused again to active leadership. It had not been very active since it sponsored the "seedling miles" in 1913–1916, which spurred the country to lift itself out of the mud. First, General Motors commissioned Norman Bel Geddes to plan its Futurama exhibit for the 1939 New York World's Fair. He did well for GM; Futurama drew 5 million visitors. The people were attracted, said Geddes in *Magic Motorways* in 1940, because his future city was "a visual dramatization of a solution to the complex tangle of American roadways." Geddes himself was acutely aware, of course, that "the city and its traffic have become rival elements" in which the "result was stalemate."

In a stalemate between traffic and the city, the city would have to give way. So Geddes set out to break the stalemate by restructuring the city—and the entire continent—around a system of super freeways with separate roadways for traffic moving at designated speeds of 50, 75, and 100 miles per hour. The urban commuting radius could then stretch 100 miles or so from the center. According to a 1943 reviewer, Geddes "appeared to assign more than three fourths of the land area to roads and their auxiliaries." Even at that he did not make sufficient allocations of land for the corollary buildup of parking and automotive services. His failure to reckon with the auto's destructiveness of the inner city was matched by a blindness to the sprawl that such a fantasy of mobility would incite.

In 1956 the Ford Motor Company made its pitch for leadership in a giant publication revealing the wonders of automobility. A battery of writers sought to enlist popular support which might guarantee the motorcar's fullest development and progress at a time when the new, expensive Interstate highway construction program was in the offing. The book was called *Freedom of the American Road,* according to Henry Ford II, "simply because we Americans always have liked plenty of elbow room—freedom to come and go as we please in this big country of ours." Apparently Ford was worried a bit—possibly as Futurama revealed at GM—about the automotive muddle putting that freedom in danger.

Detroit has, of course, always had its varied unpaid irregular forces. Less frequently does it receive the services of a volunteer general like Lawrence Halprin, a landscape architect from San Francisco (home of the original freeway revolt). Halprin, who strives to be a freeway critic, has evolved an aesthetic theory of motion to make freeways into a civic art. They can be, he says, "a great adventure in choreography," involving movement quality, character, speed, and other elements. Without doubt, with Halprin to handle enlistments from the art community, a new battalion will be added to the ranks of autocracy.

But Halprin is not commissioned by the Detroit hierarchy, whose theories of conquest all boil down to how much automobility can be sold, not to utility, certainly not to aesthetic principles. How can freeway choreography help sell more freeways and open the automotive floodgates another notch? Of course, the foundation for selling has changed radically over the years, like all things automotive. In the elder Henry Ford's heyday the principle requirements so successfully built into the Model T were durability and a popular price. When GM took the lead in the 1920's a dramatic shift took place: advertising, credit finance, a span of models to cover and penetrate the whole range of the market, and especially the annual model change. That, said Alfred P. Sloan, changed the mass market into a mass-class market. His colleague Charles Kettering put the reason succinctly: "The simplest way to assure safe production is to keep changing the product—the market for new things is indefinitely elastic."

Later, both Ford and GM responded to the highway problem, indicating that it was a bottleneck of selling. Thus another crucial though subtle turn was indicated in expanding the scale of automotive selling. It could be, then, that Lawrence Halprin (like Ralph Nader and his safety crusade) may now be demonstrating to the aging and lethargic auto establishment how to meet the critical new turn required for selling—highways that are sold like car styles.

Over the years the market was stretched as fast as the economy could be squeezed and cities could be split open to accommodate more cars. In 1955 Chrysler President Lester Colbert, speaking to the U.S. Chamber of Commerce, could be guardedly optimistic, predicting that "by 1975 the one-car family could be in the minority—and a large proportion of families may be using three or more cars. All of us feel optimistic about the long range prospect for the economy—but at the same time we all recognize that there is no ironclad guarantee that it will go right on becoming stronger and stronger. . . . All of this means that American business has its work cut out for it."

After the confident fifties some anxiety began to appear among the generals. In 1962, James Roche, soon to become president at GM and famous for hiring private detectives to harass and trip up Ralph Nader, became worried about the effect of the traffic muddle on the automobile market. In a piece called "The Public Prefers the Automobile," he trenchantly observed that "the market will expand greatly *if* we achieve the better environment for driving that is necessary to maintain the automobile's utility and appeal at a high level." The improved driving environment wasn't better choreography or a grand parkway for a Sunday outing. It was serious, nasty problems like safety and congestion.

But what disturbed Roche more than the problems themselves was the fact that some people were using these problems for propaganda to promote rapid transit. "This campaign," he said, "rejects the principle of a balanced urban transportation system. . . . It is therefore important that there be vigorous opposition to this reactionary movement. There are two ways to do so. One is to refute fallacious arguments against automobile use in cities. The other is to support urban traffic measures that will better accommodate the automobile."

Despite a continuation of good times for auto production, the Detroit generals kept finding critics in the woods who did not seem to feel that balanced transportation meant cars and buses, highways and parking. Henry Ford II, like Roche, tried hard to convince himself that breaking the city open and dispersing it with mobility was really a very popular endeavor. Said Ford plaintively to the Young Men's Business Club in New Orleans in 1966, "When so many people buy our products, the automobile industry must be doing something right."

Ford felt that the industry was obliged to help solve the safety, pollution, and congestion problems, especially if that would make it easier for Americans "to live with" the automobile. But the deeper problem for Ford was the hostile critics who, against the public interest, can get bad proposals adopted, just as long as they are anti-automobile. And these "critics would have us believe that the automobile is a monster that has run out of control and taken over our lives."

Now that the city had been ballooned to the scale and performance of automobiles and the people were dependent on automobility in both body and mind, Ford could confidently wield the weapons of democracy in the service of autocracy. Thus his argument continued: "Some of our critics seem to feel that the government should plan cities and transportation to reflect their own conception of the ideal city, regardless of what people prefer. This is nonsense. . . . As far as urban transportation is concerned, what people want is clear. They have voted overwhelmingly in favor of the automobile. . . . The purpose of metropolitan planning is . . . to develop better ways of giving people what they do want and are willing to pay for."

Naturally there were reservations, familiar reservations that guard automobility from the fatal flaws like total immobility. These Ford summarized: "In our larger cities, public transit is essential to help meet peak commuter demands. It is also essential to provide adequate mobility within downtown areas and service for those who cannot drive or cannot afford a car."

Here, then, is the auto establishment applying its formula of social engineering to achieve bigger corporate profits that sow more massive civic problems. The profits and the problems are a closed-circuit system aimed at endless expansion and unlimited success. The doctrine has solid footing in American traditions of both economics and politics. As Ford said, "sometimes people vote with their dollars; sometimes with ballots." This interplay between dollars and ballots is commanded by the auto-industrial complex and forms the basis of its techniques of social engineering. It is the free interplay that helps blind the American to the destruction and leaves him to suffer, to be wounded and killed. But he is stoic in the face of the conquest.

War Chest

Financing the growth of autocracy is a truly awesome saga in financial history. The story is little known. It is not yet finished. Its significance is not appreciated, even where democracy is still openly defended.

Most expenditures for automobility are private. They amounted to some $130 billion in 1968 (more than the national income of West Germany). Since most of the dollars are spent out of necessity they are hardly the ballots for automobility claimed by young Henry II. But neither are they the crucial dollars that make autocracy absolute.

The growth capital expanding the fortunes of automobility are precisely the government funds spent year in and year out for highways and parking. These buy the rights of way, construct the roadways, build overpasses, push back the sidewalks, install massive electronic control mechanisms, subsidize parking expansion. They do all things essential to increase human dependence upon wheels.

The phenomenon of public finance for automobility may be illustrated in California, the "most motor-wise state in the union," according to Arthur Pound, writing in a 1938 *Atlantic*. The story there began in 1909, when Governor Hiram Johnson told the newly appointed State Highway Commission, "you are expected to build with eighteen million dollars a highway system that some of the best engineers have estimated will cost from thirty-five to fifty millions." From then on California's estimated needs would always surpass the accumulating capital investment.

Thirty-five years later (in wartime 1944, when the annual highway budget was $18 million) the state's Division of Highways listed $700 million in highway needs, in addition to regular construction, "to provide an adequate highway system." When war pressures had subsided in 1947 Governor Warren called a special session of the legislature (telling them it was "human nature" to want good highways) to act on a report calling for $2.4 billion in new construction within ten years—nearly twice that which the State had spent on highways until then. As a result the yearly budget increased from $42 million in 1946 to $98 million in 1948.

But in 1952, five years and $500 million later, another report estimated that $3.4 billion would be required over fifteen years "to bring the entire [state] highway system up to tolerable standards." Accordingly a second 1½-cent addition was made to the gasoline tax, making it six cents, and the annual highway budgets jumped up into the range of $250 million per year.

Now it happened that one of the auto establishment's most capable provincial commanders was State Senator Randolph Collier, long-term chairman of the legislative joint committee on highways, known for the fastest gavel in the West and as the Father of the California Freeway System. Nor was it a coincidence that the Automotive Safety Foundation, a body created and supported by the auto-makers and accessory industries, was called upon to prepare the 1947 and 1952 highway needs reports. Through the Foundation the auto industry thus became a trusted advisor to a great state on the matter of automotive expansion.

Then in 1958 the Foundation was again called in, this time to plan a statewide freeway system. That system—12,250 miles and equal to that planned for all of Western Europe by 1968— would by 1980 put a freeway within 1.5 miles of nearly every resident in the city of Los Angeles and five miles of almost everybody in the state except those in a few ghost towns, logging camps, and cattle ranches. That system was a mighty coup: It extended "planned access control . . . to the entire state," said the Foundation proudly. And it opened the state to another quarter-century of rapid autocratic development.

Despite Collier's admission in 1955 that the state was making "huge expenditures" for highways, the new freeway plan of 1958 was billed at a suspiciously low figure of $10.5 billion. When he looked back at the accomplishments of 1947 and 1953, Collier recalled in 1959 that it "seemed as if we had been standing still. The plain fact is . . . that highway transportation continued to be hazardous, frustrating, and uneconomical. It was clear that the legislature must intensify its efforts and devise a new departure." The new departure, the freeway plan, would have to respond to estimates that congested 1958 traffic would triple before 1980. Thus, Collier continued, "we should look upon the proposed freeway system as the *first step* in the development of new concepts of highway management and finance in California." (Italics added.) And it was entirely appropriate, too, that Collier should quote Daniel Burnham's famous line: "Make no little plans—they have no magic to stir men's blood. . . ."

Well, by 1967 annual state highway expenditures were running to their first billion. More than $200 million was being spent merely for rights of way, $70 million for maintenance, and $75 million for enforcement and safety. But, as we have seen, the highway needs for 1975–1958 jumped to $23 billion—1,277 times larger than Governor Hiram Johnson's first program almost sixty years earlier.

California's story is not exceptional. The auto's grip penetrates too deeply into the political economy to permit much regional variation. At the end of World War II the American Association of State Highway Officials estimated that necessary improvements on all state highway systems required $11 billion. Then, in 1955, just prior to enactment of the $101 billion highway program (inaugurating the interstate highways), a report to Congress estimated the highway needs for thirty years after 1955 at $297 billion dollars. However, in 1968 the state highway officials testified before Congress that highway needs during the ten years from 1975 to 1985 were $285 billion. A comparable amount was asked, but within only one-third the time, despite many tens of billions spent on the system in the meanwhile. To underscore the reasonableness of their position, the state highway officials made a qualification: "However, should, for any reason, it be decided that the highway program be expanded, the justification for such expansion is well established and justified. . . ."

It is necessary to clarify the meaning of $285 billion. That is a figure to declare war on: it is nearly equal to the cost of World War II and two-thirds of the present national debt. Those dollars would build five interstate systems with a mileage equal to all existing American railroad lines, though the four-to-eight lanes make most rail lines appear like cow trails. Then too, an annual expenditure of $28.5 billion is twenty-three times more than was

spent in the good highway construction year of 1929.

Today the sky is dark with billions of dollars in highway escalation. The original 41,000-mile interstate program was a mere tactical starting maneuver. "Probably the most effective way to introduce the public to the safety, convenience, and economy of modern highways," claimed A. E. Johnson, an executive of the American Association of State Highway Officials in 1956, "is to construct the vitally needed interstate system. Such action would provide a sample of modern highways, and . . . could spark a future road and street modernization on all systems and at all levels of government." Then, to leave no doubt, Mr. Johnson cautioned the autocrats: "The fact that many persons gathered the mistaken impression that the $101 billion needs figure was being proposed as an ambitious highway program confused the problem."

The specter of escalation (recalling the "seedling miles" campaign of 1913–1916) might be considered a fantasy were it not proven to be the shadow of the coming reality. How the highway funds have been developed and monopolized within constitutional and legislative fortresses is another melancholy tale of the automobile's sovereignty in society. The strategy has revolved around "highway user revenues."

Throughout the era of the automobile, general tax resources have contributed a significant amount to highway construction and maintenance, the major part in the earlier period. Up to 1919 the auto registration fees and drivers' licenses contributed no more than 5 percent of all highway construction funds. When Oregon led off with a tax on fuel that year, the highway-user revenue percentage began to climb, to 20 percent in 1925, to 37 in 1935, reaching 75 percent in 1965.

As the highway-user taxes gained in relative importance the autocrats began to make the case that fuel, licenses, and registration levies were really road-user "charges," not taxes at all. This meant that highways were achieving special status and independence, privileged over all other governmental services except education. In states where this concept became a statute the legislature lost or abdicated its responsibility to apply its total resources to the total burden of government. Moreover, the bottomless problems created by automobility—the urban transportation crisis, for example—created burdens far beyond the application of captive road-user taxes.

When legislatures exercised their total responsibility, allocating all available funds to all programs as judged most beneficial to the general welfare, the autocratic interest groups then claimed that *road funds* are "raided," "diverted," or "pirated." Those groups have been so effective that a majority of the states now have constitutional amendments prohibiting road taxes from all but road uses. Many other states follow the same rule out of the new necessity and the political power of the road interests.

Wiping out "diversion" of user levies wherever it appeared had its greatest triumph in 1956, with the creation of the Highway Trust Fund, which financed the interstate system. The fund guarantees all federal fuel tax revenues for road uses until the slightly expanded 42,500-mile system is complete. Though Congress deliberately made it temporary, the auto lobbies sought from the beginning to make the fund permanent. California's economic highwayman Richard Zettel confidently analyzed the breakthrough in 1956: "The entirely new approach to federal highway financing made explicit by the legislature," said Zettel, "will have an overriding significance as long as highway transportation is important in our economy. We are well on the road to a national system of major highways, nationally financed through user charges, a course from which we are not likely to retreat."

These measures of automotive privilege and power are clearly aimed at the future, when highway revenues will be a much larger part of all governmental revenues. They were hardly needed in the past. Only in recent years have user taxes become sufficient to independently finance the growth of automobility. As *Fortune* described the situation in 1955, the auto interests "like to blame the highway mess on 'diversion' of some $200 to $300 million a year . . . away from road use. However, they gloss over the fact that four or five times as much money is 'diverted' *to* road use from general revenues and property taxes."

Highways have always been "subsidized," almost completely at the outset. But when auto ownership passed 30 million, then 60, then 90, and when fuel taxes were increased, the constitutionally protected road funds gave the automobile a guaranteed momentum for growth. Not surprisingly the financiers of autocracy began to talk about giving up their general tax subsidies. Zettel could then easily say that "there appears to be no more reason to provide major highways on a social welfare basis than there would be to provide vehicles and fuel" to the motorist.

For a half-century the auto was subsidized on a welfare basis while its strength multiplied. But now, when the automotive war chest holds road taxes captive, the economic foundations of auto conquest rest upon great power, protection, independence, and acceleration.

The *power* is the massive tax base which is built upon one hundred million indispensable cars (fuel, licenses, and registration). The *protection* is defense in depth against competing legislative programs, against regular close legislative review, against rebellious cities in front of the bulldozer, and against local popular movements and freeway revolts. The *independence* is the freedom of the highway establishment from the moderating, cooperating, coordinating—and subordinating—influence by the whole society on all public activities. The *acceleration* is the self-generating power of automobility arising from its growing necessity in society, which in turn steadily enlarges the resources for its expansion.

That's about the best foundation for continued conquest one can ask of a war chest.

Field Command

"The great need," wrote one of Detroit's most illustrious field commanders in 1945, "is for mixed traffic expressways right through town. These are prodigious undertakings, the full extent and nature of which the average city dweller does not yet grasp. Probably busy people with their minds elsewhere will not realize what is in store until they are disturbed and discommoded by demolition, moving of tenants, and the inevitable noise, dust, excavation and detours of heavy construction."

This "great need" was really the great plan of Robert Moses to attack America's most rugged civic bastion against autocracy: New York City. The statement was as clear in intent as *Mein Kampf.* Once the overall plan is set in motion, "the rest," said Moses, "is battling obstructionists, moving people and dirt, paving, planting, veneering and painting the lily. . . ."

It took a lot of work to build an organizational superstructure for highway conquest. The effort has been only a shade less successful than the development of highway finance. Naturally, there are still weaknesses in the autocratic due process. No one has seen them more clearly than Mr. Moses. Nor has anyone struggled more to correct them.

Strategically, the most important means of effective highway building has been the tamper-proof highway authority. Moses' own Triborough Bridge and Tunnel Authority was a progressive though still imperfect model. The more it could act without interference from obstructionists—that is, the more it could build highways as freely as General Motors builds cars—the more readily it could promote automobility. Many state highway commissions also come up to a relatively high standard.

Naturally, it was Robert Moses who won the 1953 first prize of $25,000 in General Motors' essay contest on the question of "how to plan and pay for the safe and adequate highways we need." In his prize essay Moses observes that local governments are the least dependable because they are the least tamper-proof, commenting that "democracy as we practice it is a tedious and irritating business."

To Moses, the democratic poison clearly revolves around those evil practices, public hearings. Hearings were even a requirement in the Highway Act of 1956, embedded of all places in Section 116 of the act, which was expected to do most to further highway development. Outraged, Moses fulminated in *Harper's:*

. . . every state highway department must hold 'public hearings' with respect to every 'federal-aid project involving the bypassing, or going through, any city, town or village, either incorporated or unincorporated.' This means public hearings in every city and hamlet in the country which is to be traversed or by-passed by a new road.

Just think of it! The authors of this 'sleeper' must have little sense of the difference between time and eternity. Wholesale public hearings would only delay, bedevil, and ultimately destroy the program. Routes must be laid out by competent engineers and experienced highway officials, in co-operation with responsible local officials. . . . But properly located modern highways will not come into being if the highway departments have to placate publicly every local politician, stump speaker, real-estate speculator, amateur road-builder, professional reformer, exhibitionist, and promoter.

The very thought of having to go through these shenanigans will discourage even the most courageous highway official. . . . The program cannot be launched in such an atmosphere.

Somehow Section 116 remained intact, but the public hearings hardly delayed highway construction. Since the federal government paid for 90 percent of the conquest, few states or cities could long resist the momentary relief from congestion.

Soon many realized how, in the words of a *New York Times* editorial, the administration of the Interstate "program is so neatly divided that it is a buck-passer's dream." This was autocracy's defensive parry. And it was made possible by democratic federalism, which permitted juggling of responsibility between federal and state agencies. Highway projects backed by hard money could dissipate all but the most zealous local defense as it passed through the long, tedious democratic ritual.

Buck-passing is almost a rule in the procedure of the state highway commissions. California's, besides being padded well with former chairmen of highway promotion committees, avoids analyzing the important questions of its annual billion-dollar program by loading its brief monthly meetings with bureaucratic trivia. Then, too, the state's Transportation Agency Administrator is *ex officio* chairman, and this helps assure expeditious project review and approval. Through the chairman and his control of information, the agency also controls the procedure and content by which the agency's work is judged.

"What actually exists," said a highly enlightened minority member of the California Highway Commission, "is a condition wherein the inmates run the asylum, with the Chief Inmate serving also as Chairman of the Board of Visitors." Since there is no independent staff for the commission to sustain an independent perspective, the commission members have no alternative but to have their information spoon-fed to them by the "inmates" of the highway establishment.

Despite occasional flareups, state highway commissions function as smoothly as vehicle assembly lines, producing the capital improvements for automotive expansion. Younger and more experimental are the rising tide of municipal parking authorities. They, too, now strive for independence and financial momentum. And they will be successful, of course, for they must accommodate the increasing flood of motor vehicles dumped downtown by the new state freeways. That is one consequence of immense roadways being built according to carefully measured needs but in ignorance of the measurable results.

In evaluating the offensive capabilities of autocratic organization we cannot overlook the mobilization of sophisticated planning, information systems, electronics, and basic scientific research. Action in these areas accomplishes two complementary objectives. It invokes the popular faith that scientific solutions to traffic problems are just around the corner. And there is just enough practical realization over the years to prevent a final immobility, just enough to keep the faith alive.

Currently, there is some hope that positive results will come out of the traffic and transportation institutes such as Berkeley, Northwestern, Penn State, and Texas A & M. Most of the interest, nevertheless, centers on big business and the promotional development of devices that will magically dissipate congestion.

The automakers are concerned and active, and invoke the faith in characteristic fashion. We quote Henry Ford II at New Orleans in 1966: "At Ford we are investigating a number of different approaches to the application of Space-age technology to traffic control and driver information systems. In the not very distant future, we foresee the possible development of a nationwide traffic control system based on earth satellites or aerial reconnaissance linked by computer to urban traffic control centers and finally to the stoplight on the corner and even to the radio in your car.

"As fantastic as it may seem," said Ford, "we believe such a system will be technically feasible and economically sound. . . ."

We agree that a distant early warning network may be both technically feasible and economically sound, given the fantasies that pass through R & D and the fundamental importance of preventing total immobility in American life. However, we are not certain what all the nationwide electronic information should do. Is traffic so great that congestion in Hartford is affecting congestion in New Haven or New Rochelle? Perhaps it is Mr. Ford's intention to shift traffic west a bit, to give Nevada more of its share. Adopting the network could, to be sure, set off a new round of economic expansion at a cost of some $10 or $20 billion. Possibly it might set off the alarm clocks of commuters a few minutes early on days when traffic is especially heavy. Certainly it would inject traffic control more intimately into the behavior of the driver. But we are not so certain that such industrial proliferation represents progress for humanity and civilization.

Urban Attack Plan

The signs are unmistakable. All preparations in the 1960's have aimed at rapidly accelerating and focusing the autocratic attack on cities throughout the 1970's and 1980's. The precedents, the methods, and the momentum are favorably set. The facts and needs have been established and a cloud of ignorance about knowable results prevails. The propaganda and politics have been developed to sustain an immense attacking force.

The *1968 National Highway Needs Report* made it official. In the view of Francis Turner the most crucial element of the report is this: ". . . A future federal highway program, while it must continue to aid in the improvement of intercity and interstate routes, needs to turn greater attention to urban and urbanizing areas. This is where the major transportation problems of the next two decades will be."

The report notes that auto travel in cities is growing twice as fast as the population and will double in about twenty years. It therefore proposes that the federal interest be extended to "all of the arterial systems in urban areas," a powerful new departure, if adopted. An equally significant departure is found in another urban proposal: "Federal funds for parking might be used experimentally, testing a variety of approaches to make parking a more harmonious element in the total transportation system."

Underlying the stepped-up attack on cities is the fact that cities are already so swamped by automobility they account for one-half of all vehicular travel miles. Negligible before 1944, federal support for urban highways jumped to 25 percent of the funds between 1944 and 1956, when it was raised to about 30 percent (but 45 percent of the interstate funds). The proposed changes would correct this inequity between urban and rural highway finance. They would also belatedly and finally recognize that the problem of the automobile is no longer rural mud but the urban muddle.

So now the urban highway needs are proven and financial equity is in sight. What kind of cities can we expect from the hundreds of billions of dollars that will create ever larger vessels of *urban* automobility by the year 2000? Will the city's heart give out from the heavy pumping? Or will the city just fade away into the continental vastness? Wilfred Owen tells us that "if unlimited use of private vehicles were to be permitted, existing cities would have to undergo a metamorphosis that would mean a far greater dispersal and far lower densities of population than is the case today." An administrator formerly with the city of New York said merely that "the number of automobiles increases to fill the space provided."

Notwithstanding an English observer of American traffic who in 1960 already thought that some American towns had "almost ceased to be towns for living at all," a greater metamorphosis still is in store for human life in cities. The results of that metamorphosis will be a destruction of the natural environment, a failure to develop urbanity and a loss of civility. Ultimately the results are a deprivation of freedom, association, and even human purpose (subjects we will later examine). The new programs will not merely provide new spaces for automobiles to fill. They will provide another leverage for the growth of automotive power. They may always seem to be exercised with reason, but as in both the past and present the programs will enclose upon, discipline and isolate the individual.

Freeway aesthetic theorist Lawrence Halprin clarifies the immediate issue when he observes that "the confrontation between the freeway and the city involves an encounter between motion and static mass. . . . The city, dense with buildings, heavy and massive, almost impenetrable, stands in the way of

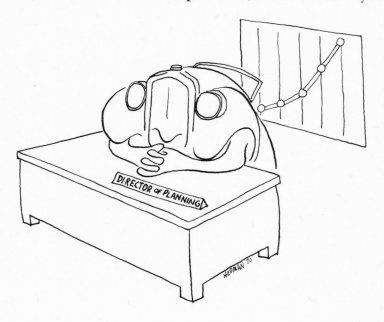

motion." Obviously, the power of our time overwhelmingly favors motion. The whole mass of the city loses its form and integrity in the encounter.

Thus while central Boston is cracked open for the Inner Beltway (at a cost up to $50 million per mile) the famous Route 128 draws space-age industries by the score, along with a deluge of nondescript housing at the distant periphery. It is all done solely to relieve auto congestion according to elaborate traffic studies in the name of naked economics, not to realize the composite of human purposes or the rich spectrum of civilized rewards attainable only in coherent cities. All the loss occurs merely as the incidental result of making way for the motorcar, because of the inadequacies of motorized motion.

It is very natural, then, that standards which relate freeways to urban population and auto registration should now be proposed. And it is natural that one of the earliest formulations is found in a report commissioned by the Automobile Manufacturers Association, *Transportation and Parking for Tomorrow's Cities*. The report calls for one mile of freeway for every 10,000 persons, or three miles per 10,000 registered vehicles.

Now, what about the cities? We know from experience that freeways charge through the valleys of lower real estate value just as armies charge through valleys in their marches of conquest. In roadmaker jargon, "culture" lying in the path of the projected freeway is rated on a priority list. Living areas, commerce, and industry are important only for their relative costs (and occasionally their politics). Schools are more difficult to deal with, and are avoided wherever possible. Churches are yet more sacrosanct. The most sacred cultural roadblock is necropolis, city of the dead.

Sometimes even they make way for the freeway. One reportedly lost out to the four-level "mixmaster" interchange in Los Angeles. But the bulldozers generally miss the headstones. A trade publication reported that the "Michigan state highway engineers showed regard for human values," when they found the grave of William Leith, who died at age three in 1859. In 1963 the grave was directly in the new alignment of U.S. 31, near Traverse City, but the compassionate engineers realigned the highway to save the dead boy's final resting place.

Henry Ford II has ample basis to gleefully report that "the basic reason why transit is declining is that most big downtown areas are not as busy as they used to be." How could it be otherwise, when the city is gorged with automobiles? With such arbitrary pressures the city slowly loses its ability to deal with economic problems in terms of any real economy. For tens of millions of dollars per mile a freeway delivers an immense automotive burden and little humanity and service to a downtown area. For nickels and dimes cars idly occupy streets fronting on properly valued at millions.

And slowly the city loses its ability to deal with human problems in human terms. The arbitrary and uneconomic competition underlying auto domination forces great stores to build great parking lots. Sometimes they leave a single residence incongruously in a barren black sea of asphalt. One house stood for years in Sears's parking lot in Salt Lake City. One remains in Hahn's in Westfield, New Jersey. Both are reminders that the motorized environment no longer responds to human sensibilities.

As the auto's assault on and penetration of the downtown becomes more intense—as route alternatives all reach high levels of congestion—the auto's intimidations take on a more tyrannical form. All local streets become congested, partly because freeways empty so many vehicles upon them, partly because the freeways and boulevards are themselves inadequate. Therefore the traffic engineers have turned back from their super roads out of a devil's mixture of success and failure and are now developing "street stretching" programs to improve the "efficiency" of humble city roadways. Hundreds of spot improvements are made, such as one-way movement, channelization, median barriers, and the elimination of on-street parking (which at least insulated pedestrians from the fast-moving road missiles). These are combined with new and very costly computerized signal systems. (New York's late traffic commissioner Henry Barnes reported that their new electronic signal system "should get off the ground" with fourteen IBM units.)

Despite the increasing efforts, traffic on the streets of larger cities is revealing a new phenomenon: *continuous congestion.* Beginning by stages with morning and evening commuting, the frustrations that were once thought to belong only at rush hours now often extend to morning school traffic and truck deliveries, to lunchtime travel between 12:00 to 2:00 P.M., to mid-afternoon school and delivery traffic, and, finally, after the late commuting, to evening entertainment. Traffic pressures of one activity merge into those of the others—and remain just below the point of complete municipal futility.

A somber consequence of local traffic intensification is the conversion of every street from a mere pedestrian's nuisance and danger to a formidable barricade. Signals are prejudiced more and more against the walking signal. Although walking is necessary even in the most motorized setting, the walking environment itself—the moving, breathing, seeing, feeling—is reduced to the bare requirements of the function.

One response to the debacle appears in St. Paul, Minnesota where a second-story pedestrian Skyway has been developed to pass through the middle of many blocks and over the streets. A certain integrity is thus returned to human mobility. But it is a patchwork reaction threatening to detour and bewilder the walker between one level and another, between the inner and outer parts of blocks, that is, between two only partly serviceable patterns of movement.

And, by offering an alternative to the walker the street signals and channelization may then be prejudiced more sharply against him. Or pedestrian street crossings may be eliminated altogether. Just as the first "side-walks" protected the pedestrian from road vehicles, they also permitted his elimination from the street. The St. Paul Skyway may give him new protection but it may also permit his elimination from the sidewalk—and from the entire ground-level environment.

Turner affirmed this intent in his "street stretching" scheme. He called for sidewalks to be converted to additional traffic lanes and "for an expressway type of traffic flow on existing city streets. This can be accomplished by restricting cross traffic during rush-hour periods on most cross streets and by constructing elevated or depressed crossovers on selected streets." The intent is not new, just the power and overriding necessity. Sidewalks have been losing out ever since New York's Fifth Avenue was widened in 1908. Of course, street stretching will not succeed any more than past efforts. It will merely forestall total failure at an inhuman price.

Here, then, are the general outlines of the new attack plan. They are unmistakable, for they are already in motion.

Paving Public Purpose

"Just take a good long look at your automobile," advised a *Collier's* piece in 1937, "and try to place it in this civilization." Today we know we should have followed that advice. For, as it was, the automobile made its own way in the world, growing powerful without essential social restraint or civil refinement. Consequently the civilized heritage, both the arts of ordinary life and the life of the fine arts, now follow in its wake and count for little.

True, the automobile, like all forces permeating a society, brings forth a new unity. We wonder, however, whether trips and trip ends (requiring freeways and parking) don't substitute mobility for man as the objective of social unity. Of course, there is a pleasure in forever breaking old records, like registering more than 100 million motor vehicles and traveling more than a trillion vehicle miles each year. But is the infinite expansion of what the engineers call trip production a suitable medium for organizing human behavior, or a sufficient reason for monopolizing the environment and terrorizing the senses?

The unifying influence of the automobile evidently steers right through almost every action of government. When we want to pump-prime the ailing economy or a depressed area we build highways. The Appalachia program initially involved $1,100 million, of which $840 million, or nearly 80 percent, went to highways. Good highways were built to declining mountain areas despite the knowledge that agriculture, coal mining, and other mountain activities cannot compete in the modern world.

When we want to improve recreation programs we emphasize the building of highways. The Council on Recreation and Natural Beauty thus received in 1966 a report recommending a national ten-year scenic road and parkway program to improve 43,000 miles and construct 11,500 miles of roads. By a peculiar reasoning, the highways—which Mumford calls those "brutal assaults on the landscape"—are proposed to *assist* an outdoor recreation program which itself cannot look forward to as much investment as the $4 billion proposed for scenic highways. The report, prepared by the Bureau of Public Roads, stresses that the program is minimal and that the more complete program of 97,000 miles costing $8 billion is fully justified.

Through the 1960's autocracy took an increasing interest in the profitability of recreation. The field revealed magnificent new opportunities to enlarge the automotive conquest during and after the 1970's. Of course, autocracy has only a special and passing interest in recreation and beauty. Otherwise the scenic highway program would have proposed the restriction of truck traffic. And since 18 percent of all scenic highways are planned at four or six lanes, recreative and scenic values will be marginal when trip production is so massive.

The proprietary interest of autocracy in recreation and natural beauty is found in the Highway Act of 1968. When $25 million had been considered minimum even to start ridding the highways of billboard blight across the country, a sum total of $2 million was actually budgeted, less than $\frac{1}{2000}$ of the federal highway allocation.

With such pervasive power it is hardly surprising that the livability of cities is studied through the highway lens. In 1968 the Departments of Housing and Urban Development and of Transportation undertook a $40,000 joint investigation of the relationships between highways and community values. Apparently highway values rather than community values were at the heart of the matter, for the study was executed by the Highway Research Board.

Then, when we get really serious about improving urban

livability, we discover, as Lawrence Halprin puts it, that "the new highway becomes the spine of a vast redevelopment" occurring "on linear principles in the city." And when freeway programs got into full swing, "renewal" along the spine displaced nearly as many persons as all formal renewal programs: 32,395 by highways, 34,003 by urban renewal.

Almost every urban freeway involves a neighborhood division, a multiplication of local street traffic and mercilessly unending noise—rather awkward renewal characteristics. The personal consequences of a "hit" or "near miss" of a new urban freeway are great indeed: expropriation and eviction, bulldozers appearing across the back fence. Complaint sessions at hearings easily turn into full freeway revolts, sometimes with civic leadership behind them. Since local revolts could spread into countrywide rebellion, and possibly invade Congress, they had to be placated through a tactical maneuver. The first move came on September 24, 1967, when Transportation Secretary Alan Boyd announced a $4.8-million contract for a "design concept team" to plan for twenty-four miles of Interstate highways in and around Baltimore. Since the persuasion had to be widely convincing, the team consisted of psychologists, sociologists, economists, urban planners, architects, and engineers.

The team was asked to answer the question: How can man make the freeway beneficial to the city? Given the inalterable traffic generation and urban scattering effects of any freeway, that task is monumental. Although the team was to use freeway development to benefit housing, community centers, and parks, only the freeways are assured of financing. Therefore the $4.8 million for planning and design represents a peculiar concern for route alignment and roadside design.

The Baltimore approach was instantly successful and is being extended elsewhere. We may now expect autocracy to rule both urban formation and reformation with infinitely greater finesse. Tactical adjustments for human values may be expected from the interdisciplinary teams. But the new order will be extremely difficult to challenge, supported as it will be by a whole spectrum of experts. Cities will be tied more firmly to highways, which will continue to bound through them at a powerful clip of $5 million to $50 million a mile.

The program in Baltimore is therefore another evolutionary precedent giving automobiles more authority to shape and occupy every city. Highways have long benefited by exacting rights-of-way reservations and setback-requirements. New frontage roads and access limitations are regularly applied to ordinary highways in new urban development, especially in California, in a struggle to make their capacities more permanent.

Since 1920 the weight of zoning has shifted increasingly to the automobile's favor. First it segregated residential, commercial, industrial, and public service areas at such distances that increased trip production was guaranteed. Zoning then introduced parking requirements for commercial establishments, to make certain that trip production and trip ends were in balance.

Subdivision regulations have been as accommodating. Road width and paving standards are among the most stringent, costly, and sacred in new housing developments. Yet children don't merit the same safety and convenience, for sidewalks are no longer required in many subdivisions.

In the area of invention, the U.S. Bureau of Public Roads has been developing a complex in-motion weighing and measuring system for vehicles. If successful, the system would obviate having trucks stop for inspection or weighing. Then, in Utah, where shooting at highway signs remains a hangover from frontier days, a motion picture camera has been designed to take movies of all those who shoot it out with the highway signs. Formerly the state Road Commission hung paint-can lids with bulls-eyes painted on them below the signs in an effort to prevent the destruction of the signs. This evidently failed, so highway signs may now join banks in commanding photographic protection.

If today we take a good long look at our cars and try to place them in this civilization, as Baltimore now places highways in its plan, it is clear that civilization is being fitted ever more thoroughly to the automobile. Currently, the automobile is developing an entirely new level of sophistication in the politics of poverty, recreation, and urban development, as well as a wide array of new practices and inventions.

Automotive Afterburner

The automobile and its infrastructure of social penetration, the highways and parking facilities, could not exist without a mammoth service establishment. This auto "aftermarket" is dependent on and loyal to automotive causes, yet vigorous and extremely varied. Altogether the automotive subordinates composing the aftermarket give an astonishing afterburner thrust to the cause of Autokind.

The fillin' station was always foremost. In the very early years it relieved druggists of dispensing spirits from the backroom. It soon became an American thoroughbred. "'Fill 'er up!'" commented David Cohn in *Combustion on Wheels*, "is a thoroughly American phrase . . . a phrase that could have been invented by no other people. There is no beauty in these words, yet they unlock for us the beauty of this continent . . . which few of us will ever see in its entirety. . . ." But that wasn't the fault of the man who put a tank in the ground and wrenched gasoline up into the snappy roadside sentinals at every prairie crossroad.

The stations multiplied into the hundreds of thousands and took their characteristic American form: an asphalted corner, a garish corporate sign, a flat tin box, and several pump islands. The station also took on a secondary facility to attract customers: the restroom. The station came to sell relief almost as much as gas.

The old fillin' station was a real pioneer for autocracy, setting out the Great American Strip. Some Strips, like U.S. 1 south of Hartford, remained hardly more than gasoline gullies. And the fillin' station was the pioneer, too, of another form of urban scar: the drive-in. Competition to serve the automobile has always been keen in America, and Moscow, Idaho, claims more service stations than Moscow, USSR. The competitive spirit often lands four stations at one corner.

Yet the gas stations could not serve all vehicles. A new specialty, the truck stop, emerged, with diesel fuel, larger service bays, extensive repair facilities, and more space. This multiplied the blacktop. The flat roofs were raised. The whole thing took on the character of a village built for elephants. And villages they are becoming. Many now boast restaurants, complete stores, lounges, barber shops, and sleeping accommodations.

Gasoline sales are highly inelastic, as the economists say. One cannot sell more than a full tank. But selling cars can be stretched and stretched. Color and comfort, power and style, all articulated by carefully calibrated annual changes, are the raw materials for the soft sell of the franchised auto dealer.

In keeping with their repair-shop origins, the early dealers sold only basic transportation of the Model T variety. But a new imperative of selling more than mobility began with the close of the first era of auto development in the 1920's. Many dealers thereupon added showrooms or transformed them into a class that sometimes bettered the local department stores. Often they shared the same neighborhoods.

But most dealers required great space and sought to make their establishment into glamor patches out of the Strip. Of course, this isolated them from everything but automobiles. In such isolation repairs required the presence of two persons, the mechanic *and* the stranded owner. Then the dealers found it necessary, if not profitable, to provide lounges and even baby facilities for a captive audience of those waiting to be plugged into society once again.

Nor is the evolution complete. Philadelphia has now established a complete automotive center in its Eastwick urban renewal area. Here the automobile is discovering an additional source of federal funds which originally were intended to improve the livability of cities. Eastwick also breaks new ground in adapting urban renewal plans to achieve a higher quality of automobility.

It was also in the 1920's that used-car dealers made their appearance and took over the selling of basic transportation. This new secondary market and the improved Chevrolet combined to kill the Model T. While doing so, these afterburner merchants made annual style changes economically feasible by creating a smooth avenue for cars to be purchased regularly and be passed from one class of owner to another.

Nearly four decades passed before basic changes in automotive sales and service began to show up again, this time in the repair field. Here clinical diagnosis of a car's present or possible ailments began to be systematized and divorced from actual repairs. Even though still experimental, the new diagnostic centers reveal the logic of vehicle development: increased mechanical complexity, rising automotive affluence (indicated by *preventive* checks, repairs, and replacements), and an inevitable penetration by Madison Avenue. Although the diagnostic centers consist of a sequence of stations which comprehensively examine the mechanical condition of a car, the centers devote as much or more space to the customer and the paperwork, notably customer consultation booths, instruments for customer viewing, and lounge and refreshment areas.

The meaning of it all is better health for cars and another advance for the automotive world. If present trends continue we may expect that systems of preventive care for the auto will outdistance preventive diagnosis and treatment of human ills. While both the repair and health professions are proprietary, the mechanics are showing much greater resourcefulness than the medics. Or perhaps there is more money in auto care. In any case, the significance of formally instituting the white frock coat with auto diagnosis cannot be overlooked. For society as a whole, auto diagnosis represents but one more step toward fulfillment of the idea (somehow misapplied to airplanes) that

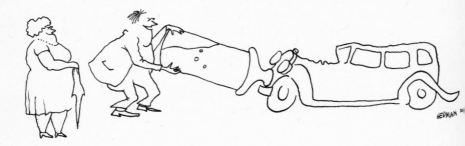

"only the [automobile] gets more attention than you."

Autodiagnostic centers could also merge with another concurrent line of evolution, mass merchandising. The attraction of big money into both diagnosis and mass merchandising and the automotive affluence behind them may well spur the development of complete automotive department stores. Naturally, many small auto shops, dealers, and stations will have to go, just as the corner grocery went, and for the same reasons. Well financed and well organized, the big auto marts would also be invited and could pay to enter the blue-chip shopping centers, as a few diagnostic centers already have.

And, with that, another cycle will close. When the automobile began attacking downtown many merchants took flight without fighting and put themselves at the complete mercy of the automobile by moving into the new cars-only shopping centers. Few automotive services themselves went into the centers. Their economics were not quite favorable, their appearance was poor, and their space demands were high. But the new affluence behind automotive buying, combined with unified departmental control of auto services, will change this. Therefore the automobile can now penetrate the functions and purposes of the shopping centers, as well as their location and form. Should they not be invited in, they will be powerful enough to establish and organize their own.

Fellow Travelers

Armies once had informal services provided by camp followers, who helped soldiers in every way soldiers need help. Today the armies of automobility have lured their own miscellaneous camp following, who scramble for the crumbs of conquest. However, it may be more accurate to describe these associates of automotive conquest as fellow travelers. And, instead of identifying ideological shades of pink, we will look for profit-seeking shades of gray.

Their variety is bewildering, and they infiltrate virtually every realm of industry, service, and government. Behind automaking are machine tools, steel, rubber, glass, lead, lacquer, plastics, chrome, copper. Behind gas and oil lie exploration and drilling equipment, refining equipment and its machinery, pipelines and tankers. Behind highway, bridge, and parking development lie construction machinery, cement, asphalt, and steel. Behind them all exist other sets of industries, other modes of transportation, and a diverse range of research and development (which, incidentally, makes current research to improve cities look like carriage research in 1875).

The manufacturing capacity serving the nation's 211,000 service stations alone (including large underground tanks, gas pumps, hydraulic lifts, air compressors, and tin houses) is powerful enough to substantially raise the living standards in many poor nations. The varied manufacturers behind road maintenance and traffic engineering on America's nearly 4 million miles of streets and highways could alone propel development to economic takeoff in many countries. There we find motor graders, mowers, sweepers (including fast new ones for the freeways), and snow plows; paints and salt; machines to paint lines and others to remove the lines; saws to cut and drills to puncture heavy concrete pavements; millions of warning and directional signs (often massive, overhead, and lit); railguards and reflectors; freeway lighting (sometimes single interchanges have more light than a small city); and immense systems of traffic signaling.

Computers are now being added to the signal lights. After being integrated into auto production, licensing, registration, and driver citation records, they are reportedly headed into auto diagnosis. As the usage grows the electronics industry may be expected to owe a great allegiance to automobility. Automatic highway guideway systems are a prospect that could raise the allegiance.

All this, we are taught, is the good story of industrial growth. Massive computer systems are necessary for massive vehicular traffic, and massive traffic is the necessity of modern life. Autocrats and economists count it all as contributions to the economy. Everything that multiplies the exchange of dollars is good for the economy. The automobile is superb in multiplication, especially in the field of surfeit economics.

Huge bureaucracies of fellow travelers have quietly been accumulating in government. It has become the duty of municipal police, highway patrols, vehicle registration and driver licensing offices, vehicle inspection stations, and the judges to perform many of the enclosure movements for autocracy. The sordid mark of tyranny in our times is that while government has been neutralized in protecting human freedoms of the environment, public agencies are very positive in enforcing the oppressive demands of automobility. In 1967 the California Highway Patrol made 1,923,788 arrests (one for every six drivers in the state, excluding all city and county traffic arrests) and gave nearly as many warnings.

Fellow travelers infiltrate finance and insurance, constituting about one in five employees—roughly the same proportion as automotive employees in the economy as a whole. Since investments and loans are made solely on calculable return, the automobile's superb history of multiplication and its solid grip on society give it a bread-and-butter attractiveness. But the weight of automobile finance and the delicate balance of financial markets suggest that everyone on Wall Street becomes solicitous of the industry any time it sneezes.

Some of the lustiest fellow travelers provide no service to the automobile at all. The billboard companies, for example, are a special brand of fellow travelers: automotive parasites. The industry is as ingenious as it is small. It can encourage man's gluttony while dulling his appreciation of the environment. On occasion, a single billboard can be strategically spotted to clutter a thousand acres for millions of people whose major form of recreation is still reputed to be pleasure driving. The industry revealed its tactical brilliance in defeating the Highway Beautification Act of 1965, not only by converting "just compensation" into a windfall, but by simultaneously using federal compensation to undermine struggling non-compensatory state and local efforts to regulate billboards, and in the end by using the windfall as a means of financing billboard expansion.

Overdrive Society

A very large and varied body of fellow travelers took their basic form from the drive-in, as evolved from the service station and the old roadhouses. From roadhouses that functioned like filling stations arose the Howard Johnson's, Foster Freezes and MacDonald's Hamburgers of today. From the cabins and auto courts of the 1920's evolved the motel.

Soon the drive-in expanded beyond services to the traveler to include services only mediated by the automobile: drive-in banks, cleaners, and outdoor theaters. As the automobile accelerated the breakup of the close-knit city, the drive-in idea also spread to all major activities of the city: industrial plants, major stores, office buildings, and even city hall. Subsequently industrial districts, shopping centers, and civic centers—all really collective drive-ins—were developed to retain a semblance of coherence and convenience. But, whatever they were, they always *required* mediation by the car.

At an early period the garage appeared in back of the family house. Then both car and garage came right into the house, making the family dwelling itself a drive-in. Both ends of every trip were eventually thus converted to drive-ins. America was a drive-in society.

Today America is adding another dimension to mobility. Two groups of fellow travelers are making dramatic progress in developing a completely new dimension of automobility. They are perfecting the plug-in, pull-out, move-on life, portending instant and portable cities. While the drive-in phenomenon reoriented the city to serve automobility, a drive-out phenomenon promises automobility of the city itself. This new mobility will guarantee a new freedom—freedom *from* place. Everyone will be as free as a particle of sand. Like sand, human relationships will become contacts dictated by the winds and waves of the faster-moving society.

The American's susceptibility to the mobilized life was noted by the *New Republic* in 1926. A car-based breed of people, "gasoline gypsies," were observed who had a passion for distance, a reverence for the statistics of mobility, and accepted overnight neighborhoods at the auto camps as readily as dust and flat tires. "You may like it or you may not, but the process will go on," plaintively submitted the *New Republic.* "The country is on wheels, and on wheels it will remain."

In 1926 the trailer house was being born, having descended from the covered wagon. Since only 1,300 units were produced by 1930, the new trailer house did not figure in the Dust Bowl drama. It did grow up to do service in World War II. But the great breakthrough came in the 1950's, when the newly named mobile home increased its width to twelve feet. This put it solidly into the urban housing picture. By 1966 4 million Americans were already living on wheels.

And what about the future? Has the mobile home reached its saturation point? Though mobile-home parks have provided the plug-in all along, now a Wisconsin firm called Skye Rise Terrace, Inc., has designed a twenty-four-story mobile-home parking "garage" to be located in central city areas. The plan calls for a spiral rampway with a slot for each mobile home unit and two automobiles which spread out as spokes from the ramp. Should such efforts succeed, the new coiled communities set in concrete caverns near the heart of the city will close another cycle of automotive expansiveness. The automobile first dispersed new urban development, returned to fragment the city center, and now threatens permanent automotive occupation of the center on precisely the same terms which the auto denied to people. Those terms were human scale, service, and relevance. Mobile homes near the center would conclude the transition to a motor scale, service, and relevance right at the heart of the city.

Now the mobilization of services appears to be gaining new momentum. The most improbable mobile facility of all has appeared: the Swimobile. Accompanied by a shower truck, the Swimobile (thirty feet by seven feet, and about four feet deep) already makes the rounds in the poor neighborhoods of several cities. Revealed once again is our ingenuity in applying mobility to solve life's problems. One Swimobile can take the place of several costly pools. It is an obviously flexible resource which can be deployed to districts in danger of rioting.

When private recreation vehicles of the affluent are are-examined, the horizons are varied and bright. The production of *travel trailers, pick-up coaches* (campers), and flip-top *camping trailers* have all been multiplied since the 1950's. More varied still are the sport accommodation vehicles for boating, racing, riding, and soaring, which themselves carry special means of mobility. The obsession with mobility in recreation and sport is sometimes seen in the kinds of travel combinations intended to compose the ideal: a camper with a motorcycle slung on its rear and a boat in tow.

The American's image of the camping vehicle is that of a second house for a two-car family—a freedom house to see this great country of ours. What possible harm could they do? Well, that's what we used to ask about the car.

Motorcars and recreation vehicles threaten open space and freedom in this country just as surely as motorcars and suburbs have destroyed open-space and urbanity in cities. Because convenience, maximum automobility, and open-space values are sought so voraciously by so many individuals, the very objectives sought are the first to be destroyed. The result is a peculiar form of anarchy requiring an unprecedented organization of men and resources.

Recreation vehicle output in the 1960's was quite parallel to auto production about 1910, after which traffic began to reshape the city. The motorcar and recreation vehicle together now promise to do the same for vacation districts in the mountains and by the water, to form temporary dispersed semi-cities.

Cars and trailers require encampments with a complete range of special services. But even that space will not be enough. Auto space demands at the encampments are too great for them to be near the scenic attractions. Additional ordinary parking lots will be required for that. This division is already occurring in the congested Yosemite Valley.

With both the "off-site" encampments and the "on-site"

parking fields, convenience and accessibility for non-automotive vacationists is reduced. More people will then "choose" recreation vehicles, just as they now "choose" a second car. Once again society will painfully learn how vehicles become an antibody to the service and convenience that first brought them into existence.

Set in motion will be a new spiral of defeat by plan.

Environmental Virus

Today automobiles not only beget automobility. Automobility also begets minimobility.

To some people the new clutch of General Motors's small experimental cars is a belated step toward automotive sanity. In 1920 or 1930 this might have been the case, before speed, weight, and power ruled the cities and countryside. In the 1970's the really small car can only fill the dead spaces created by the huge cars, mass raceways, and dispersed cities, expanding the auto necessity into a new specialized market. GM would not be interested otherwise, any more than it was in building a safe car or a fumeless car.

Golf carts have been a pioneer for minicars, opening to the wheel one of the few remaining tranquil urban reserves while robbing men of their exercise. Home tractors are also pioneers, but with a difference. The automobile has so bloated home lots in a space-wasting struggle for spaciousness in suburbia that digging and mowing have gotten to be too much for ordinary labor. So minimobility is required for yards too large to be fully usable and too small to provide real openness or a natural setting. On spring and summer weekends abrasive noises break the neighborhood peace, resounding from squatty machines toting squatty men in rectangular monotony.

Nowadays minimachines are used by metermaids, stockyard cowboys, postmen, and telephone repairmen, and in warehouses and storage yards. But these activities are not what stirs GM. The big market is the third and fourth family car. GM has admitted working on simplified controls to permit at least part of the socially disenfranchised half of the population (the young, the old, the disabled) to regain social membership. Of course, the growing automotive grip will soon require that younger people, older people, and semi-invalids be given special licenses to drive—and special routes to travel on. But this will not reduce the need for the two-ton seventy milers. And to the extent the autocrats succeed, they will once again find another reinforcement for automobility—and demonstrate another success arising out of the motorcar's failure and profound destructiveness.

As yet the minicar lies mostly in the future. But another mechanical virus of equal importance rapidly grows among us: the off-highway sport vehicles. Whereas the first seventy years' challenge of automobility was limited mostly to providing the roadbeds that overcame auto weaknesses, the new breed is designed precisely to challenge men to charge onto mountain slopes and into stream beds, or across sage prairies and over water, sand, and snow. From motorcycles and the four-wheel drive, the list has grown to include trail bikes, dune buggies, snowmobiles, and sand sailers. Now Uniroyal has introduced a six-wheel amphibian to maul shorelines and madden quiet lakes.

Excepting sand sailers, all have rugged engines and special designs encouraging a test of men and machines against nature. Winches and flotation equipment for Jeeps tell their own story about who will win. Their success will follow the pattern set by automobility over the decades.

No longer are the deep scars of motorcycle hill climbs enough. Today one challenge for the wildly increasing numbers of machines is the "hare and hound" races in which hundreds of cyclists charge across California's deserts, cutting a wide swath of destruction in one action. The Bureau of Land Management reports that in one encampment 58 percent of the vegetation was destroyed or irreparably damaged. Since desert brush is slow-growing, the destruction denies wind or water protection on the desert floor for up to ten years.

Off-highway vehicles are a new breed of invaders, intent on extending the armored conquest of the American continent to every square foot of the natural heritage, trampling the flora under tire, terrorizing fauna by roaring motors, intruding in the last habitat of game at all seasons, setting off a rampage throughout our remaining wild areas. A generation after General Patton held war maneuvers in the Mojave Desert the original scars and gullies of tank tracks still remain.

Let no one be complacent about the apparently good clean fun with the car's backcountry cousins. That was the mistake men made about the automobile itself. This new clan of destruction begins with a wide repertoire and adds its powerful reinforcement to the automotive conquest.

Maginot Mobility

Trucking is an outgrowth of an early revelation that the automobile seemed to be useful in moving goods. That was an afterthought which led to the most massive transport subsidization in history—relegating the railroad land-grants of the last century to virtually a dry run. And so today trucking is an auxiliary giant perpetuating a medieval system of transfer on a progressive people.

In 1913 it was considered a pity—rather than a contribution to the economy—that 1.75 million people were required to care for the horses of the country (mostly on the farm). In 1970 the Automobile Manufacturer's Association proudly displayed the fact that more than 10 million people were employed to manufacture, distribute, service, and use nearly 15 million non-farm trucks in the United States. That is now counted as a *contribution* to the economy which cannot be matched by the 600,000 railroad workers who handle nearly double the intercity ton miles (as well as carrying passengers and repairing their own roadbeds). The 10 million truckers carry 23 percent of the intercity movement, while 42 percent is carried by the railroads and 35 percent by waterways and pipelines.

Of course, the truck is busy within the city as well, helping propel it to overmobility. The fact is that there is one truck for every four families in America.

To be sure, the horse that preceded the truck was not really a city animal. A drayage team required as much space as the wagon it pulled. It was slow and could not pull great weights. The horse also polluted the city. And, regardless of whether he was worked or not, this oats locomotive had to be fed morning and night.

Even with such easy competition, trucking did not get much of a start before the special circumstances of World War I and the growing subsidies of good roads during the 1920's. Few then thought trucks would ever serve as more than local transfer and delivery. In 1925 the American Section of the International Chamber of Commerce stated that the "great usefulness" of truck and bus transport was "as a feeder, as a supplement of the main lines of railway transportation."

The apparent advantage of trucking, like the deceptively destructive advantage of the auto, was simply its door-to-door service. This was its rationale. Trucks could give flexibility to the inexpensive long haul by water, rail, and pipeline carriers. And they did, until the accumulating subsidy began upsetting the natural course of events. By 1940, when trucking employment reached four million, this complementary rationale of railways and trucks had seriously broken down within the major regions of the country. And since about 1960 the breakdown has been nationwide.

Today trucking is subsidized with more than two million miles of America's paved streets and highways, ten times the railroad mileage, an investment replaceable at about $200 billion. The truckers claim, of course, that they pay their way. "This vehicle pays more than $3280 a year in road users taxes," reads a sign on a truck in New Jersey. By this they mean that anything is justified in society so long as it seems to pay its share, whether it contributes to a social tyranny or not.

These taxes are good propaganda. But they don't change the subsidy by 90 million motor car owners and the general tax base. While general-fund taxes pump-primed auto and truck expansion with new highways, the growing road-users taxes were protected to accelerate the expansion. Not only was expansion and acceleration built in, but trucks pay no taxes on the roadbed, as railroads do on their trackage. Were the same advantages given to the railroads, the states would construct and maintain the railways out of taxes paid by the rail companies only on rolling stock and fuel.

The highway subsidy for 10 million teamsters—nearly one-seventh of the labor force that mans one part of the transportation system—means that the country is now investing in the greatest labor layaway plan since the building of the Great Wall of China. The high investment in labor (60 percent) and the low equipment amortization (4 percent) point to trucking as an anachronism from the paleolithic era of technology.

As a *system* trucks reveal more storage than movement, more handling than transfer. Fork lifts, bulk loading, and computer invoicing are the mere frosting of efficiency over a waste structure. To dramatize their waste, truckers have taken to riding piggyback on the railroads, thus employing two frames, two sets of wheels, two sets of loadings and unloadings, and two bureaucracies to carry one shipment.

What is morbidly fascinating is that trucking itself poses an enormous obstacle to automation. Whereas railroads already use natural guideways, train location sensing, and remote control switching, autocrats can only dream about these preliminary steps to automated operations. And should we apply money and technology equal to that applied to our moon trip to automate highways, it is doubtful that a rig could go unmanned. It would be unsafe as long as highways carry mixed traffic. Then, too, it would require human control at the congested urban trip ends. Notwithstanding the fantasies of Henry Ford II, highway guideways are as practical as building the Lincoln Highway over Pike's Peak.

Such absurdities are likely if trucking can drive its burden more deeply into the politics and economics of the country. Two precedents are being tested. The federal Department of Transportation is building a short freeway solely for buses in Milwaukee. If this test to escape traffic congestion proves successful we may expect a similar differentiation for trucks, first in special locations, then on general routes. Already the New Jersey Turnpike has made a partial differentiation on its expanded twelve-lane metropolitan section.

Secondly, buses in New York are being fitted with retractable rail wheels to permit them to escape traffic on an abandoned track between Manhattan and Kennedy International Airport. Having defeated rail transit and set back all railroads, the automobile now appears to be headed toward an inefficient occupation of both its own right of way and the tracks.

But the most serious problem of the truckers is the technological deadend imposed by the very conditions that got them going: a vehicle with such flexibility that it cannot be automated except at the price of trucking men to the moon. This they are attempting to face by seeking larger interim subsidies to tide them over until society can afford to carry out another fantasia for automobility.

Like so many next steps of automotive progress, the truckers' proposals seem reasonable. All they want is to use their potential more effectively. This means more trailer units and axles per rig, and more length, weight, width, and height. The truckers have been pressuring the federal government and the state legislatures to expand in all directions: maximum length of more than 100 feet with three- and four-unit combinations, gross weights of 105,000 pounds on nine axles—2.5 times more than the emergency weight limits of World War II. They want to increase truck width from 8 to 8.5 feet (noting, of course, that mobile-home widths of 12 feet are permitted with special precautions) and increase height another 12 inches, to 13.5 feet.

What the truckers want, of course, is more money from the public treasury. The new dimensions spell higher standards of pavement construction. The new truck dimensions—adopted bit by bit and blindly over the years—will eventually make obsolete the general-purpose highway. The car and the truck will then separate onto different paths of conquest. Highway construction costs will shift once again to a new order of magnitude, this time in a giant stride. Another increment for congestion will be set into motion, while railroads flounder along with unused capacity.

Once more, the motor vehicle will increase its domination

over mobility, work, association, and recreation, while destroying the vestigial remains of environmental relevance to the human body, mind, and emotion.

War Resources

Each successful assault by automobility takes its toll upon social rationality and humanity. Systematic gluttony itself has been raised to an economic principle and social ideal. True, Americans have always had a weakness for unlimited expansion. Nevertheless, one of those moral casualties of conquest was revealed when automen could openly brag about accelerating the gross national consumption of resources.

"Think of the results to the industrial world," boasted Charles Kettering in *The New Necessity* in 1932, "of putting upon the market a product that doubles the malleable iron consumption, triples the plate glass production, and quadruples the use of rubber! No other one artifact in history has affected so many people and so many industries. . . ."

Kettering could hardly contain his exuberance over so much consumption by automobiles: "As a consumer of raw material," he exclaimed, "the automobile has no equal in the history of the world." He gloated that 15 billion gallons of gasoline were consumed by cars each year (today he could claim nearly six times as much combustion). Rubber was an industrial infant until the car came along. But by 1932, 84 percent of a multiplied output went into tires, according to Kettering.

Today, despite the certainty of having to shift from inexpensive liquid petroleum to hard-to-get and hard-to-process oil shale and tar sands for gasoline, the principle of consumptiveness drives on. Despite the depletion of high-grade domestic iron ore (replaceable only by imports or low-grade taconite), the principle of runaway consumptiveness shifts into a higher gear.

And the principle remains virtually uncontested. Note the "Fabulous Figures on the Interstate System," presented by the Portland Cement Association, based on statistics of the U.S. Bureau of Public Roads:

+ Pavement area equals 400 square miles.
+ New right of way equals 1.5 million acres.
+ Excavation would bury Connecticut knee deep.
+ Sand, gravel, and stone would build a wall around the world fifty feet wide and nine feet high.
+ Concrete would build six sidewalks to the moon.
+ Steel requires 30 million tons of ore, 18 million tons of coal and 6.5 million tons of limestone.
+ Lumber requires all trees from a 400-square-mile forest.
+ Culvert and drain pipe equals the combined water and sewer main systems of six cities the size of Chicago.

Despite its six sidewalks to the moon, the interstate system still constitutes less than half of all highway construction, hardly any parking. All streets and highways consumed nearly 6 million tons of rock salt in 1967, and this is expected to double by 1975. The automobile itself consumes over 50 percent of all lead, 35 percent of all zinc, an eighth of all aluminum. And the same multiplication of our resource "development" goes on in the facilities to serve the car—the service stations and dealers.

Not the least resource is man himself. Nowadays the human resources demanded by the automobile are enormous. To economists the car's demand upon human resources helps achieve full employment. Measured by its effects, the huge auto employment is simply all-out mobilization.

The Automobile Manufacturers Association estimates that about 13.3 million persons are employed in producing and servicing automobiles, refining and selling fuels, maintaining and repairing public roads, and driving trucks, buses and taxis. This accounts for about 19 percent of total current employment. Left out of the accounting are highway contracting, driver education and licensing; motor vehicle registration and inspection; law enforcement and legal activities, finance and insurance, commercial parking, and, of course, endless backup industries and services. If these activities are added to auto employment, roughly 15 million persons are employed by the autocratic regime in America.

That is almost 21 percent of all workers, more than one out of five. The human input is of the same order as that required to produce the material for World War II. That war required sweated labor, which everyone understood and gave, always looking for the end. The automobile also requires sweated labor. But that labor is without purpose or end, except to accelerate an internecine chaos.

War Debris

The autocratic regime does more than claim this planet's men and resources. Waste and debris inevitably follow from its conquest. But whereas men laud the auto's claim on human and natural resources, some of the car's noxious effluents are creating anxiety among those who remember the earth in an earlier era. That was when men could struggle against nature with the secure knowledge that they could not fully win. For, with winning, waste was systematized and debris multiplied. And before men began to win they knew that the only source of tyranny was in man's soul, not in the intricate system of invention and mass production.

All in all, however, the anxiety of the elderly and the wise is but skin deep. Only in air pollution is there a real danger of popular rebellion, though from the auto's beginning it was noticed that the exhaust smelled bad. Some people learned to use the carbon monoxide for their trip to eternity. Others passed off the bad smell without much thought. "Well," said one of the more concerned in 1903, "we are glad that [smell] fades in the distance."

But today, when the hot summer air stops moving in the Los Angeles smog bowl, there is no easy fading in the distance from nearly 5 million of the world's most active exhausts. One can only leave the Southern California Sun—which converts the hydrocarbons and oxides of nitrogen into the "oxidants" of smog —and its congestion of both respiration and movement. The slow chemical immolation is so bad that sixty doctors at the UCLA Medical School broke out of their professional aloofness and advised everybody who could to move away.

Across the country, at New York's Albert Einstein College of Medicine, Dr. Leonard Greenberg speaks of a "killing effect" during some periods of heavy air pollution, when there are as many as 150 "excess deaths." Such figures should spur the National Safety Council to establish daily or weekly smog scores, similar to its tallies of holiday traffic deaths. Five thousand deaths were estimated for one black week of London smog in December 1952, and this makes the 500 or so traffic deaths on holiday weekends really worth celebrating.

Dr. Greenberg proposes that hospitals establish "smog shelters" or "clean rooms" for persons most sensitive to air pollution. That is a good pragmatic medical solution (for about $1,000 per patient). It also would be another subsidy for the automobile.

The New York City Planning Commission has calculated that 630 tons of auto pollutants are dumped into the air daily in Manhattan below Fifty-ninth Street. The concentration of vehicles produces a mountain peak of emission in the square mile

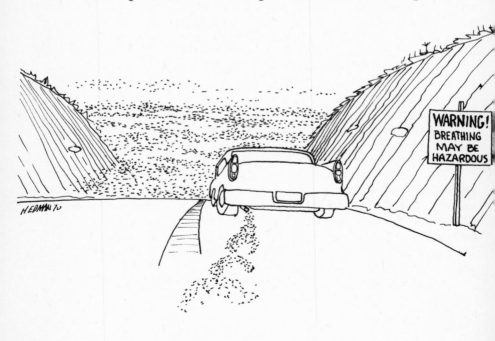

south of Central Park, precisely at the greatest concentration of people. In the entire Los Angeles basin the daily vehicular exhaust is estimated at 13,000 tons.

Autocrats like to claim that the motor vehicle is not the country's major desecrator of clean air. But the former director of the National Center for Air Pollution Control states that the automobile is "the most serious single cause of air pollution," producing more than all other sources combined. And in Los Angeles, where stationary sources of pollution are well controlled, motor vehicles account for 90 percent of the effluent.

All along it was evident that the auto industry didn't want to develop exhaust controls, any more than it wanted safe cars. In 1957 Harry Williams, director of the Automobile Manufacturers Association, made it quite clear: "What I want to discuss today," said Williams at the National Conference on Air Pollution, "is something which, so far as I know, no other industry has been called upon to do: namely, to concern itself with how the consumer uses or misuses the product long after its sale to the public." Another auto official revealed the industry's deeper sentiments about exhaust controls: "Well . . . will that device sell more cars? . . . will it look prettier, will it give us more horsepower? If not, we are not interested."

Not only were the manufacturers dragging their feet. They were evidently coordinated in their restraint. California learned that its standards for emission were very largely ignored by all manufacturers. It was a surprise, but hardly revealing, when the U.S. Justice Department initiated antitrust action, charging that all four auto producers had conspired for fifteen years to avoid competition in all phases of exhaust control.

The petroleum companies, fearing a practical electric car, spent $263 million up to 1967 to solve the problem of motor exhaust. But the results thus far have not cleared much air. Meanwhile the companies continue their own pollution. Their refineries and petrochemical plants continuously pollute streams, land, and the air. Their tankers clean their bilges of many thousands of barrels of fuel oils with sea water.

Air and water pollution are matters of life. However, the

pollution of sight and sound debilitates the means to experience and appreciate life, undermines the higher faculties of men and the qualities of civilized life.

The ear is a marvel of capacity and tolerance, ranging from a barely audible 1 decibel (said to be as loud as the sound of a baby mouse urinating on a dry blotter three feet away) to a painful 120 decibels (one trillion times greater than 1 decibel). Yet the ear has its limits. Mice die in one minute at 175 decibels. Human loss of hearing is directly related to the amount of noise one is exposed to over a period of time, even at 85 or 90 decibels. Since city noise levels are reported to have increased about 1 decibel per year for thirty years, the increase in partial deafness is understandable. How intensely noisy New York is was demonstrated in December 1960, when a heavy snow stopped all traffic. Then it was possible for normal *human conversation* to take place between persons a full block apart.

And what about the inner scars of human perception? If a thousand traffic signs and another thousand billboards (often counted at over 100 per mile) are thrown into our faces on the journey to work, if we are required to constantly respond to stop-and-go lights and the brash beseeching to fill 'er up with Mobilgas (because modest messages do not get through to cash customers at 40 mph), what sensibilities are calloused over into thoughtless compulsion? Is it possible that the environmental disarray of power and speed—of clutter and clang—gathers as a photochemical pollution of mind and emotion which, like Los Angeles' 5 million exhausts, no longer fades in the distance?

It is hardly surprising that refuge from sensual bombardment is a major preoccupation of modern man. Suburban escape is one of the palliatives. But is not refuge from our senses possibly as damaging to the good life as the relentless bombardment? The question is the quality of the environment that may stimulate us, or that we must suffer, not the necessity of immersion alternated with refuge. For it is the city that is the mother of higher human sensibilities, and it is now the defiling din of the cities that has become most oppressive and least meaningful to men.

Venice is a city of the pedestrian, even more than it is of

the gondola. Being carless, the sights and sounds of the inner passages are distinctly human in scale and relevance: the sound of voices, feet and hand tools prevail; and the sight of faces, clothes, merchandise, water, pavement, and walls predominate. The short distances of things foreclose the need for the massive signs and lights which are necessary in the auto environment. Even blaring billboards are reduced in Venice to the size of men at walking speed. Machines have made only a limited and qualified entry. The typical heavy urban din is almost absent; the sounds are clear, placeable, human, and meaningful. Despite its density of building and intensity of human activity Venice remains a serene but vital city.

The hard question about the auto's contribution to pollution is not the waste it often represents, probably not even the physiological harm that it can do, though these are formidable and urgent. The degenerative sights and sounds that count are not even in the environment. They are what have become a part of man, penetrating every person as assuredly as the automobile has made itself essential to society. What is absorbed by the senses is the corrosive experience which degrades the quality of life and thus, ultimately, the meaning of society. Pollution of the mind is the most serious consequence of the automotive conquest.

3

ASPHALT VENICE

Equilibrium for Autos

IT ALL HAPPENED very methodically. Along with construction and congestion of highways came dispersion and congestion of cities. A pincer movement—called balanced transportation development by the experts—closed in on downtown. This consisted of freeway construction, parking expansion, and local street "stretching."

True, as one expert observed, "the nation's urban centers are striving for a new equilibrium attuned to the motor vehicle." For a half-century the automobile steadily displaced other transportation in the downtown, and this has created the present disequilibrium. Now a new equilibrium may be expected when the automobile has displaced most of the downtown. This is what a piece in a 1907 *Harper's Weekly* must have meant when it predicted that the automobile "will solve the problem of overcongestion in our city streets."

Two automotive landmarks will set the stage for the new equilibrium. The first, already achieved in Los Angeles, Atlanta, and a number of other cities, is reached when the automobile occupies more land in the heart of the city than all other activities combined. The other, demonstrated at Century City in Los Angeles, occurs when the floor space devoted to automobiles surpasses the total acreage involved.

But the new equilibrium will not bring forth a benign occupation. The automobile is too aggressive for that. All downtown streets and the boulevards extending outward will become less and less negotiable for anything other than prescribed auto movements. "The system of traffic divides the people even more effectively than a river," observed Arthur Pound in a far more tolerant 1938. The intimate urbanism of shops and offices our fathers knew becomes divided and isolated between the widened arteries and larger quantities of parking. The city center is balkanized by its own mobility. Defensively, city-making reorganizes the businesses into ever more isolated groups, making each a little island. The whole city becomes a melancholy sort of Venice in which there is no movement without the automotive gondola to span the sea of parked and moving masses of metal.

The results for society are similar. If the city was once the principal foundation for civilization it is now increasingly an accessory to automotive enterprise. If it was once the fountainhead of the renaissance it is becoming an industrial proving ground.

Infantry Against Armor

By a lapse of civic sanity, autocracy was helped to defeat transit, except where transit was needed to shore up the automobile at its weakest point: at peak hours. And by the same lapse, autocracy was permitted to eliminate the pedestrian as well, except at points where the auto cannot serve: at both ends of every auto trip.

The defeat of the walker is unheralded, even unaccounted

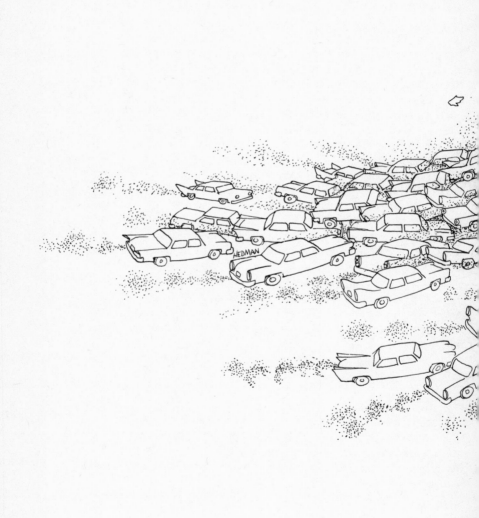

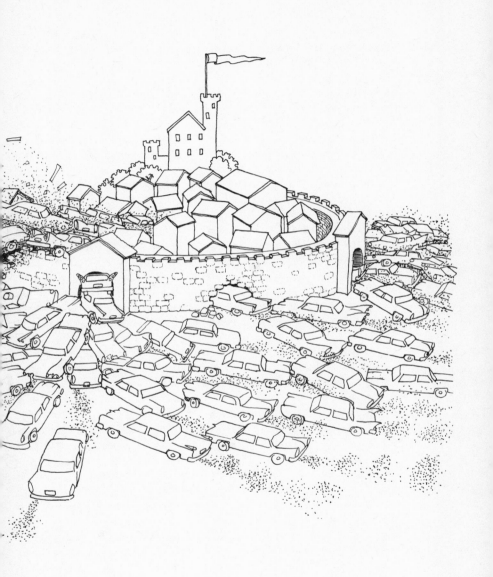

for in statistics. But his defeat is not just a sentimental pity. It is a tragedy for modern man and modern mobility. The tragedy is man's legs, his figure, his heart, his lungs. It is his senses, his nervous system, his mind. It is his freedom, his civility, his association, his society.

Mankind needs to understand a few important facts about walking. In these days it may not be known, but walking is a highly efficient and inexpensive—as well as exceedingly pleasant —way of getting about. Today one often hears "You mean you *walked!*" Yet walking is so efficient that economists are not certain how to consider it, because walking adds nothing at all to the gross national product. City planners have been intimidated as well. When they speak of access to property they always mean access for automobiles.

The forgotten fact is that the human body was made with its own locomotion built in. By comparison with all mechanical forms of movement, a man's legs are instantly available and completely responsive (if used sufficiently). Walking imposes no burden on the mind and calms the nerves. It requires no learning after the age of two, and no particular discipline of the eyes or rigor of the spinal cord. Walking poses no danger (except from cars and trains), nor does it require laws (except for cars). There are virtually no costs, as the engineering of paths and sidewalks can be absorbed easily in the costs of landscaping. Pedestrian traffic is rather a joy and makes the jaunt lively. Finding a place to stop is rarely a problem, though it would be nice if there were a few "service" stations.

Even without these the walker does not seem to pose a problem of pollution. The blight of wrecking yards is avoided, as is the investment of manufacturing. Walking requires no installment payments, no liability or collision insurance. Nor is there a precedent for licensing walkers.

Moreover, it is very difficult to congest walkers. Only where they are bunched at parades, theaters, and stadia are there likely to be delays. At that, the congestion afoot dissipates quickly. Even busy sidewalks reduced to narrow ledges seem to serve surprisingly well, despite numerous parking meters, traffic signs, and trash baskets that must be negotiated. Even an additional five or six feet in most cases would eliminate the present inconvenience permanently, whereas a roadway widened twenty-four feet but eases auto congestion momentarily.

Perhaps it is this very quality, call it human compressibility, which is the undoing of the walker. He is flexible, can sidestep and pass an impediment quickly and gracefully. A sidewalk "crowd" can be bunched at an intersection, and a moment after the "walk" signal appears the people cross and are on their way. But automobile traffic is rigid and incompressible, and therefore demanding. Given the car's political power and affluence, what can we then expect but a setback of the sidewalk, a longer "wait" at the signal, and less interesting, more barren, and more burdensome walks.

The walker may be compressible, but he is not insensitive. In Paris a study found that both the willingness and the desire to walk were directly related to the quality of the walking environment. Where it was convenient, visually interesting, and either pleasant or active, the people willingly walked twice as far as they would in other districts where their movement was intimidated or their senses were affronted. Since the latter is the norm in America, it is little wonder that walking has lost its reputation as well as its adherents.

Why, then, weren't the defenses of walking better prepared? America is acknowledged to be a corporate society. A corporate society is based upon corporate values, real values like money, hard values like steel, operating values like production and consumption, human values like employment. Ever since the second decade of this century the corporate world has realized that there could never be a better vehicle to advance corporate values in the whole society than the automobile. This idea permeated the literature after 1910 and gradually became implicit in all corporate and economic thinking.

Given the unchallenged legend of the social utility of the automobile, how could a valueless thing like walking rate any social defenses at all, except at teas for bird watchers. The huge parking lot at River Rouge was a better symbol for corporate democracy than any Piazzo San Marco could ever be. About the best that could be said about a walker, even in 1938, was that he was "a person on his way from one motorcar to another."

The real problem for Detroit's engineering assistants isn't that pedestrians get killed but that they slow up traffic. Los Angeles best revealed it, of course. An official there said humbly that "the pedestrian is the largest obstacle to the smooth flow of traffic" (despite the many miles of pedestrian-free freeways).

The police in Los Angeles have a long history of halting and arresting walkers, whether they disrupt traffic or not, whether famous or not. One psychiatrist was repeatedly stopped on his strolls. Once, after being taken to the police station, he began to take a dog along. As he later said, "everyone knows a *dog* needs exercise."

With the walker, the cyclist has been defeated by the auto conquest. A safety consultant pointed to the common moral. "Like the pedestrian," he remonstrated, "the bicyclist is his own worst enemy," because most who are killed or injured were in violation of the law. Of course. For whom was the roadway designed and the laws enacted? The cyclist is illegal on the sidewalk, restricted in the street, and an obstacle to the smooth flow of auto traffic in the intersection.

It is not strange, of course, for the safety expert or traffic engineer to say that autos and pedestrians are an "immoral mixture." What is the immoral element? Who but the walker, the man? Who should be unmixed? Is there any doubt any longer that man afoot is immoral and that the moral foundations of society rest with machines?

Rasping the City

In the early auto literature we noted the assumption that the automobile would not only decongest the city but eliminate slums and raise the standard of living. This was the propaganda of conquest. And it persists, despite severe inconsistencies with reality.

All propaganda requires a grain of truth, of course. The

auto's claim always held just enough to give its urban conquest the air of liberation. The auto did open up the countryside to the city people. But the greater truth is that congestion, danger, and the very uncivil manners of the auto helped to force people to flee the city, while its consumption of land and disorderly scattering of new development robbed the people of the delights of the countryside. Permanent auto camps called suburbs—shaped by a squatter's formula of city-making—left a squatter's level of urbanity and a miser's level of open space.

The suburbanites were refugees who used wealth and automobiles to flee the city. They were squatters and misers. Instead of applying their wealth to improvements of their environment and the building of city values in the old urban tradition, they established a new city tradition of commuting. They made a daily escape, symbolizing their distrust, ambivalence, and lack of commitment to cities. The attitudes, the escape, and the end results set up a mutual system of defeat between city and countryside.

The abandonment of fine old homes to be converted to tenements, the rasping action of car-commuting, and the corollary rise of the Great American Strip had their telling effects. The claim that the auto would decongest the city was a vision of pure fantasy, as was the belief that the auto would eliminate slums. "There will be no slums in that automobile city" of the future, crowed the automobile editor of *McClure's* magazine in 1917, "for slums are created by high land values which cannot be leveled so long as this is a horse-ruled world."

The early propagandists worked very hard on the auto's wealth-producing qualities, especially the automobile itself. *Country Life* in 1913 prophesied that "everyone will ride in an automobile, except the vagrants." But hardly twenty years later, by an ironic twist of fate, Will Rogers quipped that America was the only country in the world which could go to the poorhouse on wheels. It was sometimes a peculiar fact in the Depression that cars and gasoline could take precedence over food. The story was told of a man claiming his family was starving. "If you don't believe it," said the man, "I'll drive you over to our place and you can see for yourself that there's nothing in the house to eat."

At the heart of the problem of congestion, slums and poverty is the competition between the city and the car. A 1910 issue of *Outlook* suggested, "If the auto and the house are going to compete, give them both fair play and let the fittest survive."

However, fair play was never part of the game, not even part of the rules. We have seen how public taxation filled the war chest for conquest. The rules also dominated government. The federal government's expenditures have favored highways over transit twenty-four to one. All levels of government spent ten dollars on highways for every one they spent on both urban renewal and public housing.

Plainly, the game is played entirely according to conqueror's rules. Both public and private lending for housing massively favors the auto-refugee suburbs over inner-city construction and rehabilitation. Cities in more prudent times were built meagerly and then improved over the generations. The rebuilding of structures or whole districts was fundamental to the rise of civilization. But now the spirit is to build and move on. Improvement capital has become escape capital. Gypsy investment sooner or later results in Gypsy abandonment. Where the roadway is the foundation of urban investment and the street map (courtesy of the oil companies) is the essential guide, what else can we expect?

Today Americans are charmed by the character of European cities. With some important exceptions, the human scale and even the human relevance of those cities remains intact. Their vigor of self-renewal is also retained in those very parts—so attractive to Americans—which would have been long abandoned in American cities. Then the Americans return home and continue to accept the degenerative abandonment of the old quarters of their cities while expending unprecedented capital on anti-urban, auto-isolated monoxide manors. Only in a few spots, such as Society Hill in Philadelphia, has the old tradition reasserted itself.

Conqueror's rules govern urban development practices. Modern subdivision and zoning controls, which grew up with the automobile, certify and demand the auto's advantage in every project. They guarantee: (1) the land consumption (through barrack-like house layout, boulevard-wide local streets, and "acres" of parking); (2) the distances (assuring a motor monopoly of movement), and (3) the dispersion of facilities and services (requiring an irrationality of travel patterns).

Still, the conqueror's rules are fairer than the conqueror's tactics. For while the automobile restructures the city for automobility it simultaneously undermines the city's natural vitality, encouraging abandonment, class by class, like the used-car market, until slums are the achievement.

Those assult tactics are pervasive: the arbitrary divisiveness of traffic-loaded streets, the debilitating noises, the visual disarray, and the killing fumes. Wilfred Owen calls commercial strips the "longest slums" yet known. With every through street to the city center pressed into thoroughfare service, traffic poisons the whole pattern of urbanism. Escape becomes compulsive for those who can afford it. Depression and deterioration are reinforced for those who cannot.

Henry Ford himself felt the destructive effects of traffic. After he restored the old Wayside Inn at Sudburry, Massachusetts, he found it necessary to relocate the Boston Post Road for two miles at a cost of $250,000. According to a Ford biographer, this act "may well connote the manufacturer's effort to flee from himself, to turn against the values of an uneasy age which he had helped to found."

But the city's problems with the automobile are more complex than those of a wayside inn. And there are no sentimental auto barons able to rescue them. So cities merely deteriorate under the impact.

Urban slums could not exist in the age of affluence without wealth somehow working to defeat urban life. The automobile stands guilty of being the most pervasive and systematic factor of degradation. Owen has warned us about the destructive effects of automobility: ". . . it is evident," he stressed, "that accommodating all comers driving their cars would mean the elimination of the city itself." Ford in his quixotic way also warned us, when he said, "We shall solve the city problem by leaving the city."

If slums once existed mainly because of problems connected with urban poverty, the automobile has now helped make them an essential part of the urban process. No amount of wealth can prevent the deterioration when the rules, the conditions, and the underhanded tactics favor the complete defeat of urban life.

Urban Elephantiasis

We don't know fully what Ford meant by "leaving the city." Was it River Rouge, built out in Dearborn? Was it the bloated suburbanization of the city Ford destested? If so, urban sprawl was getting under way by 1920, when many workers already required a car to get to work.

From the outset the auto's potential for distant commuting created admiration and awe. "To the car-owner," remarked an English observer in 1903, "it is virtually the same thing whether his home is one mile or a dozen miles from the nearest railway." As a result, "our country districts will revive" when "thousands of town dwellers of today will be the country-dwellers of tomorrow."

Anything the automobile could do was praised. One we have already heard from in the chorus was Herbert Towle, in a 1913 *Scribner's*. The automobile, he observed, "added threefold or more to the habitable areas outside the cities. . . . Think what this will lead to in the course of a generation or two," speculated Towle, "and you will realize the transformation which the low cost automobile is working." To Towle, "the logic of the situation points to the growth of motor colonies" in the rural districts from which residents would commute to work by car.

Even without distinctive colonies, the auto suburbia that grew somehow seemed to infect the intellect. One social scientist was quoted in a 1933 *Literary Digest* "The automobile is making it possible for us to go again to live in quiet spots where we can have neighbors and be neighbors, as in the early days, and where our children may know those fine relationships of intimate living which once counted as our most valued possession."

The mood of the time was well expressed by Charles Kettering in *The New Necessity,* when he said that "all you have to do is drive up to a filling station, buy two dollars worth of gasoline and you can go a hundred miles in any direction and return. . . . When these tracks or roads have covered every logical course and when an automobile can travel these roads with maximum speed and safety, then we can truthfully say that the automobile can do nothing further to liberalize the people of the world."

The mood was put more bluntly by General Wood of Sears and Roebuck, who reportedly said that "historians one day would marvel at the stupidity in building closely when the decentralizing motor car was at our command."

The automobile seemed to bring a springtime of freedom to men: no longer must they build cities as they had for thousands of years. And the automobile thus sprawled the city upon every hill and dale without rationale, social purpose, or aesthetic concern—except for the street and highway access which was essential to the new order.

But in the end decentralization was an act of pure faith, a disastrous pact between the old democratic cities and the new autocracy. The result was to *centralize* physical, economic, and political power around a special machine. That power derived from the complete dependence upon motordom in which people found themselves.

Life in the suburbs turned upon men. Isolation became a stronger reality than freedom. Inaccessibility of services and institutions was stretched more than the new mobility. Privacy became more guarded, neighborliness more like protocol. Of course, rising levels of affluence made it possible to buy off, compensate or disguise many harsh realities. But most people suffered them, and accepted them as if they were as inevitable as the seasons.

Whatever the hidden deprivations of suburban life, the nation today faces the realities of megalopolis. Jean Gottmann called it "a nebulous, quasi-colloidal, structure" in his study of the Boston-to-Washington agglomeration. The futurists Kahn and

Wiener speak of three gargantuan megalopolises by the year 2000: the Gottmann "Boswash," "Chipitts" in the Middle West, and "Sansan" in California. Kahn and Wiener were modest, for Arizona, Texas, and Florida will undoubtedly count their conurbations in the big leagues within three or four decades. The ominous possibility is underwritten by a number of long established trends of motordom:

1. The tendency of the automobile to isolate every element of urban activity so that every cell of activity is related to every other only by the automobile, which in turn multiplies land requirements.

2. The continued growth of congestion and the steady loss of close-in open space, which intensifies the desperate outreaching for more distant breathing spaces.

3. The increasing number of multi-car families and rising personal wealth which encourages dispersion to advance geometrically.

4. The half-century political tradition of doubling highway construction nearly every decade (excepting wars and depressions) to maintain a minimum freedom of the American Road.

5. The steady diversification of motordom into every area of life—the mobile homes, recreation vehicles, and mini-vehicles —and the enlistment of more urban activities as fellow travelers to make life more tolerable on the highways.

6. The extension of the automotive necessity from a purely functional matter into an integral part of human nature in psychic, social, and cultural behavior (see Part IV for a discussion of this topic).

What is the meaning? Of course, an increasing percentage of gross national product will be contributed by automotive transportation. The enormous GNP will become important less for what it is than what it is based upon: the thorough dissipation of cities which Ford prescribed and helped to set in motion.

In a civic-minded gesture at the opening of its new home office building in 1958, the Connecticut General Life Insurance Company sponsored a conference on "The New Highways: Challenge to the Metropolitan Region." The conference was spiked with irony, for the new headquarters occupied 300 acres of rolling countryside beyond the city limits of Hartford—whose entire central business district covers 210 acres, cars and all.

Progress of the automobile is thus pockmarked with ironies: its evolution from a romantic toy into a despotic necessity; its ability to grow upon its destructiveness as well as its contributions to society.

Charles Kettering, speaking of industrial progress, took great pride in the idea that the automobile "has literally taught the entire manufacturing world—and we might even include agriculture in that—how to make two blades of grass grow where one grew before." But for society the automobile has taught one man to live where four lived before, because the urban environment is now pulverized and infertile. While old tenement crowding was real, the auto has now isolated and insulated men from the normal interpersonal relations that are at the foundation of civilized life. Socially the automobile has been as enriching to men as blacktop for growing dahlias.

What the early automobilists thought was the beneficial union of town and country has turned into the sacrificial spoilage of both.

New York: Beleaguered Metropolis

Just as old-fashioned war is difficult to comprehend in all of its destruction and brutality, the automotive conquest is difficult to understand in all of its devastation and lost humanity. Even with deep personal experience in wars or conquests, comprehension is dulled by narrow perspectives and the very human necessity to accommodate oneself to reality.

But when deep personal experience is combined with meaningful communication conquest may begin to be comprehended. Americans in cities such as New York, Washington, and Los Angeles are in an excellent position to pioneer that understanding of the auto conquest. A dialogue among them can lay the groundwork to resist the growing tyranny and establish the foundations for liberation.

Though the automotive attack against New York has been pressed relentlessly for half a century, and has succeeded in overrunning the outer ramparts, Manhattan itself has flourished during the struggle as has no other American city center. The outcome in New York is still in question, however. The overwhelming initiative remains with autocracy, as does the organizational strength, resources, and manpower. Only the first preparations to organize New York for counterattack are evident.

From its beginning the automobile heavily infiltrated Manhattan. Yet it was never able to mount an assault of sufficient strength to dominate mobility or control the pattern of development. At least it couldn't overrun Manhattan as it had other cities.

New York's strength rests not with leadership, which is usually inept, but on the natural defenses of its geography and the durability of its pre-auto growth, plus some inborn weaknesses of the automobile itself.

Manhattan's first advantage is that the automobile never became amphibian. Since it costs upwards of $100 million to construct a two-lane highway tube, which may bring in hardly more than 3,000 people in a peak hour, the number of auto traffic lanes into Manhattan understandably increased very slowly, from 80 to 120 between 1927 and 1957. Here, the old transit dramatizes the great weakness of the modern automobile. While 61 inbound auto lanes transport 110,000 people to Manhattan's core during the peak hour, 26 tracks and 1 bus lane bring in 730,000 people. Transit's demonstrated advantage here is fifteen to one. And since hardly 5 percent of all travel to Manhattan's most dense square mile is by car, compared with, for example, 75 percent in New Haven, the automobile certainly has not defeated that island outpost of democracy.

The Battle of Manhattan, like the Battle of Britain, hinges on invasion capacities, particularly since all routes crossing the Hudson and East rivers into Manhattan are congested at peak periods. Those capacities continue to increase. In 1962 a lower deck was completed on the George Washington Bridge, increasing lanes from eight to fourteen. Currently the new third tube of the Queens-Midtown tunnel (cost: $122 million) will allow about 8,000 more people to ride cars or buses at peak hours —adding less than 1 percent to the total commuter capacity of Manhattan. However, should 10 percent of all automobile commuters switch to rail transit, the added burden would be only about 1.5 percent.

But water crossings are only part of the necessary invasion capacities. At the Queens-Midtown Tunnel's east portal the Bushwick Expressway is planned; at the west portal the Mid-Manhattan Expressway is proposed. The bill for all three additions: $480 million. The Regional Plan Association has estimated that the new tube and expressway extensions will permit about 16,000 commuters "to switch to cars at a cost of about $22,000 per person." Upon such calculations the eminent transportation economist, William S. Vickrey of Columbia University, exclaimed that "in no other major area are pricing practices so irrational, so out of date, and so conducive to waste. . . ."

Irrational, of course, yet very pragmatic—that's the logic of conquest in any form. The secret of highway conquest is one step at a time, rarely a grand plan, for plans are susceptible to a comprehension of the consequences, comparisons of benefits, and, naturally, counterplans. But the highwaymen know that a highway wedge will eventually go through, even to split the hard rock of Manhattan.

That's what eventually happened when the George Washington Bridge pierced northern Manhattan. That's what the Mid-Manhattan Expressway will do for the Lincoln and Queens-Midtown tunnels. And that's what the world's first $100 million mile on the Lower Manhattan Expressway would have done for the Holland Tunnel and for the Brooklyn and Manhattan bridges over the East River if the highwaymen had had their way. When the Midtown Manhattan project is complete, and should the Lower Manhattan Expressway project be revived again and built, all three highway crossings of the Hudson River will pass through Manhattan as freely as a highway crosses the Mojave Desert.

The Lower Manhattan Expressway was originally planned

as soon as the Holland Tunnel was complete in 1927. But the steep price for ten lanes across 1.4 miles of Manhattan—currently $150 million—delayed actual development for nearly half a century while autocratic power increased. Then, after final approval, Mayor John Lindsay "de-mapped" the project in 1969 after an unusual level of civic protest, despite the fact that the federal government would have paid 90 percent because the route was designated as urban extension of the *interstate* highway system.

Some 1,980 families and 880 businesses would have been relocated for this gold-plated mile. Yet both the tunnel and bridges have been congested for decades. Moreover, the Port Authority, owner of the Holland's four-lane twin tubes, stated emphatically that it is "totally impractical to expand the capacity of the Holland Tunnel." Whatever this apparent hitch in the highwaymen's doctrine of build-to-the-edge-of-town now and force-through-later may mean, Manhattan may still become, like most other city centers in America, just another pass-through place.

Both penetrating and passing through Manhattan are struggles for New York's heart which, for all their assault power, cannot alone defeat the city. Defeat will come only if parking can obliterate buildings with thousands of businesses to raise the necessary garages and radically alter the commuting and travel habits of millions.

Parking is now the automobile's weakest force attacking Manhattan. The place is too big, and there is the deep-rooted strength of underground transit, however deprived that system may be. It is not easy in Manhattan for parking to get a hold on mobility (as indicated by the many huge new structures without parking) and winnow away the huge concentration. The water barriers obstruct the auto's usual tactic of gradually accelerating the dispersion of new buildings. And it is against parking that the most positive civic leadership is now directed.

Yet even on that tight little island parking makes steady and slow advances which in time could be disastrous. Despite the city's restrictions on unlimited expansion, there were 67,000 off-street parking spaces in the midtown area in 1969, distributed in 52 facilities. These spaces increase at more than 2,500 per year, or nearly 5 percent.

A faster buildup has long been sought by New York's Traffic Department. In 1960 it submitted a proposal to encircle the midtown core with 16 municipal garages having a total of 10,000 spaces costing $57 million. (One may therefore add nearly $5,700 to the $22,000 cost per person which would encourage commuters and shoppers to switch from public transport to cars in Manhattan.) The City Planning Commission fought the scheme from the outset, disapproving the application and successfully fending off a variety of political maneuvers over the years.

Although 10,000 spaces would open the floodgates of parking only a bit, that number used four times daily would mean that a significant proportion of all available midtown street space would be occupied at any moment by the newly garage-subsidized vehicles. Already it is an established fact that the streets of midtown are *congested almost equally throughout the day*. What would happen when 40,000 vehicles a day are added to the unexpandable local street spaces?

The degenerative results have been put in a formula by one of the few leaders of the anti-autocratic movement, the architect and planner Victor Gruen. His formula, based on work and research in many cities, states that *"for each additional automobile penetrating the heart area of a city, one visitor or inhabitant of the same heart area is lost."* Thus, if 10,000 additional cars come into town daily the total number of people coming to the city will drop by 10,000.

Gruen calculated that the sixteen proposed garages would require about 3.5 million square feet of building space. If the garages were built at six levels they would occupy the land area that could be used for 11.6 million square feet of high-tax-paying office space at twenty levels—accommodating more than 50,000 workers. Jane Jacobs, a staunch urbanist with some strong anti-autocratic inclinations, examined one of the Traffic Department's proposed garage sites. She found that 129 businesses, including those facing the "huge deadening garage [would be] amputated from their constellation of mutual support. . . ."

Yet the parking struggle and the entire Battle of Manhattan are but small actions in the overall struggle for the New York metropolis—though someday we may credit that battle for turning the tide against automobility. The waves of automotive pressure against the Manhattan core of 8.6 square miles are powerful precisely because the remainder of the metropolitan area's nearly 20 million people are already dispersed to some 12,700 square miles (equal to Massachusetts and Connecticut combined) and inundated by automotive necessity.

In the immense inner and outer suburbs there are more than 1,500 miles of freeways and parkways. Announced plans for the region in New Jersey, New York, and Connecticut promise that about $4 billion will flow each decade to promote automobility on the main regional network alone. Yet the terribly overloaded *old* system (much of which was completed only in the 1960's) powerfully complicates the possibilities of relief at any cost. The region's busiest artery, the Long Island Expressway, closely parallels the Northern State Parkway ("parkway" nowadays is virtually a misnomer), also congested. Can the Long Island Expressway be double-decked? Can a third expressway be built parallel to the first two?

Not many years ago Robert Moses, who initiated parkways and expressways on Long Island, spelled out the necessity for the autocratic highway buildup: "The building of roads must catch up and keep pace with the output of cars. . . . Congestion is here. Strangulation is not far off."

Washington: Open City

If New York still stands upright, proud, and undefeated at its center, defenseless Washington always seemed to await conquest by the automobile—ever since Pierre L'Enfant laid out the Capital in 1791. Even at that, its wide avenues set in a grid pattern and overlaid by sweeping radial boulevards only satisfied motordom for its first few decades. Nor did its first-generation freeways relieve the automotive pressure. Now the need to expand all highways is more urgent than ever.

However, one part of the Washington area is unlikely to get many highway improvements. It is already saturated with them. Huddling about the Pentagon's fortress-like form as if they were its outer defenses are fourteen complete interchanges. Each is comparable in area to the Pentagon itself—or either of its two parking fields. Driving south past the Pentagon on the Shirley Memorial Highway one threads continuously through seven of the interchanges, each sorting and organizing the life of the metropolis.

True, the congestion of cloverleaves offers the cartographer exciting new patterns to beautify his maps. Actually, they support the main assault on central Washington. That had been underway since the late 1930's, when the first of many underpasses was built to encourage larger volumes of traffic on Massachusetts, Connecticut, Virginia, and other broad avenues to penetrate the downtown. In classic manner, transit declined, parking pressures climbed, and then the entire lengths of these wide avenues and boulevards became congested, despite the underpasses.

Washington has thus built for the automobile. In 1947, when the district government spent less than $6 million on highway improvement, it listed a backlog of $49 million. In 1965, after having actually spent ten times as much as the entire 1947 backlog in the interim (including $74 million in 1965), it then listed $452 million in urgent highway projects.

When the pressure of traffic first appeared in the 1920's it did not take long to discover that the Rock Creek Parkway could be a natural (and very inexpensive) freeway, excellent for commuting. This magnificent canyon near the heart of the city thus became an automotive bowling alley, unfit for the high purposes set for it by the planners of 1901. Then other freeways were constructed on park lands, especially along the Potomac, and on the other rather bountiful public lands in and near Washington. Both economics and politics were on the side of the highwaymen in the early years.

In the late 1950's and early 1960's a series of plans were brought forward. One that appeared to stem the tide of the automobile was the so-called *Year 2000*, plan which called for only seventy-four miles of freeways, parkways and junior expressways, as against ninety-five miles of rapid transit. This "radical corridor" plan proposed that "most new development" be guided into some eighteen well-defined satellite cities along six major and one minor radial spokes of the rapid transit system. All of these urban centers would have fast and direct connections to the center of Washington. Large open spaces would be preserved between them.

But the *Year 2000* plan was a mere long-term guide. What counted were the short-term plans for the Maryland, Virginia, and District portions of the capital. These could more accurately reflect the automobile's immediate momentum.

Across the District boundary in Maryland the planning is solidly autocratic. Although the metropolitan transit system moves ahead, the clear logic behind it, of focusing development around a limited number of vigorous urban centers, is a dead letter. The 1967 highway plan for the Maryland suburbs calls for a freeway network which will border nearly every suburban square mile. This pattern carried to Virginia would mean that all 2,000-odd square miles in metropolitan Washington will be strangled in thirty years. The plan also calls for "major highways" within a fraction of a mile of virtually every buildable acre.

The multiplication of highways is matched by the supreme standards they command. Freeways will cut a swath of 300 feet. The more extensive "major highways" are really 150-foot expressways, with access control except where existing roadside development has precluded full attainment. Many will become full freeways; a few already are.

Washington's beltways and other circumferential routes are of particular importance. Whereas the *Year 2000* plan sought radial corridors of development to focus on and reinforce the traditional centrality of cities, the highways are both radial and circumferential. This represents the auto's power to scatter development.

The beltway idea was ostensibly evolved to retrieve some rationality for auto movement. Washington's 66-mile, $190-million Capital Beltway lassos the metropolis at the closest ring permitted by outward growth at the time interstate money became available to construct it. (Earlier other beltways had been proposed closer in, before highway finance came up to the challenge.) But in the logic of things automotive, beltways merely contribute to the irrationality of urban form by promoting more activities to spread to more dispersed places. Then more beltways are required. Before the Capital Beltway was completed an Outer Beltway was being planned some four to six miles beyond. And a third, merging into Baltimore's freeway pattern, is now planned for the more distant future.

Washington's beltway, like those girdling other cities, signifies that the city is no longer a center but increasingly a mere fulcrum for activities that go on around it, not in it. "Balance between public and private transport mainly reflects the balance between centralization and dispersion of urban activities," candidly observes a traffic expert. Washington's growth demonstrates it amply. Its beltway is really one massive interchange straddling the city, symbolizing the frenzied struggle by which modern men interact and communicate with one another.

The lesson Washington demonstrates is that automobility is impossible in cities simply because automobility destroys cities. Whatever the direct cost of highways, the resulting conquest separates men by the very means which were thought to bring men together. Apparently the reckoning will come only after the whole metropolis is hopelessly bloated and spread by automobility, totally walled and barricaded by roadways, and universally strangled by traffic.

Los Angeles: Autocratic Mistress

If Washington lay a century in waiting for the automobile, Los Angeles was bred for it. Perhaps that's why this City of Angels is the only really modern metropolis, the most American, a metropolis described by Harrison Salisbury as "nestled under its blanket of smog, girdled by bands of freeways, its core eviscerated by concrete strips and asphalt fields, its circulatory arteries pumping away without focus . . . the prototype of gasopolis, the rubber wheeled living region of the future." However, Salisbury was more pointed when he paraphrased Lincoln Steffens's comment on communist Russia: "I have seen the future —and it doesn't work."

A New Yorker's contempt? Hardly. Los Angeles' former police chief Bill Parker (Watts, 1965) said: "We are being deluged by a sea of automobiles that will destroy our economy." LA's traffic engineer Seymour Taylor said so as well: "Metropolitan Los Angeles is afflicted with 'urban mobilitis.' "

Despite the absence of tangible virtue or integrity, there once were efforts to give the young metropolis a proper upbringing. It has been said that "no other area of the country ever had such an intensive network of lines" as those of the interurban Pacific Electric. Built about 1900, when there were but a few hundred thousand people in the region to capitalize it, the automobile began forcing a reduction of services in the 1930's. All passenger service ceased in 1961 when there were more than six million people who could not keep up its expenses. Such is the fall of a sound system of transportation where the automobile has had its greatest field day.

The disfiguring of the metropolis is revealed in the trade statistics of central retail merchants, who once blundered into supporting centrifugal highway development. In the 1930's the downtown accounted for 75 percent of all retail trade. By 1946 it dropped to 50 percent, and by the early 1960's it had plunged to a bare 18 percent. The center was no longer the center. Centrality disappeared, along with unity and integrity. The centrifugal outflow and the lateral dispersion of activities effectively destroyed the *what* and *where* that make a metropolis whole, rational, and coherent, for either going, doing, or just being a worthy human place, not an unhinged nebula.

Yet the California autocrats are seeing to it that the San Bernardino Freeway, which is hardly more than twenty years old, is completely redeveloped. Before the system in the Los Angeles area is fully completed they are claiming that $100 million is required to remedy present deficiencies on existing freeways. That is a figure that rivals urban renewal expenditures in the area.

Now the struggle of fantasy has begun. The first experimental million dollars have been put on forty-two miles of freeway to test measures to maintain the capacities that freeways were always supposed to have. The capacity was undermined not by the barnacles of roadside development or the crossfire conflicts at intersections, but by sheer numbers, by stop-and-go congestion. Even at $20 and $30 million a mile, road capacity could not be assured—except by limiting how many vehicles may enter those golden freeway passages. Now all access ramps are to be controlled by sophisticated surveillance mechanisms, computer allocation of billets, and signals and radios to be certain that no car enters a freeway unless there is an assured place for it.

Road congestion originally forced the development of the freeway. Now congestion on the freeway is about to deflect its own congestion back onto the local street systems.

This goal of rationing mobility has big money behind it. And it is a goal invoking the faith that money-fed science will make fantasy into reality and reality into fantasy. That faith rejects the real world of hard questions and straight answers. It strives for a road capacity where that headway between cars will be hardly more than a half-second at 40 or 60 mph—whatever the sacrifice by the city, the family, the person, the driver.

Los Angeles has long been in the possession of automobility. Anyone who has *been* in New York and *driven* in Los Angeles cannot miss being impressed in New York by people who walk proudly with heads high. The impression is magnified if one tries to drive in Manhattan or to walk in Los Angeles. What good is it that one can reach anywhere in the Los Angeles basin in an hour when no place can be reached in less than a half-hour? That is what traffic engineer Taylor means when he says that "Los Angeles is the city of magnificent distances."

With nearly 700 miles of the freeway forge already in place, the plan for 1980 calls for 800 miles more. The extra cost: $10 billion or thereabouts. And what will the system do to the city when it is complete? Taylor predicted (to a San Francisco audience) that "Los Angeles may have as much traffic on its city streets as it had in 1960 on freeways and streets combined."

Nevertheless, the thought that cars in Los Angeles are increasing three times faster than people and five times faster than highway construction was enough to choke even *Car and Driver* magazine, whose Brock Yates reported that "Los Angeles simply cannot afford to do anything but nurture more automobiles; at the same time it is headed for a doomsday when the scene might become so saturated with cars that human life will become impossible." And it is precisely in Los Angeles where Harrison Salisbury quotes officials as saying that "the system is exhausting the elements necessary for human life—land, air, and water."

Some people have repeatedly tried to stop the race against absolute immobility by developing a new rapid-transit system. But these schemes to economize on mobility have been turned down just as repeatedly by the auto-hypnotized electorate. Yet one day it must come. "I am sure," said an official, "that it will be decided on the day when traffic stops altogether, and then it will take five years to build."

Autocracy Builds a Model Non-City

We have seen what cars can do to cities. We have reviewed the evidence of their basic incompatibility. Although Los Angeles was the easiest conquest for the auto, we have not yet looked into a case where the automobile founded its own urbanism. Not very far from Los Angeles that has begun to occur.

Partly out of its immense success in Los Angeles and partly out of the contradictions of that success, the automobile is setting out the foundation for a new kind of urbanism out across the San Gabriel Mountains in the Mojave Desert. An advance contingent of almost half a million people have taken control of about 10,000 square miles and are building the world's first non-city, 200 times the size of San Francisco. That contingent now appears to be demonstrating the epitome of automobility.

Formerly the great desert space was a challenge for twenty-mule teams to span with their grubstakes of borax. To help the teams and later the railroads and automobiles to span the great spaces, a few small towns like Barstow, Victorville, and Mojave came into being. But since 1950 the great space and the several towns have afforded the automobile the means to try out a new development.

Even Los Angeles grew up as a reasonable city should, from the center out. But in the Mojave Desert the automobile has taken a new track; it has started development almost everywhere at once. This approach was presumably the urban application of the infant auto industry's 1905 theory that "as long as man has a car he can do anything and go anywhere—*anywhere.*" So the new non-city didn't require a distinctive form at all; any urban function could go anywhere. The automobile itself could presumably overcome the dead weight of formlessness it forces onto the environment. Thus a cobweb of roads using old town sites as the major intersections offered the excitement of exercising the full capacity of 400 hp without ever leaving one's neighborhood.

Autocracy's Mojave Non-City scheme was supported by a huge contribution from the federal government. Under the Small Tract Act of 1938, tens of thousands of 2.5- and 5-acre homesteads scattered across the desert were given to individuals for a $300 "improvement." The land peddlers were also joyous at selling private desert land at city prices, and proclaimed opportunities to peanut speculators as glittering as the "exciting Gold Rush days of the 1800's." The peddlers were permitted to subdivide land in waterless, roadless, serviceless isolation at rock-bottom standards of improvement. Most could make a profit if one lot in a hundred sprouted a house, for in the desert vista a few dozen new houses gives a sales pitch the vision of a building boom. Housing the salesmen alone was almost enough to do the trick.

The sight of the Mojave Non-City is majesty in spotted disarray. A broad-sloping hillside, perhaps ten miles away, may reveal five isolated square-mile sections, each laid in rigid grid and scratched in the rocky earth by motor grader in a day. There is no boundary or center to this ghostly urbanism, only threads of county roads that carry commuters twenty or forty miles to a test station, airfield, or cement plant. Already the burdens of the isolated distances raise the challenge of life to that of an 1880's homestead. The automobile's capacity to go anywhere has set another trap. Slowly county government is pulled in to subsidize the structural waste: roadbuilding, school busing, police and fire protection, health and social services, all spread across endless wasteland. But the biggest trap is of suburbia at a vast new scale. Even traffic has begun its inflationary spiral. Five o'clock congestion appears like a desert flash flood without a cloud in sight. Congestion is beginning to appear at desert intersections with hardly a structure in sight.

Mojave Non-City has so far seen only round one of its development. The land boom of the late fifties and early sixties has waned. Round two may be expected when saturation and congestion on the Los Angeles coastal plain build up new pressures to move over the mountains. Already demonstrated is the capacity of the automobile to consume maximum acreage to build a minimum city. "Only now," exclaimed the promotional Antelope Valley Progress Association, "the search for gold has given way to the search for suitable FLATLANDS. . . ." Development may then thicken to about one house and two cars per ten acres over an area larger than Massachusetts.

Contrary to appearances, Mojave Non-City is right in the American mainstream, unfolding a continuity of events from the first 1920 auto suburbs, and foretelling a homogenous habitational pattern across the continent. David Carlson, writing in a 1963 *Architectural Forum*, suggested how it now "appears that the American region, replacing the city, can become a workable reality through the most efficient and extensive transportation systems ever conceived—systems which, as soon as they are in existence, will pose a whole new range of super-urban problems."

Autocracy in Europe

Dreadfully mistaken are those who believe that automotive conquest operates only in fertile America. West Europeans have been smug in the feeling that their cities are free of the autocratic onslaught witnessed in Detroit, Washington, and Los Angeles. But the forces of postwar affluence are radically eroding the old defenses and building a European autocracy in societies hardly better protected than the American. While the environment is different, the complex laws conditioning it for autocracy are the same.

For more than fifty years the European automobile was purely aristocratic, thanks partly to war, depression, and preparation for war. But aristocracy gave way abruptly to the first wave of mass autocracy in country after country in the 1950's. The German *autobahnen* then began expanding. Italian *autostrades,* French *autoroutes,* and English motorways soon got underway. All routes were initially only *between* major cities and, with knightly chivalry, never got too close to the tidy urban skirts. But this came to an end in 1958 with the opening of Europe's first really urban freeway in Berlin—an inward penetration of the Avus raceway of 1919.

In 1957 an American observed that "a dozen years after the war, the struggle between Western Europe and the automobile shows signs of becoming as great an influence for change as the war itself." And a dozen years later in 1969, the Rome and Paris police were openly battling motorists to prevent total paralysis. Regular summer tieups on the *autobahnen* were stretching twenty-five miles and not breaking up until late at night. And today the highway plan for Cologne resembles the freeway vise clamped around Atlanta. Copenhagen is scheduled to be musclebound with a network comparable to that of St. Louis.

A measure of the raw automotive power is the new freeway on the mountains overlooking the Mediterranean on the Italian Riviera. That seventy-mile highway from the French border is unique: there are eighteen miles of bridges and sixty tunnels; virtually all of the rest consists of huge cuts and fills.

The Dutch are now busy laying out 2,000 miles of freeway to prepare for (and to help assure) 10 million vehicles by the year 2000 (100 times their 1946 registrations). One official privately voiced the fear that the resulting *countryside* six-mile grid pattern will make all Holland like Los Angeles, where the *metropolitan* grid is about four miles.

Though Holland registered only its second millionth vehicle in September 1968, congestion had already reached absurdity. One bright Sunday that September a Rotterdam family set out for the beach at The Hague. Upon completing the trip of sixteen miles in 2.5 hours the family found that there was no place to park, and so returned to Rotterdam (in an expeditious one hour) without getting out of their car. They didn't follow an alternative plan to visit a park because the radio reported a six-mile lineup of cars at an intersection they would have passed through. How, then, will Holland ever drive and park 10 million vehicles? How will they have enough money left to pay for the parks and other places to drive to?

The crucial test for Europe is whether automotive dispersion and necessity will build up into a new wave of autocracy.

Europe still seems to ride in the rumble seat of the roaring twenties. Enough pedestrians are still around to challenge a driver's skill at intimidation. Entrances to houses in villages passed by major national highways are often within four or six feet of traffic moving at fifty miles per hour. Drivers are still excited enough to fistfight for parking places. Street parking regulations are unsophisticated. Everywhere, it seems, drivers invade sidewalks to park all day, often forcing walkers into the streets to get by. Narrow trafficways often expand themselves by direct scraping and abrasive pounding of vehicles against old buildings, especially at medieval corners.

Sudden mass automobility has provoked some peculiar accommodations. In Spain many vestibules with wide, double oak doors having polished brass fittings have become garages for small Fiats. Occasionally original paintings still adorn these brightly tiled "garages." (Predictably, that incongruous vehicle in the vestibule is a powerful motive for a family to build a single-family house in the town's first suburb.)

Many of the most famous plazas, squares, and courts, except St. Peter's in Rome and St. Mark's in Venice, have been pressed into parking service. Both the grand entrance and the huge court of the Christianborg Palace in Copenhagen have lost their majesty

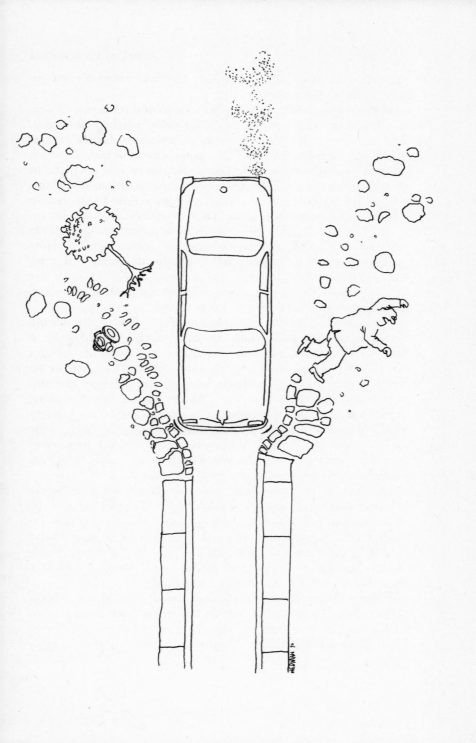

to a smothering vehicular occupation. In The Hague, the fine arched entrances of the Binnenhoff (Parliament) are a through trafficway, its large plaza a storage place for several hundred vehicles. Brussels' Grand Place, one of Europe's most exquisite public spaces, is violated to its vehicular capacity. Bordering the Grand Place is the spired Hotel de Ville and its beautiful court—whose capacity is revealed to be twenty-five motorcars. Bern's Bundesplatz, fronting on the Parliamentary Palace, seems to be a very commendable space, though its merits are nearly impossible to discern when standing in a sea of metal.

No city spreads its beauty before the automobile more than Paris. At the Place de la Concorde there is a traffic circle of about ten lanes around its obolisk, almost as large as that isolating the Arc de Triomphe. Similarly, the plaza at the Palais Royal, a very handsome space, and the monumental Place de Vendome both suffer from capacity parking. Loitering on foot—in the spirit of their creation—is simply dangerous. Although Notre Dame was scheduled for a 290-car garage under Square Jean XXIII, protests won the day and the project was abandoned in 1970.

Yet beyond these wholesale invasions, Paris has a mammoth underground garage construction program—including plans for the Place de Vendome and Place de la Concorde—and requires 1.5 parking spaces for every new housing unit, assuring increments of about 10,000 spaces annually. But Paris drivers even now reportedly can move only 32 percent of each driving hour.

Nor are France's provincial towns exempt. Cambria, near the Belgian border, enjoys a very large town plaza. No trees or vegetation are in sight. But the plaza, totally asphalted, parks about 260 cars, the peripheral street another 100. The scene displays all the grace of an American discount store parking lot.

The sudden flood of vehicles upon Europe's compact cities provides an insight into the depth of the automobile's real power. There are relatively few wide streets or handy spaces, such as Cambria's, for the auto to freely claim for its moving, stopping, and storing; that is, there is a very meager "natural" environment for easy auto expansion, unlike the United States.

Somehow, every city or village accepts vehicles as an article of faith in progress and roots about to accommodate them. Congestion evidently begins in many towns when as few as 5 percent of the families own automobiles. Bit by bit, the congestion is sufficiently relieved by both public and private means (e.g., the Spanish vestibule) only to encourage more vehicles to be put into circulation. Consequently the town begins to be changed —not to suit the automobile's most effective or realistic role in urban life—but in response to the urgent driving and parking pressures.

However, Europe is still relatively fortunate. Its cities are hard nuts for automobility to crack. The checks on the automobile have a clear though limited effect. Downtown pedestrian malls are springing forth in many dozens of cities; some will evolve into complete networks. Virtually all of the English new towns provide protected walkways. And, more important, new or expanded subway (metro) systems are blossoming in Rotterdam, Munich, Hamburg, Frankfurt, Zurich, Paris, Stockholm, London, Oslo, Brussels.

Yet all these efforts together cannot be considered more than just stop-gap measures. The malls are safety catwalks in a setting rapidly becoming intolerable for pedestrians. The subways may help maintain the integrity of urban form, but they also protect the automobile from its familiar excesses.

Europe is a bit like Zermatt, Switzerland. "Yes, it's true— there are no cars at Zermatt," announces an official Swiss travel brochure. But each year the Swiss government constructs a few more very expensive miles of modern highway up the canyon toward this resort town below the Matterhorn. Its main street may always remain off-limits to cars, as we are now told, but that will not prevent the rest of the town and its high mountain valley from vehicular innundation.

The British have raised more fundamental questions about the automobile than any other people. One English planner pleaded: "Why destroy the rest of the environment in an attempt which is, in any case, doomed to failure?"

4

OPPRESSION
OF MANKIND

War Dead

LIKE ALL CONQUEST, the controlled chaos of the auto undermines the basis of life.

Whereas we have emphasized the nature of the auto conquest and the environmental destruction up to this point, we will now focus upon the human results.

The direct consequence of war is injury and death. Harry Truman had good reason to label the automobile "the most deadly weapon man has yet invented," despite his tenure during the first years of the Bomb. Though he barely missed being in office at the time of America's millionth military battle death in 1952—176 years in the making—he was still president when our millionth traffic death occurred—52 years after one H. H. Bliss was run over by an electric taxi at Seventy-fourth Street and Central Park West in New York City, on September 13, 1899.

Bad recording must account for the superb safety record

between '96 and '99. But by 1905 *Scientific American* was concerned that accidents were "threatening to work injury to automobile interests . . . and provoking prejudice in the public mind." From that time onward the auto's inflictions upon men seems to have been managed quite well, for the first 1.5 million auto deaths do not seem to have noticeably prejudiced the public or otherwise harmed auto interests. The mushrooming fatalities did not seem to matter one whit, whether the 4,500 auto deaths of 1914 were one-sixteenth of all accidental deaths or the 32,900 of 1930 were one-third of the total.

When the automobile was still in its industrial infancy, Anatole France predicted that it would be worshiped by Americans and that the machine would, in turn, destroy them. Now an insurance executive has predicted that auto accidents will become the largest cause of *all* deaths for persons under sixty-five by the year 2000. Will this be the fulfillment of the prophecy?

There were 55,225 traffic deaths reported in 1968. Every year 13 million accidents produce about 4 million injuries, which means that the total present population would be injured every fifty years (discounting the 2,761,250 persons who would perish in the same period). The government reports that every new car has a 25- to 40-percent chance of causing personal injury to someone. Yet animals are hit far more: the AAA reports that 365 million died in 1968, nearly four for every car going.

Annually we report new crests of the crime wave. But Judge Alvin Goldstein reports in *Traffic Quarterly* that auto accidents take a "far greater toll in our society in one year than organized crime could account for in one hundred years." (And besides the crime in which automobiles are accomplices, some 500,000 vehicles themselves are objects of criminal behavior each year.)

The wave to be concerned about is the toll of the motorcar. The 1950's saw about 365,000 die violently from ruptured spleens, kidneys crushed by shattered pelvises, hearts punctured by broken ribs, or just plain shock. The 1960's saw the figure rise to about 473,000—an increase of nearly 30 percent. Will the 1970's see 615,000 doomed, the 1980's 799,000, the 1990's 1,039,000?

Well, how can we reduce auto casualties—short of hurting

Detroit's profits? Old-style military wars must be ruled out, even though the restrictions imposed on road travel saved at least 40,000 lives in World War II. Both Korea and Vietnam have revealed that war no longer reduces auto accidents. The Air Force got shook up about this in 1951 and again in 1969, when it discovered that more of its men were killed and injured by automobiles than in combat. The auto now has too deep a grip, and, beyond that, gas rationing could not improve safety very much without bringing the country to a total standstill.

There are three ingredients in every accident: the driver, the vehicle, and the roadway or roadway environment. Pre-Nader experts focused almost wholly on the driver, for it was widely believed that only new scientific knowledge could make cars safer and only a larger slice of the GNP could make highways safer. Blaming the driver was the way GM wanted it. That's why the industry set up the Automotive Safety Foundation in 1937.

The driver started getting the third degree soon after J. C. Furnas' inflammatory article in a 1935 *Reader's Digest*, "And Sudden Death," enraged the country and sent out evangelists and traffic police to put the morbid fear of sin into every driver. But the evangelism, along with expanded enforcement and paperwork, was of little value in reducing the crimson statistics.

Driver training was rapidly extended throughout the country in the high-school curriculum, with little effect. According to a U.S. Public Health Service doctor, "no conclusions can be drawn as to whether driver education is or is not effective." But in Texas a Board of Insurance report showed that drivers trained in the Texas schools were involved in 12 percent more accidents than those who were not. A debate grew as more school-trained drivers became traffic citizens, and the accident rates pressed on in their irresistible course.

Driver enforcement was also tried with increasing frequency and intensity. But the general results were dramatically sterile. "Unfortunately," observed Daniel Moynihan in 1959, "there is no evidence that cracking down on speed has much effect on traffic safety." In 1955, Moynihan reported, Connecticut Governor Abraham Ribicoff set out to reverse his bad first-year accident rate by increasing the suspension of licenses for thirty days from 372 in 1955 to 10,055 in 1956. The results: Accidents increased again over the "bad" year; injuries rose "sharply"; only the death rate dropped—slightly.

Moynihan then pointed to the dilemma always confronting those who strive to raise driver behavior to an exacting and safe level: "The significant personal characteristics seem to be so personal it is hopeless to think of doing anything about them for the limited purposes of traffic safety." Only a rigorously disciplined automaton could become a really safe driver.

All along it was known that drivers without accident histories were the biggest killers. Furnas himself described them in a *Collier's* article commemorating the first million deaths as "staid fathers of families, hot-rodders, grandmothers, drunks, salesmen in a hurry, pretty girls meaning no harm, truck drivers bullying through. . . ." They were, in other words, almost anyone who gets behind a wheel. But efforts to get at the driver continued.

Research also piled up, and in 1966 Arthur D. Little, Inc., studied the mass of it and concluded: ". . . there are, at present, no well-supported scientific data regarding driver behavior that can be applied to the reduction of accidents."

The second ingredient of an accident is the vehicle. In 1946, when car motors had only about 85 hp, Bergan Evans noted that "things are getting worse . . . and if the manufacturers make good—as they surely will—on their promise of more power and more speed, they are going to get very much worse." And they did, as engines were souped up to the power of pursuit planes. More power for accident promotion is but one example of automotive practice in the wide, wide field of vehicle safety.

Other examples appeared in succession. Many years of persuasion, pressure, and, in the end, legislation preceded the installation of standard seat belts on all vehicles. The vehicular dynamics of the infamous 1961 Corvair reveal the cold calculations behind profits. So do the eight safety features built into the prototype Mustang in 1963—since all were eliminated in the first promotional model.

Calculated, too, is the industry's open disdain of designing vehicles to carry people through collisions alive, in the face of varied proof that the human body *can* survive crashes at very high speeds if given a reasonable chance. The industry didn't even bother to redesign the simple common ornaments and protrusions that crush and impale people, sometimes in accidents at slow walking speeds. Style was too important to let safety intervene.

Profitmaking appeared again when it was learned that not only were the results of auto safety research being ignored, but critical research carried out at the Cornell Aeronautical Laboratory was kept fully anonymous concerning makes and models, although 60 percent of the research funds were federal and almost all of the information came from public bodies. And then, when Ralph Nader, a critic more substantial than straw, appeared, testified at congressional committees, and wrote *Unsafe at Any Speed*, he was shadowed by a General Motors agent trying to gather personal information to discredit and undermine him.

What it boils down to is that the automobile is "public health enemy number one in this country." That, at least, was the consensus of three Yale public health doctors. Yet the industry is very fast to scream "Big Brother" and "bureaucratic tyranny" when society considers even the most elementary remedies—alarms it hardly bothers to sound when repressive measures for drivers are legislated.

And what about the third ingredient of an accident, the highway and driving environment? Could there be a profit motive in the state highway engineers' offices prompting the design of highways with less safety than money permitted? It was a Bronx TV repairman, Joe Linko—the highwaymen's Ralph Nader —who, with his camera, demonstrated to the public that their highwaymen had been systematically building thousands of fixed objects, ditches, and embankments into even the newest freeways that demolish vehicles out of control. Soon the backup data showed up: single-car crashes into fixed objects accounted for 18,830 highway deaths in 1966, over one-third of the total. Sixty percent of all fatalities in single-car accidents on the Interstate system run off the road; three-quarters of those vehicles hit obstacles, one-quarter ditches and steep embankments. Federal road chief Frank Turner confessed to Congress that the removal of these roadside hazards would cost more than one $1 billion, an admission of great error or great unconcern for safety extending over fifty years of experience and research.

Well, when the people become enlightened, the profitmakers, engineers, and lawmakers somehow seem to learn awfully fast. So in the coming decade we may expect safer vehicles and safer highways to do much of what efforts for safer driving could never do. But what can we expect from a truly comprehensive frontal attack on auto safety?

If new, more penetrating programs of driver training, discipline, and punishment are inaugurated—and they will be, regardless of the rest—we can be sure of a tyranny of man's physiology and psyche. If passengers are "packaged" more thoroughly, particularly if the seat belt grows into an elaborate harness, automobility becomes simply auto imprisonment. And if highways are made safe only when there is a wide skid pan on both sides all along the raceway, how much more will this tyrannize the environment and extend the limited access principle to Balkanize every quarter-section of man's earthly abode?

The removal of every obstacle to automobility opens to automobility a new round of growth and a more binding necessity. Safety is not an exception. While a low level of safety did not noticeably stalemate automotive growth, a rapid improvement in safety could be another one of those new and powerful reinforcements the automobile has found in every aspect of its existence.

Nader's service to democracy and the manner of his one-man attack on the autocratic establishment is highly commendable. Yet he has forced the industry to take political castor oil when that industry was too childish to take the stuff itself. One day the industry will privately thank him because it has made them stronger. Because of it they will be freer to move more forcefully in promoting Autokind toward its endless opportunities.

Shell Shock

Conflict creates strain among men. While the struggle continues, human values, traditions, and organizations are sacrificed or suppressed to sustain the mobilization. The result is shell shock. And today the rancorous confrontation between youth and the establishment, the irrational protests and riots, and the nihilism of the hippie may be partly explained as states of shock induced by the conflict of Mankind and Autokind.

The powerful forces of machines, money, and organization are too much for human tolerance. But, since these now dominate society—and define the terms of rationality—the only immediate response to the overorganized world is negative, irrational, and anti-organizational. As the meaningless conflict continues over the years, men simply enter into various forms of collective shock.

Heavy highway casualties and the losing fight with congestion and pollution are but the most superficial of the automotive factors undermining the emotional stability of the populace. Behind them is the steady intensification of the automotive necessity, making more auto travel more necessary more frequently. Regimentation and suppression intensify accordingly.

Where there is a strong social tradition underlying the personal stability of men, these trials cannot cause significant disorder. But for some inexplicable reason men began to retreat from their social tradition as soon as they first invited machines into their lives. Men lost control of city development within a quarter-century after the automobile's introduction. We have come to the point where the environment no longer accommodates people except through the mediation of automobiles. Similarly, institutions increasingly respond to men only via the profitability of machines and mobility.

The vehicle that was thought to bring men together—the

city man and the country man, to make all men neighbors again—methodically alienated one man from another. The car was a social hoax, a system of human dissociation.

When men become alienated and lose their sense of one another, they lose their sense of history, tradition, and place in the world. Then the loss reaches to man's psyche, to his sense of purpose and identity, and, with that, to the meaning of even very ordinary things. The latter is demonstrated when driving etiquette becomes the most important ethical foundations in high-school instruction.

Just as the car has put distance between places, it has built barriers between people. Distances are spanned, to be sure, but only for necessary contact. Contacts are controlled, by appointment only, for "important" matters of business and self-interest. The chance meetings that enriched life between familiar persons in the past are closed out by walls of steel and glass and by the calculated contacts so dear to the modern institutions. The human faculties that might excite a fusion of art, association, and intellect are preoccupied with calculating a profitable pattern of contacts.

Consequently men have forgotten how to like each other. They only know how to use each other. That is what they are taught and how their lives are organized. And when one expresses a liking for another person, one is merely suspected of making use of him. That is the consequence when relationships are hybrid and calculated rather than socially free and natural.

Here, in capsule, is the alienation that drains man's psyche. A driver's license takes precedence over puberty rites or even a high-school diploma. The physical setting of the home is a split-level command post for licensed drivers to chauffeur the non-licensed young to engagements at the four winds.

What room is there for traditional human relationships or values in a society designed for the transient, portable, mobile, and trade-in qualities of every article or event; where vehicle access and parking determine the worth of land and structures; where "can you drive?" is the prerequisite of work; where auto ownership is the basis of a successful courtship? The automobile even helps explain the social abandonment of those too old to drive.

When the outburst of shock comes, it takes many forms, all unpredictable. Besides the repertoire of group insanity, instant dogmatism, and flowered, barefoot fanaticism recently demonstrated, we must also look afresh into social problems inherited from neolithic times: alcoholism and common neuroses. Science has now begun to study the influence of both on "accident-prone" drivers. This research is supported by the auto manufacturers. But science has hardly begun to speculate about the role of the overmobilized, overorganized society in increasing both alcoholism and mental disorders. That research is unlikely because the autocrats are not expected to support it.

To do so would imply an admission that the automobile is not only a very lethal weapon in the hands of all persons of unstable character (British researchers have even found a relationship between women's accidents and their menstrual periods), but that motorcars may just as effectively upset personal equilibrium, either directly or via alcohol. Some incriminating clues are found in the work of Dr. Melvin Selzer, who specializes in the psychiatry of vehicular accidents at the University of Michigan. Selzer reports that high-accident individuals reveal a "frequency of social stress and social maladjustment." Their personalities "displayed poor control of hostility, less ability to tolerate emotional tension, greater dependency needs, and extremes of both egocentricity and fantasy preoccupation." Selzer then noted that "many of these traits are independently also ascribed to the alcoholic."

If so, the condition of "chronic suicide" ascribed to the alcoholic by Karl Menninger is highly relevant to the use of automobiles by both alcoholics and the mentally disturbed. That is the thesis of Selzer: automobiles are weapons for unconscious suicide.

Since social stress contributes to alcoholism and mental disturbance—and is a natural result of the environmental conquest by the automobile—we indict the automobile as a treacherous double weapon against man: it is simultaneously a varied source of psychic disturbance and a device for the disturbed to act out their destructive tendencies. Today 'the motorcar is too monolithic and penetrating not to figure in both sides of the neurosis.

Psychic disturbance and emotional release in a man are exactly parallel to the automobile's dual role of destruction and escape in cities. In each case the automobile answers the alarm for the fire of its own making. And in each case the response only magnifies the cycle of destructiveness, accelerating the dizzy spiral of human defeat. It does not really matter whether the defeat lies in the environment, or in the psychic or social conditions of man, or in death. The real loss is man's ability to live a good life.

Nor are the autocrats squeamish about directly exploiting the social neurosis of the car's own making. "Are you driving bumper to bumper?" asked radio station WNEW in New York. "What you want is a new Chevrolet."

If the automobile was originally considered to be important for the recreative life—as when President Wilson's aide would drive through Washington's parks for relief from his tensions— the release has not always been so composing. Speaking of his racing, Walter White (of the White Motor Company) once described his feelings: "There is one thing I never get over when I race," he confessed. "Once you are off you see nothing but the road and you have a maniacal desire to run over everybody and everything that comes in your way." And if neurosis appears in this admission, a public neurosis of a very different order was set off when J. C. Furnas wrote his inflammatory 1935 *Reader's Digest* article suggesting that "every time you step on the throttle, death gets in beside you."

In America a love-and-fear schizophrenia permeates the literature on life in autocracy. Love of cars is seen in *Fortune* and *Business Week*, representing the economic establishment, and *Hot Rod* and *Car and Driver*, representing the sport subsidiary of the manufacturers. Fear also runs through the periodicals, though regular and thorough representation is repressed by potential cuts in advertising. Corrosive anxiety shows up regularly in articles on casualties, congestion, and pollution.

Subconsciously man is becoming wary of the automobile's social subversiveness. He is a bit wiser knowing that the spark setting off the Watts riot was an ordinary traffic citation in the most motorized city on earth. The civil rights marchers at Selma, Alabama, knew that a critical *human* question could not be associated with the neurosis-producing automobile. Cars would submit them to the overpowering material rationality supporting the status quo and the establishment. So they *walked,* as did Meredith in Mississippi, to insure the *human* meaning of the event.

Regimenting All Mankind

"The revolution in American life did not take place when the automobile appeared," concluded Cleveland and Williamson in *The Road is Yours* in 1951, "it came when the motor vehicle was a necessity."

True to their own rationality, the autocrats describe the revolution in autopian terms. Repressions arise in the name of safety, mobility, and freedom; automotive deadends are rationalized as proof of abundance and are overcome by a rape of the environment; contradictions are explained away as responses to the popular will; outrageous burdens upon men are lauded as contributions to the economy.

But whatever the deception, the revolution means tyranny, in the end as raw as fascism. The procedures are the same. Both the subtleties and the stark power pursuing conformity are the same. The social and psychic penetration are the same. The physical, social, and cultural deprivations are the same. Even the superficiality of high public purpose, progress, excellence, and morality are the same.

The steps toward tyranny are simple. Reason never departs. Pragmatic responses to immediate problems are its necessary foundations. The automobile progresses from a luxury to a convenience and then to a necessity. The roots are found in the transformed city, absolutely dependent upon automobility. Those who would not own one *must* own one if they are to continue to participate in society.

Second, automotive necessity impels an arduous reorganization of society to suit its growing requirements and capacities. The automobile's resounding problems *must* be resolved if society is to remain physically or economically viable.

Third, the solutions themselves place progressively more powerful demands and restrictions upon every driver, every walker, and the daily pattern of every person. Laws, regulations, procedures, and circumstances close in upon the individual. He *must* establish a complex conformity within himself if he is to survive or simply retain his license to drive. Outwardly, only his behavior must be regimented. But no widely based authority stops there. By virtue of incessant presence it moves inward to the base of personality.

The social rationale underlying the automotive progression —necessity, problems and solutions—is that *tyrannous enclosure of the individual is justified in his own best interest.* There is no necessity to formally invoke the authoritarian "will of the state," not even the profitability of Detroit. All that is required is to fully believe that "the life you save may be your own."

Repression is necessary when cars are built and advertised to be dangerous at cruising speed (and when cities are laid out so that one cannot drink without driving). Then, too, the life you save gets to be repressive when the tedium, restraint, and discipline required for it all go without honor, a thank-you, or even the knowledge that a life *was* saved.

The states are there, of course, helping in every way they can. When the automobile first showed signs of becoming both necessary and dangerous, they began to charter driving as a privilege. That eliminated the youth and the obviously unfit, but did not stem the pile-ups. So the states intensified the process, testing eyes, knowledge, and skill—and made no bones about their intent to mold proper attitudes. While doing so they established an autocratic identity card to make arrests routine and to record one's failings as a traffic citizen (as well as to prove one is old enough to drink).

And the arrests multiplied, first through the organization of highway patrols and speed traps, then through the use of radar and aircraft. Now it is proposed that highway patrolmen warn drivers and give them instructions on radios that cannot be turned off. A talking speedometer has been invented.

Some years ago California tested "talking freeways" by which recorded warnings could be radioed to cars. "The potential of the refined system is almost without limits," crowed *California Highways* magazine. "Cost would be staggering," they said in 1965, "but if the public believes the benefit worth the price, such an elaborate system could become a reality." Just as ominous are proposals for instruments in each car to automatically record lawbreaking and notify traffic police.

Somehow the relentless destruction of family, community, and cosmopolitan life, and the loss of a genuinely free mobility (of choosing whether or not to travel, or when and how), have been transformed into virtue. Americans drive approximately 33.3 million hours each year between the disconnected segments of their lives. That means forty eight-hour days of 100 million drivers are bound to the wheel, nearly 20 percent of a normal work year. What rationality for tyranny could be more imperative than the struggle for safety when the central element of social action, the automobile, operates as effectively as 100 million squirrel wheels?

Like old-theory totalitarianism, modern autocracy displays a withering range of laws, regulations, devices, disciplines, and propaganda. A road sign at its state line says that "New Jersey Likes Safe Drivers," not people or even good people, but safe drivers. Tampa, Florida, has constructed a million-dollar Safety Village to indoctrinate children with proper driving attitudes. Florida also boasts of more than seventy high-school driving ranges as large as elementary schools. General Motors has developed a highly articulate driving simulator for instruction. Under the Highway Safety Act of 1966 the states are obliged to adopt uniform traffic codes, stipulating that every driver give implied consent to take an alcohol test.

It is at this juncture that old-theory totalitarianism best enlightens us. No man understood the web of tyranny better than Alexis de Tocqueville, who more than a century ago wrote of a "new specie" of political oppression. This power, he said, "takes upon itself alone to secure [men's] gratifications and to watch over their fate. That power is absolute, minute, regular, provident and mild. . . . Thus it every day renders the exercise of the free agency of man less useful and less frequent; it circumscribes the will within a narrower range and gradually robs a man of all the uses of himself. . . . The will of man is not shattered, but softened, bent, and guided. . . . Such a power does not destroy, but it prevents existence; it does not [overtly] tyrannize, but it compresses, enervates, extinguishes, and stupefies a people. . . ."

But how does the tyranny progress in practice? Examine a statement about the parking "congestion level" in the long-range plan for the campus at Detroit's own Wayne State University. Since the planners see no way to fully meet the parking demands, "this concept of 'congestion level' is important, for at Wayne history has clearly shown that students and faculty become accustomed to any reasonable level of congestion so long as it is consistently maintained . . . therefore, it becomes imperative to maintain a consistent relationship between parking spaces and the campus population. If such a ratio can be maintained, the program will be deemed successful." In conclusion the report admits that "while this program for accomplishment may not be considered 'ideal' by everyone, it is a practical response to an existing and increasingly critical problem."

Robert Nisbet has said that the steps to tyranny "can as well be racial equality as inequality, godly piety as atheism, labor as capital, Christian Brotherhood as the toiling masses." Yes, and they can just as well rest in the profitable relationship between consumer oriented technology and responsive bureaucracy as in a conspiratorial ideology.

Tocqueville did not know modern autocracy, but he understood the invidious nature of oppression which establishes "itself under the wing of the sovereignty of the people" and makes itself appear normal, popular, and progressive. Doesn't autocracy make itself the mediator of our gratifications, representing every model change and every freeway extension as the ultimate value of good living? Doesn't it represent its suppressions as necessary for the common good and administer them through the absolute, minute, regular, provident, and mild authority of the state? Doesn't it slowly render man less useful to himself, and less a free agent? Aren't the frustrations of mobility—with its isolation of people and congestion of vehicles—enervating and stupefying to the human will and mind?

Totalitarianism works best when its control is pervasive, quietly influencing the lines of communication, the direction of ideas, the work of organizations, the flow of money, the pattern of living. In America the force and form of events assure that some things acquire integrity and some do not: today Autokind does and Mankind does not. It is this form and force of events that compress, enervate, extinguish, and stupefy Americans at a time when the possibilities of life should be bursting about them with human excitement.

Auto Perfection and Human Obsolescence

It couldn't have happened, of course, without Detroit achieving a psychic dominance over man. The case is very simple.

After more than a half-century of deep probing, advertisers have convinced Americans that cars improve and men do not. Over the years Americans have become reconciled to their own progressive obsolescence through comparison with the annually improved auto styles and performance. Deep down, all Americans know this. It is part of their way of life.

General Motors is the acknowledged master at controlling human obsolescence. The first strategy was enunciated by founder Bill Durant: "I want a lot of different makes so I will always be sure what people want." By 1957 GM had 75 body styles and 450 trim combinations. By 1969 it produced 175 body styles and 918 trim combinations.

However, annual model *changes* were more lucrative additions to the strategy. Both were ushered in during the watershed twenties, when, as Alfred Sloan put it, the mass market gave way to a mass-class market. "Many may wonder why the automobile industry brings out a new model every year," said Sloan. "The reason is simple. . . . We want to make you dissatisfied with your current car so you will buy a new one, you who can afford it." First by rapid mechanical improvements, and then by rapid changes in style, the automobile industry did just that. It could keep automobiles constantly on the mind and optimum pressure on the pocketbook.

"Dynamic obsolescence," it was called by Harvey Earl, GM's pioneer stylist from California. And GM made the most of it, particularly after Earl's first "styled" LaSalle appeared in 1927. From then on, style and change were used in a delicate interplay. "The changes in the new model," confided Sloan in *My Years With General Motors*, "should be so novel and attractive as to create demand for the new value and, so to speak, create a certain amount of dissatisfaction with the past model. . . ."

Sloan's view was managerial. Stylist Earl's view revealed the subtle variations of execution: "You can design a car," said Earl, "so that every time you get in it, it's a relief—you have a little vacation for a while." And with such fine bits of advanced social engineering the industry could proceed to sell more car per car up through the 1950's and then diversify models once more, this time promoting the second family car. Steadily the strategy of style has been extended to all visible parts of the car. *Motor Age* reported progress with tire styles as early as 1965, predicting confidently that "tires tailor-engineered to match the personality and performance characteristics of each U.S. passenger car are not far off."

Then, with a complete line of models, annual model changes, and styling to prepare the way, advertising could effectively exploit the person. Detroit's annual half-billion-dollar alliance with Madison Avenue could even help mold life styles through manipulating class ("you have arrived!"), sex (with a shapely female on each fender), or psychic insecurity (compensated for by power, speed, comfort, exhibitionism). The definition advertising gave to man emerged right from the basic elements of the strategy. A new car—being modern, being in style, and having a model marginally distinctive from all others—could make a man new again, strengthen his character, give him the lift of renewed membership in the mobile society.

Transportation, of course, was virtually irrelevant, as the strategy emphasized. "Half the joy of motoring," perceptively observed a letter to the *Scientific American* in 1905, "consists in driving the machine oneself. The ability to do so competently means a delightful independence, an absolute freedom of thought and action. It gives one a feeling of self-reliance, of perfect confidence in one's power to guide the machine and regulate its speed at will with consummate safety." And if the machine was an astonishingly good mate to personality, if it could underpin ego and enhance one's sense of self-determination in 1905, how much better would it be sixty years later, when the whole rhythm and change in society, personality, and automobility were attuned to exploiting such human proclivities.

Over these years, obsolescence has corroded the human psyche. The automobile is renewed. Man is not. And in a society demanding modernity, man can only refresh his ego by episodic engagements with new cars. "Are you looking for a love affair with a new car?" asks Chevrolet. Dependable and ostensibly servile, the gracious power and beauty of newness seem to expand the dimensions of personality, bolster it with willing friends, even cast for it a new purposefulness and sense of destiny.

The results are hardly surprising. It must have seemed a valuable public service when the California Federation of Business and Professional Women's Clubs put up a billboard on a highway which read: "Obey Traffic Signals: Your Design for Living." Nor is it surprising to hear a psychiatrist say, "A man drives as he lives." Today that is just a basic fact about modern personality. But the reverse is becoming more significant: "A man lives as he drives."

The automotive grip on personality may be judged by the

kinds of justifications given for automobility. Addicted to the auto's omnipresence, Roger Starr concluded in his book *Urban Choices: The City and Its Critics,* after visiting the Lijnbaan, Rotterdam's highly regarded central mall, how he "missed the tempo of traffic, the variety and shapes and colors of automobiles, trucks, taxicabs, motorcycles; instead of relief at having escaped from them, I found myself thinking that I was not in a city, but a summer resort, a place which, for all its charms, I would not want to transact serious matters." It did not matter, apparently, that the rest of Rotterdam afforded ample nuisances, roars and rumbles, road dangers, congestion, and fumes to satisfy his addiction. Starr felt compelled to inject automobiles into the most human and urbane design arising out of the nearly complete destruction of central Rotterdam by the Germans in 1940.

Yet the automobile has other important influences over man. Auto movement simply dulls the mind.

Charles Kettering once observed that "next to the World War, the automobile has done more to make America a nation of thinkers than any other invention or agency." Combining the broadening role of travel and the thought-provoking qualities of the machine itself, the automobile should have stimulated an instant renaissance in America. But what happened?

As soon as the car could not be repaired with bailing wire and pliers, it became too complex for ordinary men to fool with. Then the car could no longer stimulate their thinking, and thinking fell into a kind of obsolescence.

The earliest suspicion that a fuzziness of mind arises out of mobility itself seems to be that of a Spaniard, Ramiro de Maeztu, who in 1924 observed that "there is nothing like a swift-passing landscape to monotonize the mind." Psychologists have not tackled this question so far as we know. But in 1957 a sensitive South African noticed how in heavy California traffic "it is the movement, I suppose, that paralyzes the mind: One could imagine cars, just cars, stretched out indefinitely, but set them in motion at sixty or seventy miles an hour, set them moving three or four abreast, set them moving in two directions, and the imagination simply retreats and despairs; the mind is numbed."

Marcel Proust discovered that movement, sometimes even very slight movement of the limbs, destroyed or at least interrupted memory and involved thought. Motion all too easily reduces the thought processes to action responses. Travel, of course, is not the same thing as movement. Yet somehow the automobile steadily narrows travel to a monotony of movement. Everywhere the auto environment is the most uniform, and it is what modern travelers are most exposed to. Perhaps that is partly why Skokie, Illinois, high-school students who acquired automobiles dropped in scholastic standing. According to a study done there, the brighter the student the more sharply his performance dropped with regular possession of a car.

Is it that constant motion—meaningless and useless motion —both dulls the mind by its presence and filters out the perceptive content that provokes thought?

Well, there is some current recognition that a monotony of movement is deadening. Highway choreographer Halprin now asks that highway designs register "movement quality, character, speed, involvement with the mobile (or static) elements and progressive spatial relationships. . . ." If this idea is carried out, the entire environment of movement may then become a dynamic geometry of motion, a visual symphony of passing imagery. But what will that do for men when movement is largely forced repetition, a long-playing record run forward and backward in a deadly monotony of daily commuting?

Rise of Car Culture

Of course, the automobile finds ways to compensate for its destructiveness in America. It must offer *something* of value to raise its status above that of a barbarous conqueror. It must also help the masses accommodate themselves to the increasing severities of auto occupation. And so it is now attempting to overcome its rude origins as mere transportation by moving into the domain of culture.

At no place outside Los Angeles has the car done better than in New Jersey. Though the state has a large population near the heart of Megalopolis, it is without its own metropolitan core. Consequently its economics are divided, its politics fractured, its culture parasitic. Known as the Garden State, New Jersey is becoming more familiar as the Corridor State. Across it cut the Garden State Parkway and the New Jersey Turnpike. Both have been extremely successful in generating traffic since they were built in the 1950's, and they are now being widened to ten and twelve lanes.

Tom Wolfe once observed that vehicular life is the only uniquely American culture devoid of any old-world heritage. Apparently New Jersey's inferiority complex about its cultural heritage was too much for the Parkway's well-heeled Authority. It therefore created the $7 million Garden State Arts Center at Telegraph Hill with the same free enterprise that General Motors uses to initiate a new model.

Even the emergence of *Arizona Highways* magazine from a highway bureaucracy was not as significant. The Arts Center is dedicated to mass consumer culture in autocratic captivity. The center's theme stresses cultural segregation: "For Those Who Create—And Those Who Appreciate." The location and access guarantee the captivity: The 5,000-seat amphitheater, exhibition mall, nature trails, and projected drama theater set in 350 rural acres nearly fifty miles from Manhattan are locked into more than 2,000 parking spaces and an interchange with the parkway.

Since the *only* access to this drive-in Chautauqua is from the toll parkway, there can be no arts without the automobile. That is natural, says the parkway's director of public relations, because "the revenue thus generated from cars using the toll road to get to and from the site is part of the feasibility of this project." Legally the Center is a "roadside development."

Garden State's new subsidiary is not likely to be the last enterprise in the arts by the highwaymen. Culture founded on ten lanes may now become more feasible than culture founded on a population of 100,000—roughly the size of ancient Athens. Cars and tolls will be the prerequisite to sampling the finer things of life.

Though culture is the professed objective of the Telegraph

Hill project, automobility is clearly the underlying purpose: The amphitheater will not function on Sunday evenings in the summer—to avoid complicating the congested parkway traffic returning to New York from the Jersey shore.

Until recent times highways were precious connections between centers of human activity called cities. They were for movement only. Now movement has risen so high in the scale of power and value that it is becoming *the* important concentration of activity, able to string out human activities along its length. The contribution of the Garden State Parkway is to make highways the foundation of man's highest endeavors and, by implication, to demote the city to a museum of man's less mobile past. But what can we expect in a populous state without a major independent urban center?

With wealth also stirring in the vaults of turnpikes in Pennsylvania, Ohio, New York, and elsewhere we may expect Lincoln Centers to pop up on almost any Telegraph Hill. It is more than symbolic for the future that while the wealth and initiative of the highways rises impressively the impoverishment of cities continues apace, and without a turn in sight.

1994: *The Final Solution*

The motor conqueror shows no signs of slowing just because it has achieved a simple domination of mobility, land, and people. A study by Resources for the Future, Inc., *Resources in America's Future,* predicts that "[b]y the end of the century, more than one vehicle for every adult is a definite probability, and we may have as many as three vehicles for every two." As a minimum, RfF predicted one car for every .94 adults. More likely, production will reach 28.8 million annually, with 243 million cars on the road (one per .85 adults). Production could reach 73.7 million and registration 372 million (one car per .65 adults). Given Detroit's power and uncanny ability to find new reinforcements for growth every decade, the RfF projection may be considered realistic and objective.

In 1910 *Scientific American* exclaimed in awe how all the

automobiles in America would stretch from New York to Pittsburgh. However, if the 300 million motor vehicles (including 30 million trucks) predicted by RfF were lined up on twelve-foot lanes the vehicles of the year 2000 would make a solid swath a half-mile wide between New York and San Francisco.

With "objective" scientific projections of car ownership to back them up, the highwaymen's projected requirements of $285 billion for the 1975–1985 period then become equally realistic and objective. Scientific research and the planning for the public bloodletting are thus in harmony and mutually support each other.

"When I came to power in 1933," said Adolph Hitler at the laying of the Volkswagen plant cornerstone in 1938, "I saw one problem that had to be tackled at once—the problem of motorization." However, no such external authoritarian support is needed today. The autocrats are accomplishing the same results on their own power.

Nor are there limits to the influence of automobility on man's perspective on all things. Rocket scientist Werner von Braun predicted as early as 1959 that roads will be built on the moon "within fifteen to twenty years." So far, he is right on schedule. NASA ordered its first four lunar jeeps—at $19 million —in 1969. The Asphalt Institute has been alert to prospects on the moon as well, noting an estimate that there may be enough asphalt inside the moon "to form a sixty-foot lake over the planet's entire surface."

What will automotive life then mean in 1994, one century after the motorcar's American birth?

The precedents and proposals are already before us. Freeways will be specialized, one way and automated, regardless of costs or results. Truck and bus freeways are already in the experimental stage. The first one-way freeway is planned for Chicago. The automated freeway will be an admission that not one ounce of pleasure remains in driving and that society is absolutely dependent upon Detroit.

The demise of pleasure will be matched by the loss of freedom. We now see events in Los Angeles leading to the control of *access* to entrance ramps of freeways to protect the free-way's frail capacities. But when total capacities have been raised with new freeways, local streets downtown will become so fright-fully congested that *egress* control from the freeways will be-come equally necessary. A pass system will then be necessary for one to drive into intensely overcrowded central districts. The dilemma will open an entirely new arena for political pressure, influence peddling, and graft.

The present trends toward vehicular specialization and con-gestion suggest that four types of vehicles will be necessary by 1994: (1) automated trucks and buses; (2) automated highway cars, (3) manual street cars; and (4) local access vehicles. Each family will have to own at least one manual and one automated vehicle. Parking lots will maintain small cars to transfer patrons to and from the private vehicles in the mammoth lots.

Alternatives to supplementary vehicles for access are high-rise garages, minitransit, and walking—or a combination of all three. Minitransit and walking will be adopted only with re-luctance because the establishment knows that transit and walk-ing could have done the job alone if cities had been adjusted to man rather than motorcar. Nevertheless, by 1994 the environ-ment will be so fully in the grip of motordom that such anomalies can be fit easily into popular belief.

By that time insurance will be available at fleet rates for all families owning five or more vehicles. Rescue helicopters will constantly hover about to make instant physical and photo analy-ses of accidents and quickly remove mass wrecks and casualties to central accident recovery centers to prevent total traffic freezes.

Naturally the autocratic powers will celebrate the automo-bile's numerical superiority over all adults as a new era of free-dom, flexible mobility, and unparalleled affluence for men.

In reverence for the long struggle to achieve mobile abun-dance, Thanksgiving will then be rededicated to the motor age in America. In 1994 the feast will be taken in drive-ins: Carhops will serve carved turkey on a bun, with cranberries and French fries dipped in giblet gravy. Mincemeat and pumpkin pie will be optionals. The feast will be warmed in the car's instant heater. Since superways will permit eating and drinking while driving, Thanksgiving dinner can be finished while driving home, to avoid traffic congestion and high charges for the drive-in stalls.

Then, too, superb communications will be available during the long hours of mobility and queued immobility (which together may then be expected to average between 30 and 40 percent of one's workday). Rich cultural programming combined with in-car teaching machines will permit the frugal to improve their human resources and maximize their contributions to production and consumption.

Since the automobile will be absolutely essential to sustain life (that is, to be either a producer or consumer) the ethics of mobility will take on the same importance as horse ownership in the nineteenth-century West. The law will be very severe about safe driving. But jailing deviant drivers won't be necessary. The authorities will impose a tougher punishment: They will merely take their keys, leaving the offender alone in the auto-isolated suburb surrounded by freeway fences. That will deny him social membership just as surely as prison bars ever could. Nor will it be simple to bum rides with friends. Everyone will travel long distances in all directions. One man's path in the disunited society will be of use to no one else. Therefore, banishment from mobility will be as harsh as imprisonment. But it will be necessary.

When that 1994 comes it will be Orwellian—Big Brother and all—a bit late perhaps, and a bit different, but more real.

Challenge of Occupied Society

When the love affair between man and auto first revealed clear signs of being reduced to brute conquest during the middle 1920's, one Edward Martin asked in *Harper's*, "Don't you wonder where this phase of civilization . . . is leading us all to?" Forty years later freeway-design critic Halprin expressed a kind of anguish uniquely symbolic of autocratic society: "Dissociated, encased in speed, you have nowhere to go but forward."

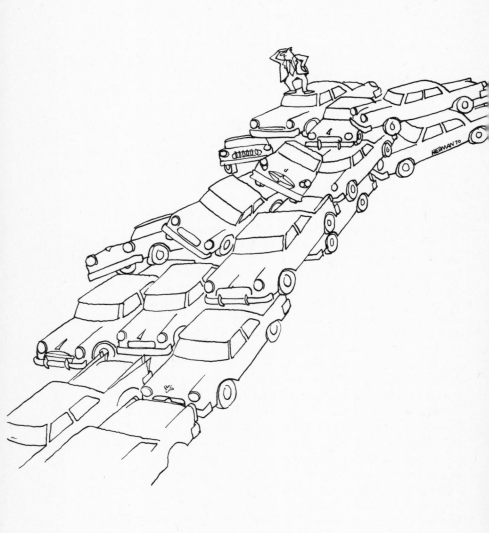

Why did man ever let it happen!

What went wrong? Why didn't democracy have an intelligence system warning us about the tyrannical potential of the automobile and freeway? The evidence was there, disparate and scattered at first, but increasingly forceful, more rude and coercive as the onslaught came on, wave after wave, depressing the human prospect. Still, no one really warned us.

The car always had many critics, of course. But in the end they were all apologists. Safety critic Nader fits as comfortably with the autocrats as aesthetic critic Halprin. Only two—Louis Mumford and Victor Gruen—have taken on automobility frontally for what it is. Even they have not always been sure of themselves. Their voices have been drowned, not so much by fortified opposition as by the pragmatic problem-solvers who are too blind to see and the moneymakers who don't want to see that some forms of transportation bind a city into an operative whole while other forms promote dispersion and disintegration.

Still, occasionally, there are isolated insights. Paul Sears in a 1965 *Atlantic* asked why men became enslaved to the motorcar. "First steps to captivity," he observed, "can be acceptable, or even disarmingly agreeable, whether we speak of plants and animals, marriage, politics or inventions." Recall that the whole meaning of the automobile is that while it was introduced as the plaything of the rich it became the necessity of the poor.

Easy it is, then, for *Fortune* to be confident that "the automobile can survive the problems it has created. The real strength of the auto market is that the ways of life of American society, having been shaped by the car, must have the car."

The setting of America's particular weakness for auto enslavement is traceable to many old myths and spent traditions: the migration and homestead complex re-enacted in suburbia; the output fixation, represented in auto production; the myth that men move mountains, reflected in building the interstate system; the habitual willingness to put up the environment for sale and to evaluate the future as a commodity. More deeply in the social subconscious are the American's doubts about living in cities; his readiness to measure living conditions and human value in terms of numbers and action to the exclusion of form and character; his ingrained prejudice which allocates to corporations the initiative on social opportunities and to government the response to social problems.

It is, indeed, a low reality perception which we must blame for the many steps leading to our conquest and captivity. So we still remain blind to the car's monstrous effects.

Consider war. Vietnam protestors riot about the inhumanity of government policy intended to contain communism and help assure self-determination of peoples. Yet there is no protest over the inhumanity of a half-century cf government policy forging annual highway deaths of 55,000—five to ten times the American battle deaths in Vietnam. Nor is there any "peace" in prospect.

Consider how federal, state, and local governments are ensnarled in the urban crisis. Yet their laws, subsidies, and capital expenditures have for two generations systematically created a transportation nightmare, making cities not only unworkable, but unsafe, unhealthy, and depressing.

Consider how the nation has become concerned that population growth will drain the natural resources, overcrowd the cities, dilute the standard of living. Yet it is precisely the automobile that consumes the great quantities of ore and oil, creates intolerable congestion while destroying urban form, degrades the human environment, and openly threatens the very *quality* of life that might be attained through affluence.

Consider how the conservationists point with alarm to the destruction of our natural heritage. Their cause is urgent. Yet the decisive instrument of destruction is the automobile, with its special assault capabilities: access roads and parking; the rude car services that soon follow, the travel trailers and sport vehicles, and the off-highway marauders.

Consider how the federal government has struggled to prevent monopolies. Yet both conservative and liberal administrations alike have conspired to create one of the most invidious monopolies of all time—that of automobility—defeating not only trains, subways, and bicycles, but the free use of man's own two feet.

Consider how each successive wave of hippies glory in rebelling against the entire establishment. Yet they have failed to rebel against the most pervasive and restrictive department of the establishment, the auto/highway/service complex.

Consider how the liberals warn us about emergent tyrannies. Yet they fail to take note of the only species of tyranny presenting a clear and present danger: that of automobility.

This, then, is the case against the automobile. And now we face the challenge: to make modern man environmentally free; to give him the full benefits of science; to give him the reins of powerful technology; to redesign the establishment to expand his *individual* opportunities and *social* integrity, and—eventually —to return to him the joy of motoring.

The challenge will not be easy, for at present we "have nowhere to go but forward." Our minds, our knowledge, our behavior are slaves to automobility. Our technology, economy, and institutions race forward, but toward no clear *human* goal. Our cities are dispersed and desolate; they dis-integrate human group life and raise defensive privacy to an ideal; they wastefully consume the countryside; thus they eliminate the very qualities we so dearly seek. This is the deep rut in which we race.

Our struggle to recapture social sovereignty for man will, particularly when we begin, grope and appear irrational to some. The perpetual motion of modernity will make most proposals for social renewal appear at first to be uneconomic and regressive. This must be expected since rationality in society is captive to the automotive necessity. But these doubts will be illusory.

Our first advances will not please those who measure life in statistical escalation. But gradually new goals will become clear and new challenges will become more constructive. Then the varieties of human excitement that are unleashed will expose the compulsions of a captive psyche.

Therefore we will now consider our campaign against Autokind.

5

MANKIND'S STRATEGY
FOR VICTORY

Strategic Handicaps of Humanity

OUR IMMEDIATE BURDEN is to plan the counteroffensive to reclaim the environment for man. The environmental reclamation will help stimulate us to consider how to *humanize* the environment, the final task of this volume.

Since man's greatest inspirations often arise out of struggles against oppression, bringing him to broad and unforeseen visions of the human possibility, we may expect widespread social inspiration, possibly a renaissance, to radiate from man's emergence from environmental totalitarianism.

But Mankind faces an enormous challenge in seizing the initiative. And because the momentum of autocratic conquest is far from spent we must expect conditions to deteriorate further before anything more than isolated progress is possible. While the Bay Area Rapid Transit District in San Francisco will spend about 1 billion dollars to prevent a transport collapse, another 4 billion will be poured into the area's freeways and major highways. Yet, because of the great odds against him, man's hope for victory against the automobile rests in turning automobility's ungainly massiveness to its own disadvantage. Numerous opportunities will appear by thoroughly evaluating the strategic and tactical strengths and weaknesses of both Autokind and Mankind.

Recall first that there are nearly 15 million full-time mercenaries employed by and for Autokind and an indeterminate number of reservists in the varied support activities. They will be loyal to automobility because they will preceive their livelihood as directly threatened by any automotive retreat. Then, too, we know that there are more than 100 million card-carrying vehicle operators, most of whom are captive to the auto rationality. The remainder of the population, mainly children, invalids, and the elderly, are hardly the human resources to weld into an effective fighting force.

This is the manpower strength of motordom. The mechanized strength is equal, with nearly one car or truck per driver, while the vehicle ratio continues to rise. This is matched again by the automotive defense network built deeply into the terrain: the freeway, the Great American Strip, the shopping center, the truck-organized industrial district, the massive central parking facilities.

Autokind's strength is Mankind's weakness, of course. Urban land in some places is more than half automotive. The city itself is wildly dispersed, assuring dependence upon cars. Dispersion also assures that local government, man's potentially most effective servant, has degenerated into a crazy-quilt, poverty-stricken disarray, while the state and national governments, which build most of the freeways and assure the integrity of automobility, are well coordinated and have ample finances for automotive growth.

The awesome strength of autocracy is best revealed by its infinitely diverse technical, bureaucratic, economic, and political power base. The one-sixth of all American businesses which are automotive carry the influence throughout the grass roots. The half of the largest twenty-two manufacturing corporations which

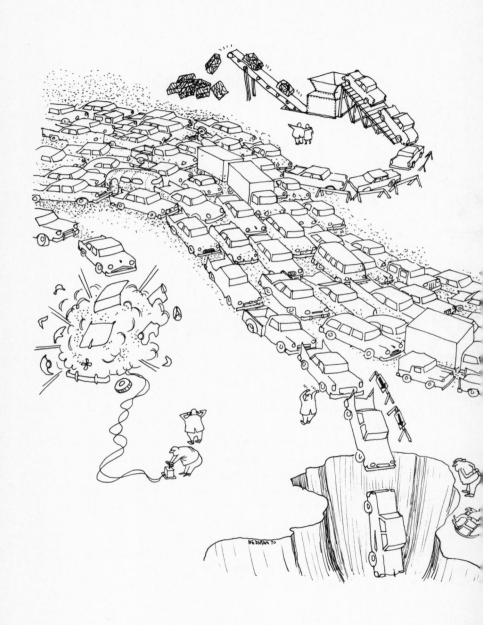

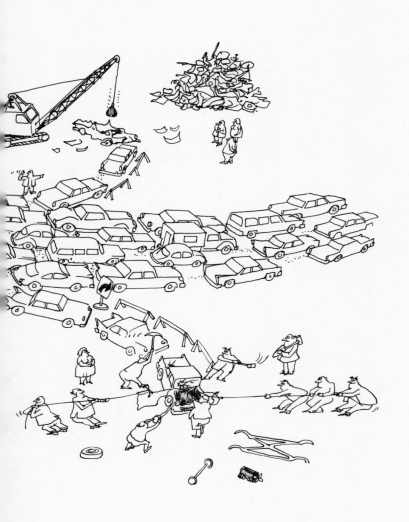

are automotive carry the influence to the centers of power. The fact that there is almost constantly an ex-president of an auto manufacturing firm in the cabinet (Charles Wilson, Robert Mc-Namara, George Romney) is more than symbolic of the immense influence of the automobile in the political structure of America.

More openly the auto interest is carried to the capital by the Automobile Manufacturers Association and hundreds of other trade groups, ranging from the Auto Utility Trailer Association to the National Wheel and Rim Association. While these play directly on the instruments of political power, the United States Chamber of Commerce, apparently devoid of self-interest, speaks a subtler form of propaganda. Behind the scenes a bit are automotive front organizations which penetrate the White House (the President's Committee for Traffic Safety), use safety as a means to safeguard automotive interests (the Automotive Safety Foundation), and participate in the formulation of vehicle and traffic laws (National Committee on Uniform Traffic Laws).

The autocratic defenses are deep and flexible, backed by the oil producers and distributors, construction industry and highway bureaucracies, law enforcement systems, insurance and banking interests, and a ragtail array of unbelievably varied fellow travelers. Their forces are capable of enormous retaliation against anyone who challenges the dictates of automotive necessity. What is democracy when such a range of establishments are united for their own institutional welfare?

How weak democracy really is shows up in the American Automobile Association. As if freeways of eight, ten, or twelve lanes would make motoring more enjoyable, the AAA today supports the indefinite extension of highway building, defends the Highway Trust Fund, and accepts unquestionably the new emphasis upon blockbuster freeways blasted through cities. With a miser's logic the association opposes the use of any road user taxes for mass transit, though that could improve motoring more than any freeway ever could. The AAA enigma exemplifies how the establishment's automotive rules of rationality permeate all cells of society.

In the face of such a massive, organized force, democracy

must fall back on the arms, methods, and moral fiber of the American Revolution. For tactical support it must depend at the outset upon such bodies as the Hide and Leather Association, bird watchers, shoeshine parlors, and news and flower shops. The main body of soldiers must be drawn from children under sixteen who are too relaxed to drive, the incapacitated, and those too old to take the strain of the wheel. But we may expect their numbers to grow in time, right out of the ranks of autocracy itself.

Autocracy's Critical Weakness

For all of man's apparent disadvantages and for all of autocracy's real strength, our long-term human prospects are very good.

Clues to a great inner weakness have been showing up increasingly since the onset of the muddle, even while auto strength has outwardly increased gigantically. The fact that automobility becomes more ponderous and perpetually accelerates suggests the possibility of collapse. A preview was observed in 1966, when during the New York transit strike a taxi driver reported that he was able to drive only forty-one miles in twelve hours. Another was noted in non-strikebound Los Angeles, where a newspaper editor remarked, "I know this metropolitan area is interrelated because if a dog crosses the freeway in downtown Los Angeles, a woman in Anaheim twenty miles away crumples a fender."

The highwaymen are worried and contribute further evidence of our good prospects. Even their own literature points to the dramatic conclusion that *the automobile is technically impossible for basic urban transportation.* No one piece of evidence is definitive or conclusive, but together they set forth the hard, clear lesson of modern history.

The inner contradictions of automobility become more apparent with every new automotive advance. "The very success of the machine carries with it the seeds of its own destruction," states Victor Azam, editor of *World Road News.* What do some of the experts say?

"Apparently, no matter how many new super roads are built connecting outlying areas with the downtown business district, auto-driving commuters still move at a crawl during the morning and evening rush hours." This is the proposition Anthony Downs made in his "Law of Peak-Hour Expressway Congestion." That's what happened with the $50-million-per-mile central section of the Boston expressway, built at six lanes with a design capacity of 120,000 vehicles per day. Soon after it was completed in the 1950's the estimated 1975 traffic was put at 300,000 by the traffic forecasters.

Planners in Atlanta reported that without mass transportation 120 expressway lanes (20 6-lane freeways) would be required to carry the commuter peak loads to and from central Atlanta. At San Francisco the planners for the Bay Area Rapid Transit system reported that freeways with an equal peak load capacity would cost more than five times as much to build, eat up four times as much land, and require double the operating and maintenance costs.

These figures raise the next big question: how and where are the local streets and parking caverns to come from to accommodate this influx? Victor Gruen calculated in his classic 1955 Fort Worth plan that for the stagnant (but congested) city center to recoup by 1970 the business it had lost, it would require 16 million square feet of local street space, more than three times what was then available downtown. Gruen actually planned 60,000 parking spaces for Fort Worth, 12,000 more than there were in central Los Angeles at the time, and stated that even this would be "adequate only with a highly efficient rapid transit system" to back it up.

These pessimistic views are from an economist and the planners. What do the highwaymen themselves say? For many years a powerful undercurrent of defeat has built up among them as well. Let us quote a few selected from the *Traffic Quarterly*.

1. "Those who study and work on planning and design of expressways, particularly urban expressways, realize that the supply of adequate facilities will probably never catch up with the demand" (Herbert Elder, 1949).

2. "The problem is already tremendous and it doesn't appear to be approaching maturity" (Wilber Smith, 1951).

3. "To be perfectly frank, the measures we are taking in all big cities to relieve traffic pressure have given only temporary relief" (Harry Casey, Jr., 1956).

4. "A realistic appraisal of our highway transportation problems compels us to warn against any illusion that the ultimate solution is now within our grasp" (Richard Zettel, 1956).

5. "Traffic congestion is a condition which appears to be accepted as a part of our present way of life" (Julius Henry, 1962).

6. "All over the world—from London to Los Angeles and Capetown to Copenhagen—the motor car has become the number one problem confronting urban and metropolitan authorities" (S. S. Morris, 1966).

7. "The fact that better roads mean better living . . . tends to becloud some disturbing consequences of the trend toward motorization" (Victor Azam, 1968).

Parking, even more than traffic, has long been recognized as "a need that grows heavy by feeding on itself," as one entrepreneur put it in 1951. Only with automobility can a despair of action be transformed into programs to accelerate action. That is, simply, its rationality. "Because of the very nature of the problem," admitted the manual *Parking* in 1946, "it will be almost impossible to bring about a complete solution in the oldest cities. Even in the newly planned and developed cities it is not likely that complete solutions will be brought about. It is therefore necessary," pressed the manual with typical autocratic logic, "that public officials and private interests devote their resources to the most effective techniques and facilities for meeting parking demands." Like socialist realism, auto rationality thus drives ahead through the obstacles of history.

The persuasive logic moves on with bulldozers, money, and immense human resources. "The nation faces an urban transportation crisis," exclaimed a 1967 Automotive Safety Foundation report, which in the same breath proposed that "it must begin to plan the street and highway *system that will have to be built* between 1975 and 1985" (italics added). What is a crisis? A need to rethink the nature of programs, systems, objectives? No, obviously, it is the need to plan for the next stage of acceleration.

Naturally, by 1968, the urgency of auto reasoning had become all the greater: "One obvious conclusion resulting from any reasonably careful review of the problem is that the highway program must be continued at a high level after the Interstate System is completed. . . . Optimistic as one may be about continued programs of construction, we must accept that they will not be enough," reported the policy planning director of the Federal Highway Administration, with a straight face.

Upon such evidence Mankind's prospects of regaining its sovereignty are surprisingly good. Human weakness and auto strength are real enough. But the automobile carries the seeds of its own downfall.

In a society priding itself on competition, the automobile has multiplied under the nation's most powerful protection racket. Automotive tax subsidies, guarded by the Highway Trust Fund and comparable statutes, pay solemn tribute to technical insolvency. The urban dispersion and deformities are in effect subsidies paid to the auto industry. Take the protection and subsidies away and the rationality will falter.

In a society taking pride in individualism, every personality is strapped to the dictates of the wheel, the circumstances of the road, the styles of Detroit, the disciplines of road law—or it is deprived of participation in society. In a society priding itself on equality before the law, the auto is given legal precedence in subdivision development; integrity of auto movement is legally protected, while integrity of place is not. Return a measure of individualism and equality and automotive power will surely decline.

But the automobile will defeat itself mainly by its multiplication. Convenience of movement is defeated by increased distances. Speed is lost by traffic congestion. Flexibility vanishes with massive parking deficiencies. Enjoyment of motoring disappears with the strain, costs, and fear of accidents. All that the car originally had to offer is killed by the car's own excesses.

Our general assessment is that the automobile's own weight and unwieldiness is the best foundation for an effective strategy against autocracy. The automobile's built-in contradictions, the experts' own diagnoses, and the highwaymen's blatant irrationality all point to this conclusion.

Strategy: Three Stages to Revolution

Obviously, the raw power of autocracy rules out immediate action directly against the automotive power centers. Mankind's total lack of preparedness requires a careful plan, unfolding in three broad stages, to stop the meaningless movement and mechanized despair.

Stage 1 will make preparations in four areas. First, the strategy must be developed, refined, and amplified into hundreds of special action plans. Second, a campaign of enlightenment must win a very large number of able-bodied recruits and supporters who understand the capital-intensive irrationality of auto tyranny. In particular, we must recruit many persons directly from the auto establishment—just as Marx relied upon converts from the bourgeoisie—who understand it thoroughly from the inside. Third, cadres and anti-automobile organizations need to be established to prepare the attack. Fourth, many existing public-spirited organizations must form a militant team for concerted action against the automobile. Simultaneously many not-so-public-spirited organizations and corporations require convincing that their long-term interest lies with men, not autos. This, then, will constitute the American liberation front we require for action.

Only when all preparations are well advanced will it be advisable to initiate Stage 2 and openly challenge the auto occupation of America. The first strikes must be very carefully selected and well planned. Their primary objectives are to test and strengthen Stage 1 preparations and to win large numbers of workers and sympathizers. Therefore action should be undertaken only where victory is almost certain and where dramatic demonstrations will result. Very gradually the number, extent, and daring of all-out offensive operations can be increased as our strength grows.

Stage 3, the struggle to eliminate auto occupation of society, can begin when the separate actions reveal that Mankind is capable of sustained frontal assault in all theaters of action. Whereas early engagments necessarily must be selected for their isolated effects, Stage 3 will strike out for major and comprehensive realignments of the environment and of transportation—and of the institutions that shape them. Consolidation will follow and be nearly as important, embedding every advance into law and custom, work and organization, economics and industry.

As a starting point we will use a production of 10 million vehicles per annum and a registration of 100 million as the base to judge our progress. Both figures may be expected to rise during Stage 1 and possibly in Stage 2 before they begin to decline in our favor. These figures may serve as barometers of the balance of autocratic power. The 42,500-mile Interstate system will also provide us with a rough gauge, and this too must be expected to rise before the high tide of the automotive Pickett's charge is finally turned back.

And desperate charges must be expected. Already the Asphalt Institute has put on record its readiness, saying, "we must . . . fight against diversion of highway revenues for non-road-building purposes whenever and wherever it occurs." Other larger autocratic outfits will certainly increase their armament and supplement their fighting strength as soon as they perceive a threat to their power.

The major content of our strategy is also defined by the three stages. The strategy in Stage 1 is intended to gain control over the terms of rationality. It will rid society of its *ad infinitum* complex whereby men are led to believe that driving more miles requiring more consumptiveness and more production for more money is the highest good. *Ad infinitum* thinking is automotive, technological and institutional, not human. The rationality we seek will be founded upon *human* purpose using a *social* logic that, above all, will guarantee *personal* freedom and enlarge *individual choice.*

The strategic objective of Stage 2 is the city. The automobile has effectively demonstrated since 1920 that the city is uniquely susceptible to defeat by thousands of small changes. Our strategy will use the same approach at the outset. This will also permit men to limit their first points of attack to those places which are most certainly attainable and will yet have the greatest impact: a mall, a minitransit line, more "walking" time at traffic signals, a park in a parking lot, a natural area protected from auto access, and, of course, seats, fountains, rest rooms, and a favorable land-scape setting to show men the pleasure of being human and walking again.

The Stage 3 strategic objective is to take control of the in-stitutions to see that their laws, budgets, programs—and, yes, their very existence—conform to the needs and the desires of personality and interpersonal life, not simply to the good of the organization. Although transformation of the environment will be a very critical accomplishment, it is through institutions that human sovereignty will be secured. Only after the automobile is dethroned in law, economics, city planning, mass media, and education, and especially in the politics of public decisions, will we be able to say that revolution is underway. No longer will organizations constitute themselves as the establishment. They will lose all rights but those required to serve men.

Let no one be fooled. The three stages only lead to revolu-tion. They are not the revolution itself. The revolution will start when man begins to realize his human potential. Dangers will remain, of course, as always. But one danger will disappear: No longer will man lose his sovereignty to what he produces, nor, hopefully, to what he organizes.

Stage 1: Offensive Defense

Unfortunately, the positive objectives of our campaign against automobiles will be difficult to convey at the outset, and a certain amount of misunderstanding appears to be inevitable. Since it is first necessary to cut Goliath down to size, many people will judge our efforts to be only negative or even destructive.

The auto rationality has so pervaded men's thinking that they perceive no other way to move (or live) in society except by continuing to multiply the ton-miles. Henry Ford knew better, as we will show. And as our strategy progresses all men will know better. Furthermore, the positive nature of our goals will not only permit but promote the automobile. We agree with Leon Mandel, editor of *Car and Driver,* that "the ultimate use of an automobile is a ride in the country—on a side road or a race course." We will promote it, *for pleasure.* Our objective is to eliminate it as a necessity for any man. For it is the necessity that kills the pleasure.

Yet the tough business of breaking the grip of Goliath is necessary. The auto's hold over us must be broken. Citizens who daily suffer the auto necessity feel this deeply even as they claim that there is no alternative. Therefore, we are confident of an early realization that more varied forms of transportation will decidedly improve safety and—moving to the very heart of the automotive claim—convenience and flexibility, while yet reducing environmental debris and destruction.

In the early years we must concentrate on those areas where further auto damage will be greatest, in the cities. For example, freeways now seem destined for a massive new scale of expansion. And the greatest expansion will be aimed straight at the heart of the cities.

To protect the vital cities we must initially give ground elsewhere. We must be prepared to make a measured retreat on the *inter*-state system and permit a degree of expansion there while seeking to prevent expansion on its *urban extensions.* At the right moment we can point out that the 42,500-mile system is not at all a complete national network.

Using the engineers' own arguments we can show how the northwest and southeast are badly connected, especially from New Orleans to Dallas and on to Salt Lake City. Other shortcomings readily show up: Houston-St. Louis, Buffalo-Washington, D.C., Minneapolis-Denver, New Orleans-Little Rock-Kansas

City, Chicago-Columbus, Birmingham-Memphis. To concede such regional extensions at the "expense of the cities" will not make sense at all in the automotive rationality, of course. Nor will it to the conservationists. But the human rationality will unfold as we progress.

And while we retreat we should also strive to correct another highway shortcoming: the form of the highways themselves. All betray deformities of alignment and design, and deficiencies of landscaping and billboard protection. In the wealthiest society no less than the best parkway standard should be permitted for *any* highway.

The same offensive defense can apply to parking. As we want to protect the city, we want most to protect its center. We can at least strive to reduce or eliminate municipal zoning *requirements* for parking with new structures. And where more parking is forced upon us, we will fight for shielding and landscaping.

Our strategy will call for strikes all along the soft underbelly of motordom, wherever vulnerability is revealed. Zoning and subdivision ordinances may be attacked. Headway may be made against the protection racket of highway-user-taxes. We would benefit by changes in the property tax assessment and home financing practices, which now favor escape to the auto suburbs.

Properly armed with thorough studies of both economic and social costs of the automobile, we will seek to have charges put on size, emissions, and noise. Wherever we can reduce size, transfer traffic to buses, or convert the traffic to bicycles or motor scooters, we will do so as preliminary steps against motordom. Streets or lanes can be reserved for buses and (small) taxis. We can strive to charge for contributing to congestion: tax parking garages for congesting downtown streets; charge car commuters on freeways (inversely to the number of passengers).

As our strikes increase and the campaign gains momentum, we will be able to emphasize more positive projects of reconstruction. These we must plan with extreme care, for they will reflect upon our ability not only to meet problems but to raise the human outlook. Initially this may be our greatest problem, because the environment is so totally automatized that the very isolation and novelty of our first projects means that they may be only partly usable and incompletely understood in the beginning. Then, too, reconstruction projects must fit into long-range plans for each main element of transportation: an attractive walking environment, varied and flexible modes of public transit, and relaxed recreation driving.

We now know all too well that cities designed solely for automobiles do not work for people. The most exciting challenge for planning, therefore, will be the coordinated reformation of the city to assure more urbanity *and* more recreational open space, more accessible commercial and public services *and* freedom from their bizarre or dour effects, more kinds of convenient transportation to more places *and* freedom from the domination of transportation. In short, our plans will achieve many diverse values which auto rationality makes contradictory. Our larger struggle is not against the automobile; it is simply for humanism of the environment.

This we must remember above all: It is not enough to consider the automobile, or even transportation, all alone. That was our critical mistake in the past, and it continues to underwrite auto tyranny. That is the trap of specialism, of pragmatic specialism without farsighted goals. We must think of the whole setting of life, constantly consider our goals, and bring those goals to bear upon the immense technical powers of society. The central goal of our campaign is an environment that works well and, above all, is congenial to the human body and its senses, to group life, and to *social esprit.*

Renewal of Rationality

Before Americans can start to break the auto tyranny they must ask themselves—in every way they know how—"is it possible to be urbanized and motorized, and at the same time be civilized," as Wilfred Owen puts it. This is the real option, but it cannot be understood so long as we remain locked within the closed cycle of automotive rationality.

Parallel with the larger struggle, we will renew and reinvigorate human rationality and resolve that it will serve life—all of the excitements of living.

We will begin by presenting facts: the casualties, the debris, the resources consumed, and the urban and rural destruction. We will agree with the highwaymen to call highways a crisis. But we will not permit the highwaymen to slip us a fast one by demanding continued and expanded programs to ease traffic. We may agree with *Fortune* that "the U.S. highway problem, succinctly stated, is that the most mobile nation on earth is in danger of becoming immobilized." But we won't permit the failure of fifty years to be used, unchallenged, as an argument for expansion.

We will challenge the highwaymen not only with their own facts but with their own statements. We cannot seriously quibble with Henry Barnes, New York's late traffic commissioner, who once said that "the automobile is a supplement to, not a substitute for mass transit." We will challenge his successors when they make demands upon the public treasury to convert 95 percent of all travel in New York to the motorcar, as in other cities.

We will challenge the highwaymen and use their own prognoses, their own descriptions of automotive contradictions. No longer will we watch in idle wonder while they use their studies to extort another $200 billion worth of construction, threatening to foreclose on society if it reneges in the next acceleration. We will underscore the contradictions by drawing each to its inevitable conclusion. And we will match proposal for proposal, dollar for dollar, transport benefit for transport benefit, and social value for social value to show how automobility fails while it destroys.

We will challenge the highwaymen's irrationality wherever and whenever we find it. When federal highwayman Turner says that his duty is to "accommodate the choice which the people have made," we will dramatize how choice is denied by automotive necessity. And of those who claim that the anti-autoists are killing the goose that lays the golden eggs we will ask, "What price autopia?"

Of those who defend the highway-user taxes for road use only, we would ask "Do you think that cigarette taxes should be reserved for the promotion of smoking, that liquor taxes should be set aside for the promotion of drinking?" As with the logic of auto taxes, cigarette and liquor tax resources would be dedicated first to promotion, then to dealing with the problems arising from the promotion.

There is already an uneasiness in some quarters of the auto establishment about how solid its grip is on the conventional wisdom. "If the public ever catches on to the fact that a new car every two years is not a necessity," confessed an auto executive, "we are sunk."

Our case, then, has many starting points, many levers, and a wide variety of appeals for all who seek enlightenment. But the case against the auto is only the starting point. Enlightenment will not occur until there is a bright new vision, perhaps like that which motivated the early automobilists.

Possibly the prevalence of automotive logic in society is like the situation described by Plato in the Allegory of the Cave. The people he depicted lived in a deep blackness and knew not the use of their eyes. Their only reality was through touch and sound. One day a venturesome person saw a dim ray of sunlight penetrating a distant part of the cave. He followed it and the light got brighter. He climbed toward it, and the brightness nearly blinded his unused eyes. He persisted, and soon emerged from the cave to find an entirely new reality which pointed to a new breadth of life. But when he returned to the cave and reported the existence of the new dimension of reality to his people, they only laughed at the story. Reality in darkness was what they knew; their aspirations of life were self-restricted to the darkness. So the adventurer was ostracized for his mischievous deed.

Plato's lesson is sobering. However real, however critical our case may be, it is impossible to expect that society will easily accept ideas which are not conventional and do not correspond to the auto rationality which frames our perception of reality. Nevertheless, we know that some persons even now, quite independently, realize how the darkness of auto rationality continues to close in upon men. They will readily join us. And we have wide evidence that many, many others are approaching the same threshold of perception, and require only minor assistance to begin their enlightenment. Both groups will furnish the crucial starting momentum we require.

One who never required such a boost to enlightenment— Mahatma Gandhi—gave us the simple foundation for our growth when he said, "There is more to life than increasing its speed."

Partisans and Political Action

To inject more human vigor into life—without at all decreasing speed where speed is good—maximum *planning* will be complemented by maximum *improvisation.* This unity of opposites points to a more basic principle: simultaneously increased *social order* and increased *individual freedom.* The power of motordom operates on the opposite principle of starting with chaos and always struggling to make minimum order out of it. That imposes arbitrary discipline and denies choice to individuals. Our movement will strive for *responsibility and discipline for institutions* while maximizing *social opportunity and liberty for the individual person.*

Most existing public-interest organizations respond to one problem, establish one goal and follow it to absurdity. The specialism we have inherited is simply anti-social. It splinters and confuses human behavior as forcefully as the automobile disperses and scatters the city. Its method therefore confounds and constricts human purpose. Our starting point will be one problem —motordom—but nothing less than the broadest possible conception of society will guide our responses to it. This will help us (and society) realize the Greek ideal of "nothing in excess"—the denial of which modern man suffers so deeply.

As the movement grows, a number of major endeavors will emerge to assure the results we seek throughout our three stages. Support and guidance for spontaneous local uprisings will be the first area into which we will channel the earliest volunteers. Although revolts have occurred since the first row of sycamores lost out to the bulldozer, few such efforts have been very effective. Most bubble and burst without facts, tactics, leaders, allies, and they lack an understanding of the automobile, as well as a sense of their own purpose of direction.

In 1966 a "wheel-in" was staged in New York by thirty-five persons on motor scooters to protest parking regulations that were biased against them. Though all thirty-five parked vertically to the curb in space reserved for five automobiles, vertical parking is illegal, and they were soon flushed out. The protest was a flash-in-the-pan, only a little publicity. A few months later students at City College sat down in front of a grader which was cutting up the lawn for a new parking lot. Construction momentarily halted and about 100 students carried stones from the site to a paved driveway and to the president's office. It was a nice start but today the parking lot is now as firmly established as the city's parking regulations.

The Provos (provocateurs) of Amsterdam have been more astute with their anti-auto campaign. They even got one of their members elected to the city council in a more comprehensive effort to "Fight lies, be human, resist the power structure." But they failed to develop a broad-based program and establish an effective coalition, which was necessary before they could make real headway.

The lesson is clear. It shall be our task to provide an infrastructure to guide all spontaneous outcries against autocracy. And from them we can then build our strength.

Once a spontaneous uprising reveals signs of permanence our next endeavor is to unite it with our program. While the foundation for action will be specific grievances, the purpose, strategy, and tactics will be fit into a whole. Only when the many groups are operating effectively in concert from thousands of neighborhoods to the nation's capitol can the strategy ultimately succeed. Independent action will continue, of course. Each local body will develop its own understanding of the automobile's particular circumstances in its area, initiate its own attack plan, and evolve appropriate civic recovery plans.

These efforts will require research, not only to gather data and analyze the political, economic, and other strengths and weaknesses of automobility but to reconstruct human rationality and prepare it for contention in the public arena.

Extensive planning will naturally follow from the research, as action on the frontiers of automobility reaches its critical stages. In keeping with our philosophy, we will resolve that planning will serve nothing less than the whole society, the full compass of human values.

Our struggle will require a literature to point the way to an ethic of social renewal. Some will call this propaganda, but propaganda will be just the starting point. All arts from the cartoon to the theater will be included. But writers who can make us laugh and make us cry and who can inspire us to liberation will be in the vanguard. We know already, thanks to Bob Hope, that freeways and smog, along with the girdle and Crosby, are always good for a laugh. And if we can laugh as we roll back the auto armor, we will even then be restoring one of the casualties of the autocratic era.

Next we will unravel the automobile from its primacy in public decision, in the statute books, and in the capital budgets. That may be long, tedious, and tough. Only a few minor advances will occur in the early years. However, when the earlier endeavors begin to pay off and some demonstration breakthroughs prove the great merits of our cause, the statutes and budgets will then begin to fall back into man's hands once again.

We must be prepared to build institutions that renew mobility, widen choice, and free the environment. These organizations will vary widely, and they will challenge our imagination. While one of our development groups, for example, may be burdened specifically with providing transportation or improving the local environment, we will also want these groups to respond to popular demands on a wide front—such as assuring a superior human environment—thereby serving men not only in what they do but for their total impact on society.

Finally, we will consolidate the new heritage through education, just as we now attempt to consolidate political liberty through instruction in history and politics. The high purpose is to develop an appreciation of environmental democracy. Through studying the social portents of land and space, the *value* of men and the *functions* of machines, and the specific conditions that induce tyranny or democracy, we may lay the foundations for full social democracy.

We will not make static blueprints. Nor will we impose them. We are simply stating priorities that set forth the interlocking requirements for victory and, more importantly, assure for men the broadest benefits of victory.

Alliance for Progress

Our movement must build alliances if it is to overcome the auto's accumulation of powers. The horizon is full of promising allies. They will join us if we can identify our purposes with theirs and prompt them to action for the common good.

We should not be surprised if many of our most vigorous supporters are the sports-car enthusiasts and their clubs who see in our struggle the possibility to make the world safe for fun at the wheel. An ethical alliance will thus be formed between good driving and good living. However, there is no such possibility in racing. Those people are bought and paid for by Detroit. Theirs is a non-ethical alliance between fantasy and money.

We may woo and eventually win over the auto clubs, now so inebriated by mass autoism. The professional hierarchy of the clubs is clearly reactionary and deeply entrenched. But the AAA clubs are, after all, associations of people, and people cannot fail to be alarmed at the multiplication of cars and highways. From the grass roots the membership can call insurgency strikes in their clubs against endless autoism. One by one the clubs will then join us.

The ladies and their clubs can make immense contributions if they can be convinced that their dreary home work, their hectic family routine, and their calculating cosmopolitan life all follow the pattern of existence designed for motorcars. But they must dedicate themselves with more than teas and sympathy. Where vigorous women cannot steer their club through the dead weight of Robert's Rules of Order they are advised to leave and join the regulars.

Our cause is singularly united with urban renewal organizations and rural conservation societies. If with these movements we can open a dialogue an extraordinary force can be shaped to counterattack automobility. When farmers also begin to realize that urban sprawl undermines their most productive regions they too may join the insurgents to struggle against wanton automobility.

As knowledge of environmental tyranny spreads to the institutions claiming to defend democracy, our movement may grow to include the Center for the Study of Democratic Institutions, the American Civil Liberties Union, SNCC, and SDS. This may seem a questionable melange. But their diverse talents are likely to make yeomen contributions to our struggle.

Churches may be ready recruits. The rising pressure upon them to provide massive parking with slim budgets should work in our favor. Inspiration may come to them when we show how the splintering of family activities and the disintegration of neighborhoods and whole cities due to the car has worked against church attendance, if not faith in general. Perhaps a new stirring will arise from the pulpit with the reaffirmation that society is the commonwealth of Mankind, not Autokind.

Labor assuredly will be highly antagonistic at first. Not only is a car or two a grand if wilted symbol of their striving for the American Dream. They also feel that the car is their best guarantee for employment. And indeed it is. But there is hope. We will begin by convincing the unions that the lesson of automated production is increasing leisure and wealth, not work. Jobs there will be, even as work declines. As soon as they understand this we can open joint strategy sessions with them.

There is almost no hope for the corporations, for they have weak democratic foundations and therefore little basis for enlightenment. Their rationale is based on calculation, not reasoning, and they will support automobility as long as it multiplies dollars in the GNP. And so we will fight them, massively at first, then less, as the economic calculations change their logic in our favor. In the end, they will be with us too, but not a part of us. And that is how we would have it, because as they become more productive they will fade—like farming—and become almost unnoticeable in human affairs.

Stage 2: Popular Revolt

The sure sign that Stage 2 can be initiated will be a groundswell of doubt by the man in the car about automobility, a growing awareness that cars mean captivity rather than freedom, social disintegration rather than advancement. When Stage 1 has brought society to general doubt, our struggle will still be almost entirely *against* automobiles. When Stage 2 is concluded our efforts will be almost entirely *for* man.

The difficult first steps of this transition will be led by specially recruited shock troops: the flower people and peace marchers. Bare feet and marching are unmistakable clues of a willingness to enlist with us, as is psychedelic auto artistry. Indeed, feet blackened by asphalt and cars blurred by tattoos may become the campaign symbols. Possibly they will become, along with bare bodies, our uniform of combat.

You see, this war will be entirely different. It will be a revolt for peace. Unlike the car, we won't kill 2 million people to regain control of society. This war will be waged by those who don't kill and aren't willing to die. Our goal is to vanquish conquest itself. That is why the flower people and peace marchers will be our shock forces.

And in this war against autocracy we will not ask anyone to give up even so much as his car. Cars will diminish in number only when they are not wanted and not needed. That is the meaning of the car tattoo: to demonstrate that it is not wanted and that it will go when it is not needed.

Unlike past wars, we will ask little of most men, certainly not personal sacrifice. The greatest burdens will be put on institutions. No longer will we permit the establishment to throw the onus of morals upon the conscience of individuals while organizing an autocratic and immoral society. In our plan, organizations will be made responsible not only for their own moral behavior but for creating a climate that makes ethical relations among men natural, respectable, and rewarding.

As the promise of Mankind improves, men will raise their heads, hold their shoulders straight, and walk erect with increasing self-confidence. To those who must remain enclosed and wait for liberation, the manner of the free may seem haughty, even arrogant, especially when they tap victory ($\cdots$—) on the hoods of the cars they pass at crosswalks. And where cars violate those crosswalks the free walker may pound the victory symbol as in drum-like warning for all to hear. Or, in the most serious cases of blocked pedestrian movement, walkers may crawl over the hood or pass through the back doors—to make certain that men's determination is not misjudged.

The troops will undertake a number of simple shock demonstrations to dramatize how ineffective—and vulnerable—the car really is. Coordinated traffic stoppage during crucial hours is one possibility. In 1967, civil rights protestors threatened to run out of gas on New York's Long Island Expressway, but this fizzled when the police made counterthreats. Unless a very large number of people are to be involved it will probably pay only to act, not to make threats. Some persons may be taken prisoner for a time, but the authorities will always hesitate to take on the welfare of large numbers of detained demonstrators. When their numbers increase sufficiently, the use of autos can be dispensed with in favor of dances and parades, music and laughter along the raceways and on the mixmasters.

Demonstrations serve only to focus public attention. But the main objective is the improvement of life in cities. This is attainable in countless small ways, like widening sidewalks. Taking our cue from the automobile itself, we note that despite the fact that 35.5 percent of Manhattan is paved roadway, hundreds of streets are widened into the sidewalks every decade to expand traffic. As our demonstrations become more powerful and sophisticated we will reverse the process and do the same for walking.

Protestors closed San Francisco's Haight Street in 1967 by

simply passing out a leaflet that announced: "Sunday, April 2, 1:00 P.M./Haight Street is ours to play on/till we feel it beautiful to stop." And that was all it was, a day with Haight Street. Goals were fuzzy, methods unrehearsed, alliances weak. And so the closing of Haight Street, and that of Telegraph Avenue in Berkeley a week later, came to little. The value of the demonstrations was largely lost. Our aim will always be a permanent improvement.

We have it on the reliable authority of a traffic engineer that the best way to get pedestrian improvements is by confounding the very delicate signal systems that maintain traffic movement. When pedestrians tie up vehicle movement the pressures become unbearable. Then pedestrians will get *their* improvement. Persistence, clear demands, and the threat of escalating immobility will force the concessions. Nevertheless, we should never try to bollix up traffic without expert advice. A few traffic engineers should be kept around (those "human animal trainers," as they are called by Victor Gruen) to advise in planning such ground strikes.

Fighting from Street to Street

Autocracy will be given no quarter. The only peace we will accept will be cities that are completely human. Auto entry into the future city will be possible only on these terms.

We know well that wider sidewalks do not themselves make a new city. But they will get us started, giving us new space for benches, trees, fountains, and lots of people; and they will give us the tactical experience for bigger strikes—to take entire streets. Although some downtown streets have already been converted to malls, some with excellent results, these have all been achieved through dangerous concessions to automobility for new streets and parking facilities near the malls. A totally new strategy is needed: we must liberate the streets without making *any* concessions.

Preliminary investigations suggest that Eighth Street in New York's Greenwich Village may be the appropriate objective of a first strike to establish such an instant and permanent mall. That strike could have the same morale and propaganda value for our struggle that the Doolittle raid on Japan had in 1942. Even today Eighth Street is a busy and delightful place with dozens of bookstores, galleries, theaters, and the usual array of clothing, convenience. and gift shops. But it is a narrow street, congested and barely usable for cars, and very inconvenient for walkers.

The strike advantage we have is that since Eighth Street goes from nowhere to nowhere and carries only circulating movement. Its closure to vehicles will not provoke full autocratic power or seriously alienate the many who still believe they must drive in New York. Our case is powerful because only about eighteen feet of the approximately fifty-four feet between storefronts are devoted to pedestrians. Even the nine-foot sidewalks are burdened by street lights, wastebaskets, fireplugs, parking signs, and parking meters.

Many critical issues are at stake on Eighth Street. Could it become a new Bastille? Can the hippies and other protestors of the establishment create an urban life more suitable to Mankind than that shaped by the auto? The question is whether this new society or that older model is better suited for Mankind. Will Eighth Street be a valuable demonstration project? Certainly the strike should not be undertaken until we are confident that it will dramatically prove the human ability to act intelligently, constructively, and forcefully without falling into the vice of bureaucracy.

Preparations will begin by studying the experience of the landless urban migrants in Latin American who in one night have built *colonias proletarias* (proletarian colonies) and *barrios clandestinos* (clandestine villages). Large numbers of *paracaidistas* (parachutists) take land in the dark and present the authorities with an instant city by morning. Plans, layouts, and parcel allocation are done (sometimes with the help of experts) beforehand. Only a civil war can turn them back, as the settlers are armed and ready to fight.

Our interest in Eighth Street concerns less than a half-mile between the Avenue of the Americas and Broadway. We will be careful not to block traffic on Fifth Avenue or University Place (at least at first) because we must never take more than we can hold or justify at the time. The space gained will make possible one of the first clear elements of a very new way of life.

First it will permit a great increase of walkways and several hundred new enterprises—arts and industries with both production and sale directly by the people—in the former street area. There are reasons to believe that the established merchants will quickly grant their approval (based on increased foot traffic, i.e., shoppers and tourists). Both old and new merchants may then organize an Alliance of Merchants and People. This group will prepare legal defenses to supplement the hastily built people defenses in the streets. The principal of the case will be that the right of way was recovered to guarantee passage of *persons* who were being arbitrarily blocked by parked and moving vehicles. Autos are but accessory means of movement and cannot be permitted when they disrupt the free movement of the majority. The street enterprises will be defended on the basis of accommodating movement (that is, making it unnecessary to journey so far for goods and services) and of concentrating foot movement where it will not be in conflict with vehicular movement.

Both points are eminently valid, age-old, and nearly forgotten principles of transportation: First, pressures on transportation are eased when the need for travel is reduced—and this is a concept we will increasingly employ in our rejuvenation of cities. Second, ever since the right and left sides of the road were divided for improving traffic flow, it has been known that separating the conflicting kinds and simplifying the lines of movement improve the flow. Fewer streets can carry more vehicles if there are fewer intersections, especially fewer between cars and people. Manhattan would carry even fewer vehicles if it were entirely one flat roadway surface in which every vehicle and pedestrian traveled in a straight line between points of origin and destination. Thus—ironically—we will improve the flow of auto traffic while we improve the conditions of life. Every strike against the auto will reveal this more forcefully.

Our case is enormously strengthened by the phenomenon of disappearing traffic, which is exactly opposite to the phenomenon of traffic that mushrooms whenever a new freeway opens. For decades now the traffic engineers have been constantly underestimating potential traffic on new highways (thus, "no highway can be said to have been overdesigned to date," reports one national authority). Often they miss by 100 percent or more. The Greeks seemed to have understood this long ago, saying that what flourishes in a society is that which the society nourishes, prizes, and celebrates.

The way our engineers have nourished automobiles is not unlike a story reported in a 1926 issue of *Country Life* in which an automotive engineer asked a machine operator what he was making.

"Huh," said the operator.

"What are you making there?" the engineer asked.

"I dunno," the man said.

The engineer was surprised, and asked, "How long have you worked here?"

"Five years."

"How long have you been at this machine?"

"Four years."

"Do you know the way to the pay window?"

"Sure," the operator said with a smile.

The knowing author of the 1926 piece then commented: "Not only is this an amusing commentary on our modern factory system, not only does it show how very unskilled, almost automatic, in fact, human labor can be, but it suggests an analogy in our daily life. . . . How many of us who have driven a car, or been driven in one, for four years know the fundamentals of the automobile?"

Indeed; and how many engineers have learned about the fundamentals of the automobile in society? "Huh?"

The fact is that the principle of vanishing traffic was demonstrated just two short blocks south of Eighth Street, in Washington Square Park. In the late 1950's an extension of Fifth Avenue passing through the park was closed under public pressure. Parks Commissioner Robert Moses and his engineers had insisted that the closing would result in impossible congestion. But, as Jane Jacobs reported, "every traffic count taken around the park perimeter since the closing has shown no increase; most counts have shown a slight downturn." The avenues to the east and west "did not seem to receive an extra load," said Jacobs. Where did the traffic go? Probably to the same place it would have come from if the park road and Fifth Avenue had been widened.

Copenhagen made the same discovery. Its main shopping street, Strøget, was temporarily closed in November 1962 as an experiment, against the advice of the planners, police, and economic experts. Within four months the project had proved itself such a success commercially that it was extended indefinitely. And something mysteriously happened: total traffic counts in the area dropped by 2,000 cars a day.

Where do they go? This embarrasses the engineers. They don't like to speak about it, any more than they like to be reminded that traffic opening day on the New Jersey Turnpike was what they had predicted for twenty years later.

That represents utter failure, not success, and it is a failure of the auto rationality. Yet the engineers continue to underestimate the traffic they always generate. The job of our street fighters is to turn the process around. The degeneration of traffic will be a primary tactical maneuver.

Yes, we partly agree with Waldemar Kaempffert, who wrote in a 1917 *McClure's:* "Compared with the Fifth Avenue of tomorrow the Fifth Avenue of today will seem but a mere alley. Our great grandchildren will . . . smile at its quaintness and narrowness and wonder not only why we admired it, but why we endured it." With our new prospect Fifth Avenue will seem to grow larger, as it does even now when the people take it over for the Easter Parade and on trafficless Saturdays. People will have the use of the whole street, not merely the bordering ledges. They will then indeed wonder why they endured it so long.

Stage 3: The Massive Assault

Territory reoccupied in Stage 2 will be relatively meager. But upon these demonstration grounds the whole population will dramatically realize the critical importance and—above all —the *possibility* of eliminating the automobile as a social necessity. People have long held the desire but thought it was impossible. For every street fighter we will therefore assign another to psychological warfare to assist in this understanding and to convert the insurgency into general revolt.

Wide effects will follow from the rise of popular understanding and support in Stage 2. First, there will be changes in the buying of houses and cars. A downturn in the number of second, third, and fourth family cars will be noticeable. And a few who select their home locations very carefully may dispense with car ownership altogether, using rental cars for those travels where autocracy retains its grip.

The growing enlightenment and the first economic indicators of declining automobility will change the climate for business investment and jolt the money market. A cold eye will then fall upon risk investments on the Great American Strip and in the distant reaches of scattered urbanism, reversing the trend foreseen in 1903 and dominating urban development since 1918.

From this point on the initiative will be ours. The forces of development will then be constructive in intent and may be guided to become constructive in form. And from this point we will confidently inaugurate Stage 3, to end for all time what Gruen calls the "murder plot against our urban areas." And we will also break up the same plot against the countryside, because the saving of the city will itself be the first step toward saving the natural beauty of our countryside.

While privately organized action will characterize Stages 1 and 2 the emphasis of Stage 3 will shift more powerfully to the public sector. As our purpose begins to prevail in the citadels of power we will start rooting the car out of its thousand privileges. But our burden is enormous, for overcoming seven decades of rising autocratic dependency will be complex, costly, and slow.

The first breaks in the legislative barrier will permit us to infuse new life into all remaining systems of transit. No longer will the public, having overcome the drug that rationalizes auto necessity, vote against building the transit spines of their cities. Simultaneously we will carry out a crash program to develop varied, lightweight, attractive transit systems (on the order of models used at Expo 67) which will be capable of spanning many auto-made suburbs within a few years' time. These two actions will virtually eliminate a half-century of cumulative auto congestion and allow us time to develop a city heartily congenial to man.

Since at this point vehicular traffic will drop precipitously, precluding highway expansion, fuel taxes may then be applied to transit improvements and to heal the highwaymen's countless urban wounds. As auto defenses are further weakened by continuing disclosures of misspent billions, vehicle and fuel taxes will be used exactly as those on liquor and tobacco. The taxes will be raised to cover social costs, expecially to underwrite the renewal of cities. They will also stimulate us to drive less. The desire to drive less will in time help magnetize the distant suburbs into more complete and coherent centers for community (which will also reduce the need to travel) and centers for transportation (which will reduce the costs of movement).

Our method will force automobility back to a level of enjoyableness, using the same tactics the automobile used to conquer society. We will progressively revitalize every auto-penetrated cell of the city, emphasizing the center and working outward. But unlike the automotive advance, which knows not where it goes but forward, we will be guided at all times by the widest perspective of human ends and the best possible balance of social means.

Except for historic sites we will not be satisfied with mere restoration. Beginning with a few lonesome malls, whether Eighth Street in New York or Fulton Way in Fresno, we will develop systems of walkways, promenades, and plazas that join the qualities of a park with those of a fair throughout entire urban centers. Above or below ground, minitransit will travel quickly and quietly to varied centers of interest, and its stops will be closer at hand than most present-day parking garages and lots.

Those parking garages and lots will be converted one by one to more worthy activities. The atmosphere will rival or surpass the best of Disneyland; business functions will be dispatched easily, even casually; they will be interspersed with personal meetings and activities; living will become once again more important than mere doing.

As we work outward into the suburbs the ecological tragedy wrought by man will call for gargantuan corrective measures. Here the automobile so ravaged the natural orderliness of men's work places in the city that society reacted fitfully by segregating the suburbs into giant zones which isolated naturally coherent functions and sterilized social behavior.

First we will preserve the remaining fragments of openness. By selective programs we will then open grand new vistas onto meadows, woods, parks, and golf courses; we shall build imaginative clustered dwellings with variable multi-family common spaces and conveniences to help us relearn the graces of free and open-ended human association. All clusters will bring a multitude of activities, services, work places—and transportation to the fingertips. These will be the community centers. Yet each activity will be shielded as desired to avoid annoyance and assure privacy. No car will be necessary, but any person may own one—should he wish to. Everywhere we will combine the pastoral advantages offered by great open spaces with the social and cultural opportunities offered by intensive development.

Stage 3 will be arduous, but it will magnify our horizons and set us on a positive course. While it roots out automotive supremacy it will build the human environment with a care now afforded only to those going to the moon. Our goal is complete urbanity. We will inspire men to cherish their environs, all forms of beauty, friends and neighbors, the contributions they can make to society, and the inheritance they receive and pass on.

We will solve the transportation crisis by eliminating forced overmobility. A freer mobility will arise even while our attention shifts to the higher human potential.

Striking at the Roots of Autocracy

Our struggle thus far, whether building our forces, fighting in the streets or campaigning in the legislatures, has focused on the ground conditions of the auto conquest. But the fight must also be taken to the industrial sources of the automobile itself. Until we have effectively struck there all previous advances will remain in jeopardy.

It is a sorry commentary on the blindness and irrationality of man in America that he campaigns singlemindedly for birth control when the major arguments for birth control indict the automobile far more than men: resource depletion, environmental pollution, transportation breakdown, unworkable and unlivable cities. Aren't the family planners really reacting in abhorrence to miserable auto-made cities when they call for a limitation on the number of men?

Worldwide, the arguments for man to limit his own number are real enough, of course. In the struggle to eliminate poverty, economists calculate that rapid population growth limits the means which can be applied to economic growth and wipes out most benefits of increased production. In the halls where international development is discussed, a special urgency is attached to moderating the quantity of life so that the quality may be improved.

This contrasts sharply with our generous view of endlessly multiplying automobiles. The outpouring is clearly considered as the blessing of industrialization. But what is it when reshaping the environment for mobility has become a war against the diversities of nature, against the rich intimacy of old cities, and against the liberty of men?

Today in America birth control is aimed at the lesser threat to the good life. Isn't a constant population of 200 million human beings who energetically support industrial devastation of both cities and countryside the more direct threat to human worthiness than a population of, say, 400 million people, who follow the Greek admonition for moderation in life?

Throughout history most men have lived in powerless poverty. Now wealth is coming to man. His own numbers are multiplying as well. But the important fact is that man's new wealth, while highly organized, is totally unrestrained. The salient force is the automobile, which makes a tragicomedy of the human struggle for worthiness.

In India people love children almost as Americans adore cars. Indian children are cherished out of love, for the help they give in the fields, and for security they give in old age. Their parents don't realize that their numbers are the source of a serious national problem. In America, cars are cherished, if not from love, at least for emotional release through luxurious appointment and horsepower, and for the new mobile necessities of life: commuting, shopping, and chauffeuring children off to babysitting institutions. Their owners don't realize that their numbers are the source of a most serious national problem.

The Indians are now coming to the painful conclusion that they must find other kinds of field help than numerous children, other kinds of old-age security than sons and daughters, and other forms of emotional expression besides filial love. They are accepting the necessity for birth control.

Indians now understand that too many children—which but multiply poverty, disease, ignorance—are immense obstacles to social and economic growth. As yet, while we self-righteously urge acceptance of human birth control in India and at home, we have not questioned whether our high standard of living and the automobility it multiplies also promote their own version of human degradation—mobilized poverty, technological psychosis, and induced ignorance.

The thesis is this: While human birth control is chiefly necessary in the newly developing countries to overcome the finite limitations of natural poverty, automotive birth control is necessary in the advanced economy to help overcome the infinite disarray of technological wealth. The two propositions are the same: Unlimited multiplication of anything challenges the worthiness of what is created. The failure to achieve industrial wealth is no more harmful than the failure to prevent the debilitations of industrial excess.

Recapturing the Civic Ramparts

So now we will demand that Detroit take the pill. Ironic, yes. Radical, possibly. Anti-modern and un-American; well, when life is plagued by a gluttony that undercuts the value of property, undermines social tradition, diminishes the benefits of science and industry, and usurps freedom, then the clichés must go. It is the system which has become radical, alienating men from their culture, their communal associations, and themselves. The irony is that the system has turned against man. Yet, while doing so, it inherited a clutch of the deepest American myths (mobility, spaciousness, ownership, individuality, enterprise) and obtained the protection of the conservative tradition. What has been conserved is not man but raw momentum without direction or purpose.

Our fight will not end until Mankind has unconditionally defeated Autokind and regained total sovereignty. We need not look far for a plan. The "family planning" required for the auto industry has been pioneered in agriculture by the soil bank and has already been fitted comfortably into the practice of private enterprise. If its operation has made *enterprise* a little less free the *individual* has gained a new measure of freedom and security. This is as it should be.

The soil bank is the government's way of moderating agricultural output by paying for non-production. The concept holds great importance for us. In broad outline an Auto Production Bank would roll back output, assuring the financial resources for urban reparations, increased leisure time, and a steadier income for workers, as well as transitional assistance for the corporations.

The plan will be put into operation over a period of perhaps ten years and operate as long as necessary. Special reparations levies on vehicle sales will be applied in annually increasing rates of 4 to 8 percent. These levies will be adjustable to assure that the decline in output will not disrupt society. As a transitional assistance measure, the levies on taxis, rental cars, and farm vehicles will follow some years behind those on other cars and trucks. All revenues will be placed in the Auto Production Bank, applicable only to programs that free society from autocracy and reconstruct the environment.

Transitional assistance may be given to corporations, as we intend to be far more considerate of organizations than organizations have been to the individual. The country could well *give* GM, Ford, Chrysler, and all dealers their profit on lost sales from the Trust Fund—perhaps as much as $600 on each non-car. The payment might drop one-third on each non-produced unit each succeeding year until the adjustment to a lower production and sales level shall be deemed complete.

Fortunately, since the promise of technology is the reduction of toil among men, society will reduce a man's allotment of years to work while it increases its benefits to him. That is, government will then strive to reduce work as assiduously as it now seeks to increase it. After all, the automotive necessity not only binds men to oppressive mobility, it just as arbitrarily binds men to the assembly line and gas pump when they might be enjoying the fruits of industrialization for larger parts of their lives.

Men will be more creative and produce more lasting benefits for society while punching the time-clock less. Less work will permit men to allocate more wealth and time to activities that give vitality to life. Recapturing human sovereignty will be most valuable to men in combining time, wealth, activity, and association into unlimited varieties of personal stimulation and challenge.

With our immense technical and corporate productiveness we are certain that the government can manage the details of reducing work while increasing our wealth. Where the discipline of work symbolizes the values of Autokind, the challenge of leisure supported by increasing wealth will symbolize the values of Mankind. Industry, like agriculture, will become more productive as we push it into the background of our lives.

While retaking the last civic ramparts we may expect autocracy to counterattack in a final, desperate Battle of the Bulge. Money and resources will flow to stem the human tide. Propaganda will bombard people, arguing that wealth invested in automobility should not be wasted. Detroit will attempt to renew and restore auto rationality to its former position. But the best they will do is create confusion, for once the people have begun to taste freedom, as the Czechs did in 1968, things can never be the same again. Looking at history, the resilient spirit of humanity is what has always counted most. If man becomes determined to enjoy democracy and the simple excitement of his own free behavior away from the wheel, he will find a way. But the confusion can be dangerous, nevertheless, because the people will not yet understand the many possibilities of being human, which they will have only begun to enjoy.

Therefore, at the earliest possible date we will take steps to minimize the force of the final counterattack. Since most men will be inexperienced with wealth, leisure, and the larger span of freedom, some special protection will be necessary for a time. Measures to inhibit powerful legislative lobbies and large interest-group representation may be enacted. But when the people have regained their strength, the only lobby they will tolerate is their representative.

We will anticipate appeals promoting organized gluttony, especially for persons still dependent on advertising for their image of the good life. Levies and restrictions therefore may be put on ads selling the consumptive life style. For some years an Automobiles Anonymous Association might assist those who are susceptible to automobility cravings to inaugurate a new pattern of life and to experience genuine freedom at first hand.

But soon the last counterthrust will be spent, and the salient of our drive will overwhelm the last effective defenses of motordom. Automobile production will be brought back down to a level consistent with inherent human desires; no longer will it respond only to that deceptive trap of necessity called consumer demand. Nothing less than a renaissance will accompany the rollback and final capitulation.

The evil that made hermit crabs out of men will then be done away with. All energies may become constructive. The industrial legacy may then be reorganized to do what it was always supposed to have done: serve men efficiently without ever so much as disturbing a chat or a stroll.

A Stillness on Forty-second Street

Every decade of automobile history has seen the meaning of automobiling change. If the last decade of the old century was experimental and the first decade of the new was developmental, the teens demonstrated the marvels of mass production and the twenties demonstrated the marvels of mass marketing (styling, annual models, the trade-in, and credit). Highway completions of the thirties made the country mobile while the grip of auto-mobility was still light. Even with the distracting war years, the 1940's consolidated auto advances. The fifties were times of great new penetrations, in the auto suburbs and city centers, especially with new freeways. It may be too early to say, but perhaps the 1960's saw the climax of the tyrannous motor grip and the 1970's will witness a powerful reversal.

That, at least, is our intent. And we look toward the 1980's —which are really not far off—as the era of our greatest advances. We now set 1994 as our target date to completely overcome society's first mechanical addiction. Then perhaps we will be able to look to the twenty-first century with as much hope as our forebears looked to this century for the freedom they thought the automobile would bestow upon it.

And how did the hope of 1900 turn out on New York's Forty-second Street? The scene is, even as Henry Ford would have admitted, a disgracefully inefficient mechanical shambles. The straight lines of buildings and curbs give a false impression of precision and efficiency. What is achieved is a rigorous system of waste (through motorcar consumption of land) organized into a system of conflict (between autos and all human activities).

The street is constantly congested. The dismal blacktop is flanked by narrow tattletale grey sidewalks—sterile, artless, and unequipped. Auto congestion has limited the sidewalk widths to a point that even they approach congestion at peak hours. This eliminates the possibility of street furniture, fountains, and planting. Yet to step off the curb at the wrong moment is virtually as dangerous as stepping off a cliff. Still, Forty-second Street and most of Manhattan's sidewalks provide some of the best urban walking environment in America, simply because they are busy with people and contain the interest that makes walking wonderful.

Yet, to rest anywhere on Forty-second Street, one must try to rent a seat on a bus, which wheezes and roars forward in 100-yard dashes. The average speed of bus movement has slowed in a half-century to a rate ideally suited to make it a billboard on a public right of way. Typically most of the ads also tell us how to escape: Duval Vermouth; Whitehead Scotch; TWA, "Up, Up, and Away."

The mostly dingy and dented trucks crossing Forty-second Street—delivery, repair, dump, or nondescript—look as if the world is not worth the image set by Madison Avenue. That is also true of the distracted drivers. Truck and driver together function hardly better than the wagons and teams they replaced. Money is the only fuel that keeps them moving, for there is no other human interest (save miniskirted groups of secretaries during lunch hour), no other human purpose to motivate either driving or passing through.

The taxis, painted freight-car yellow, are profitable only because their meters move whether they do or not. Of course the drivers still seethe all day in barely subdued frustration at every red light and every pedestrian insistent on his crossing rights. At turns they must bulldoze through pedestrians or miss the extra fares that make the day worthwhile.

And so, one day about 1994, the roars, whines, and rumbles on Forth-second Street will just fade away. Decibels will drop to the human scale in the revived hearts of all our cities. Curbs will lose the fright of cliffs. Collisions between bodies in motion will be resolved by apologies accompanied by smiles, for human bodies are not themselves very lethal.

Walking will become exciting because the renewed environment will pronounce a man relevant and whole again. His senses will perceive more while being burdened less. He will go or stop or congregate freely because movement and non-movement by foot do not create serious conflict. There will be more interest in the going and more interest in the stopping and more to congregate for. Going, stopping, and congregating will merge in a wholesome involvement that will make all theories of origin-destination, all science of traffic generation, and all manuals of traffic capacity as irrelevant as medieval disputations. An atmosphere of festive leisure will prevail, even in the centers and routes of most intensive "traffic."

The unnatural segregation between movement and stationary behavior, which forces a more unnatural segregation between human activities and human association, will all but vanish. There will be no need for keeping to the right, staying in lane, speed control, no-left-turns, no-stopping, synchronized traffic signals, warning signs, or traffic police. All of these deny free will more completely than thought control or brainwashing. The burdens of travel will fall upon technology: public transport will become so effective that men will choose to drive only for the car's special qualities of recreation. And when the auto oppression disappears the isolated parts of the city can then be rejoined; the organic relationships between working, living, and playing can be re-established; doing and watching can intermingle freely.

When there is a stillness on all of America's Forty-second Streets, except for the wholesome sounds of people, we will have broken the steel shell that has hardened about the body. Gradually we will dissolve the calcified deposits in the mind and relax the brittleness of interpersonal behavior. Out of it may grow a fresh gaiety that is today best exhibited by New York's newest immigrants, the Puerto Ricans.

The stillness of victory over the motorcar will not blind us to the larger modern problem of Mankind, the mechanistic power-centered economy that Lewis Mumford calls the megamachine. The megamachine subdues men with the same rationality it uses to serve men. Imperceptibly it raises its own welfare above men, converting them to servants of corporate attainment, wards of corporate culture.

We will use our experience with the automobile to set a course toward the broadest foundation for renaissance, restoring an older tradition of man in an organic, life-centered economy. "The mark of a life economy," writes Mumford, "is its observance of organic limits: it seeks not the greatest possible quantity of any particular good, but the right quantity, of the right quality, at the right place and the right time for the right purpose. Too much of any one thing is as fatal to living organisms as too little."

6

MAN, SOCIETY, AND THE
RENEWAL OF DEMOCRACY

Revolution of Rising Expectations

OUR STORY is about the automobile. But we must recognize that the real revolution will occur after the struggle is over, when man has reclaimed his sovereignty and realized that his life is his own. Society will then burst with excitement. Only the ancient Athenians enjoyed the social enthusiasm we expect. Only children now claim it, before the age of knowing.

Lost joys of life will emerge through a youth-like discovery that today eludes even the hippies and the dropouts. When man gets his science, technology, and bureaucracy to do what they always should have done, the organization of life by wage work will seem but a miser's career.

What is implicit is that the real liberation from autodomination will occur in our minds. Liberation in the streets will be merely the forerunner.

Our purpose here is to demonstrate how a renaissance of

the environment arising from the struggle against autocracy can lead to a new renaissance. The task before us is to elevate all the *human* opportunities of life, not merely to rid it of functional tyrannies.

Let no one underestimate the benefits of a new kind of living environment on a human scale built through advanced technology. A new tradition of living design will change even the definition of the word *modern.*

Each living environment will be unique. Each will encompass a small population, a wide range of activities and services, and an immense open space. Life will be exciting right at home, for these living environments will accommodate a variety of life styles as diverse as the life on Noah's Ark. Furthermore, each living environment will be internally as efficient (for the citizen) as a computer, connect almost instantly with the metropolitan center, provide the conveniences of a resort, combine the coziness of a medieval village with the spaciousness of a country club, and save enough annually for a trip to the Caribbean.

Imagine, for example, a castle complex—like the spired St. Michel on an island by the coast of France—as the image for a community design. Portions of the complex would extend out into the gardens, parks, and playgrounds, and lie close to the golf courses, lakes, meadows, and woods. Large private and community verandas, verdant as the hanging gardens of Babylon, would look outward to the protected countryside or inward to lively plazas or quiet squares. Each plaza would be sided by clubs, schools, shops, restaurants, and offices—all of the activities inviting congregation. Beneath it all, deep in the hold of the living environment, will be the utilities, industries, storage, parking, and transit station.

What could a living environment mean?

Consider the Adamses, a family of three who live in Brighton Center, a group of forty families who share a large lounge and veranda as well as laundry and play facilities on the eighth level of Huntington Community, and participate together in community affairs. When the weather is fair, Mr. Adams gets up at 6:30 A.M., takes the elevator down to the ground floor, walks 200 yards,

and tees off on the lower nine with his regular foursome. At 7:30 Mrs. Adams rises to prepare breakfast. She dials for milk and fresh morning-baked rolls, which are dispatched and routed automatically in minutes through a tube system connected with each dwelling. When Mr. Adams returns at about eight they breakfast on their private veranda—also their garden and out-door living room—with nine-year-old Freddy.

About 8:45 Mr. Adams and Freddy leave together for work and school. At Level B, Freddy takes the community's main promenade to the youth plaza and school, located with the library, gym, and pool, and close to the outdoor playfields. Adams cuts across the central indoor-outdoor plaza and stops for a second cup of coffee with friends who gather informally. By nine he is at work two floors below, in an automated printing plant, one of the community's principal "export" industries. With travel time about three minutes flat, lunch is usually home, though Mr. Adams takes it frequently at the plaza. Occasionally the Adamses meet for a picnic by a small lake across a little valley a few minutes from their community structure.

Evenings are rich. Between five and six almost everyone is to be found in the main concourses of activity, inside or out, walking, sitting, or chatting in the grand manner of the Spanish *paseo*. Ample indoor spaces are available in winter for all to continue their active approach to relaxation and their casual approach to association. Some of the spaces, like the central plaza, can be covered with giant adjustable shields to give protection from rain, wind, heat, and cold, while maximizing light and fresh air.

At night and on weekends, the halls, gyms, pools, classes, and clubrooms create an atmosphere of a fair in the making. The fair is the community itself, and everyone celebrates that fact frequently.

The Adamses' life is full and active, encouraged by almost everything in the environment. An immense choice is available within three or four minutes of their door. Consequently there is little time for the lassitude of TV. The Adams are more likely to watch the live performances and competitions of those they know. Yet they are but fifteen minutes by transit from the center of cosmopolitan life, where some neighbors travel to work. While life at home is varied and challenging, the diversity of the entire metropolis is quickly accessible.

Since most of the metropolis is focused in strong centers such as Huntington, each connected by fast and frequent service from "basement" to "basement," there is no need to own an automobile. When shopping, the Adamses send their parcels home in the same tube through which they receive their morning milk and rolls. And these parcels arrive home as soon as the Adamses themselves, guided by the same credit card used for the purchase. All major recreation centers in the vicinity are served not only by transit, but by the tubes as well. Picnic and beach supplies deposited in a box at home meet the Adams family when they arrive at the beach. And the going itself is great, since many in the community go to play and laugh together. Living together, it is easy to plan together.

Yet occasionally the Adamses rent a car. All kinds are to be enjoyed, and all are available around the clock in the basement. About one-fourth of their neighbors remain owners, though use of a car is hardly more frequent than that of a yacht. The Adams usually take a car when they want to visit friends who have not yet left the auto-isolated and socially sterile suburbs.

The radically efficient use of land afforded by the compact living environment permits not only large playgrounds and parks but the leasing of several hundred "farms" to interested residents. These will vary from 1000 square feet to twenty acres. The farms are part of the living environment, a link to man's past, a choice of recreation, a dimension of educating the young, a source of fresh foods in season, and essential to a balanced experience with animals, crops and all forms of nature. Similarly, a "play forest" at Huntington Community permits children to freely explore, camp, climb, dig, and build: to have the untethered experience necessary for healthy growth.

Other possibilities include an alley of craft workshops (reviving old traditions, but adding modern materials and machines); a large center for arts and celebrations, with a heavy calendar and a public budget; a constant Chautauqua (or liberal education) as diverse as a university. Together, all of these possibilities will make urban life of the city into what Barbara Ward calls "schools of civilization."

The importance of the living environment and what makes it urbane is that more things are available to all people in their home setting. More choices assure more freedom, especially when some seemingly contradictory things like urbanity and open space can only be achieved through the same means—compact clustering of human activity shaped by creative design. Our design will insure that the highest *human* interests are organized right into the environment. That will set the stage for social development to "take off"—for a renaissance close to the hearth.

Let's look at some of the possibilities more closely.

From Passage to Place

When men began to travel they learned the deprivations of isolation. With the decline of the automobile men will learn the decadence of distance.

The fast new movement of trains in the 1830's and 1840's gave men a novel experience of perceiving the environment in motion. But that was mostly novelty, for movement can also blur vision, rob perception of depth, and become a chronicle of distraction.

Today Americans travel over 1 trillion miles annually by automobile, enough to encircle the solar system about forty-five times, 22 billion miles each time around. But Americans didn't do it in outer space as a distraction to themselves. They did it in fifty states—in front of my house, by every school and church, in Central Park and Yosemite, on Broadway.

As man travels more he loses his sense of locality. As movement and the rush against time gathers momentum, place loses value and permanence loses meaning. With the decline of motordom, we will restore to its place the excitement we once sought in passage, though our aim will be a provocative balance between passage and place.

Place is where men are, live, and have roots—and it is good because it is there. Place is man's environment, natural and man-made, to identify with, to absorb and enjoy, and to build with value. The foremost place for modern man is the city, for that is the repository of his experience and belief in himself, his society, his environment.

But in a country believing more than France that transportation means civilization, it is little wonder that the American city became subordinate to movement. Americans were always ambivalent about the cities they flooded in quest of fortune and built aimlessly and expendably. Cars could get a grip on the city's form with relative ease in a few decades.

The car's needs were of course always easy to understand and always demanded solution. The city's more human needs were complex and easily lost to the louder demands of movement. So much energy was taken up in solving problems of auto transport that the city planners were stunned. They could not follow through on the "city beautiful" movement that blossomed around the turn of the century and broaden the base of the urban ideal. Instead, subdivision ordinances were refashioned and zoning emerged as tools to expand distances and facilitate auto flow. Only nomads could put a higher premium on passage.

But one bright day men will value instead the goodness of place in each part of the city. As we will demonstrate, a paradox will be discovered: mobility will improve. Then another paradox will be slowly perceived: passage will begin to achieve some of the qualities of place. Men will then learn to build value into every square foot of plaza and walkway, and in every other place which is to be honored by the presence of people.

One small and delightful example was the recent creation of Paley Park, a single lot of only 4200 square feet on the north side of Fifty-third Street, just east of Fifth Avenue in Manhattan (and once the site of the Stork Club). A quiet and serene retreat by tall structures in the hard and fast midtown setting, Paley is both a visual surprise and an environmental relief, as well as a place to sit down. The idea may be catching on. If proposals for arcades through the middle of the two blocks to the south are carried out,

Paley Park will be the first gem in a chain of man-sized places in the heart of the city.

The value of a city is the value and honor built into every nook of it, with love. European cities prove with their anachronistic patterns of circulation that passage itself is secondary. Urban value seems to increase as both passage and place intermingle freely. What is important is that everything there is human in scale and character.

When cities are designed man-size, then continuous movement by mammoth mechanization can be largely avoided. But today the deranged and overextended urban spaces have become an organized burden requiring massed movement. Massed movement itself further separates urban activities and deranges urban form. Stretched urban space and massed movement together therefore make the city but a system of conflict. Congestion is only the most obvious element of the urban crises.

"Men come together in cities to live," said Aristotle. "They remain to live the good life." Until now Americans have but come together. They have been slow to perceive cities as the setting for the good life because of their ambivalence about them. That has limited their vision and commitment. That has allowed them to destroy or derange places that might have become cherished.

Aristotle's observation also reflected the natural history of cities: to grow tentatively, to gradually become permanent, and then to become a wellspring of the highest aspirations of civilization. Somehow Americans have confounded the process, building permanently at the outset, injecting into it a system of decline, and then fleeing. Slums are assured, first in the inner city and afterward in successive rings of suburbia.

When a family moves into their new suburban home they are soon saddened by each new subdivision and its wave of newcomers. The pastoral idyl they sought is lost. Through planned sprawl—through mass grasping for private minispaces —the larger spaciousness is utterly destroyed. The highest possible level of congestion through the lowest possible density of people and cars is the costly achievement. That, of course, provides the preconditions for decline and escape into motion.

But with our new vision the impact will be reversed. People will relish every step leading to complete development of their community within the city, for every community will offer a rich local pattern of life that grows by successive stages of development. And with it will be preserved a great spaciousness —plazas, playgrounds, parks, and natural areas—now impossible with barracks-like subdivision of land.

Place will be the foundation of our renaissance. The primordial place will be the man-made community, a man-size society in the big city. Change in the community will mean improvement, not an enlargement of turmoil and conflict. Danger, congestion, and pollution will have no basis to exist. The endless, formless, consumptive, anti-social urbanism will give way as the new vision and commitment shape urban life for Mankind.

Truth about Mobility

No doubt about it, Henry Ford was a brilliant pioneer, perhaps more brilliant than he knew. He revealed the principle we will use to plan for both passage and place.

He also gave us a philosophy to judge the significance of both. "I think," said Ford in the introduction to *My Life and Work*, "that unless we know more about machines and their use . . . we cannot have the time to enjoy the birds, and the flowers, and the green fields." And what about industry? To him, "power and machinery, money and goods, are useful only as they set us free to live." We agree with Ford, but now his words echo against the hard pavement of the auto environment.

Reflecting on his principle of transport, Ford lamented how "the old oxcart weighed a ton—and it had so much weight that it was weak!" He also decried the railroads: "To carry a few tons of humanity from New York to Chicago, the railroad builds a train that weighs many hundred tons. . . ." Ford's ideal was the lean grace of material and energy. "The most beautiful things in the world," he said, "are those from which all excess weight has been eliminated." He was right, even if his cars typically carry one-tenth or one-twentieth of their weight.

But Ford's brilliance was truly revolutionary when he showed us how to eliminate the need for transportation, as he did while developing the assembly line. His search for better methods of mass production was really a search to eliminate all unnecessary movement. That is, of course, the brutal lesson we are now learning from autocracy.

At first Ford produced his cars by stationary assembly. Parts were carried to an assembly point and put together. In one department four of every nine hours of work were spent moving from place to place in making the assembly. The first step toward revolution was to rid the factory of its frenzy of movement. Tools and workers were placed in the sequence of production, instead of zones according to the kind of machines and kind of work. As we know, zoning by class of activity enforces mobility.

Then other innovations arose quite naturally. Slides or short belts deposited a part finished by one machine effortlessly at the work place of the next. Movement was short, direct, and virtually automatic. Only with the shortest and simplest movements could the assembly-line idea be put into effect: the assembly line was, in fact, the fruition of the rationally coordinated location and movement of parts. Work was taken to the men instead of men to the work. Ford initiated the assembly line with the flywheel magneto in 1913, and soon followed it with the moving assembly of the whole car.

It all seemed as insignificant as a rearrangement of living-room furniture. But the distance a cylinder casting traveled during manufacture was cut from 4,000 feet to slightly over 300. Soon it was found that the Model T could be assembled in one-tenth of the time previously required. That *was* significant.

The factory itself had become a highly tuned machine, far more important than the sum of its parts. The savings were immense. Though he more than doubled workers' wages to the famous $5 per day, Ford reduced the price of the Model T from $950 to $360 in seven years.

Ford was not loath to brag of the accomplishment—or what it meant. "We put more machinery per square foot of floor space than any other factory in the world—every foot of space not used is an overhead expense. We want none of that waste." He set the rule that no man should have to take one step if it could be avoided. Things moved; men stayed in place. And things didn't move very much. Ford later reported that in a new plant "The greatest distance any material has to be trucked is twenty feet, this being the distance from the incoming freight car to the first [automatic] conveyor."

Ford put his principle on the line: "Hiring two men to do the job of one is a crime against society." We agree. And we will vigorously pursue just such crimes of automobility against society by the same methods Ford used to eliminate criminal waste in his factories. We also agree with Ford that "Modern business—modern life—cannot afford slow transportation." Let us see how Ford's own principle of orderliness of work and movement will contribute to our renaissance.

Lessons on Urban Geometry

Although Ford saw his factory become a productive marvel when compactly organized to reduce movement, he built his biggest factory out at River Rouge, where many workers had to commute from Detroit. Some 40 percent were forced in the 1920's to travel between ten and twenty miles every morning and night. His principles in the factory were reversed outside of it. And across the country his automobiles, as if by command, seemed to execute his will to leave the city. But all they did was maximize the occupation of land and minimize the efficiency of cities.

Our lesson is not to bulldoze the countryside into an endless refugee encampment if we are to enjoy the birds, flowers, and green fields. We will no longer stretch a man between town and country in a process that denies him both openness and urbanity. We will bring town and country together for him.

By extending the principle behind Ford's assembly line to the city, we discover the axiom of urban geometry. According to this axiom the city is inherently a concentration—a compact man-made environment that elevates the human experience—bringing all things together that need to be together and work together. That environment serves men best when everything is as easy for him to reach as it is in the modern kitchen.

Undifferentiated growth to a massive scale defies the natural geometry that exemplified urban life of past centuries. Overcrowded buildings then existed; sanitation, light, and air were often insufficient; land was overbuilt. Yet the city was both efficient and urbane, even without the aid of advanced technology. But modern technology, rather than ridding the city of its old problems and elevating the charm of people living together, endlessly spreads people apart, and then binds them together with the massive, cumbersome ligaments of movement. This but accelerates wasteful production and consumption and corrupts the human qualities of the environment.

All society is put to work to overcome the marathon of miles. The automobile and land speculation, abetted by city plans, build the city into a mammoth system of conflict, as formidable as law, money and modern systems theory can manage. When men are separated from work, women from shopping, children from school, and everyone from plazas of public affairs, life itself becomes disjointed, dissociated, and costly. Separation requires more effort. More effort assures more conflict. That is where our urban and transport crises stand today.

There are two corollaries of the axiom of urban geometry. *Corollary 1:* Large parks and open spaces are available to people only when the people do not stake millions of individual claims to wasteful and selfish bits of open space, and then set aside almost an equal part of the city for the automobile. A person living near Central Park in dense New York or Golden Gate Park in San Francisco has more usable, attractive, and diverse open spaces available to him than most residents of White Plains or Redwood City.

Corollary 2: The amenities of the city are fully beneficial to people only when they are immediately and completely available, that is, when no formal means of transport at all are required to make them accessible. The "flexible" automobile, far from improving access, is a burdensome intermediary of access requiring time, effort and money. In particular, the massing of automobiles isolates the place it ostensibly serves, as when four-fifths of a shopping center claimed for parking means that the nearest residence is a quarter-mile distant.

The dynamics of urban space reveals a greater potential than cracking the genetic code or conquering cancer, for the benefits will accrue to everyone everyday in countless ways. The succession of innovations bringing Ford to the assembly line will be piddling compared to the discoveries we expect from three-dimensional urban space. Ford dealt with production in factories. We deal with life in society.

Through astute planning and design, the central values of both urbanity and openness—of built spaces emphasizing the social or man-made environment and of unbuilt spaces emphasizing the natural environment—will be simultaneously magnified. They will present to men the seemingly contradictory values of nature *and* society, privacy *and* participation, security *and* opportunity in great variety, as they choose. All will be close to their door.

Now, a social awakening is not easy. The hard question of a renaissance, like the hard question of crisis, is whether we can break myths of futility and dream anew. We have questioned the car and we will overcome that crisis. But we haven't questioned the deeper myths that made the auto conquest possible and so penetrating. This we must do now. Specifically, we must challenge the self-defeating ideal that excited the first automobilists to live in the country and commute to the city. The arithmetic of land, population, motors, and money simply does not permit it en masse, and never will.

Our question is hard, but our answer is simple. We will think small, think man-size, and apply the rule of economy so daringly exploited by Ford. We will build or rebuild the city to suit the demands and desires of men six feet high. Distances will give way to places of value. A shopping center parking lot for 1,000 vehicles alone affords space enough for 1,000 Japanese gardens.

Yet today our urban population densities are still dropping, accenting further the "*sub*-urban" nature of modern city development. As the gross consumption of land rises toward one acre per family in many localities, we still hear ominous warnings of the "disease of high density." The modern disease, however, is not high density but the consumptive waste of land and the system of conflict that is now the American city. The average density of people per square mile dropped from 6,480 in 1920 to 4,230 in 1960. New development now averages around 2,500. At this density the 300 American metropolitan areas of the year 2000 would consume an *additional* area of seven-and-a-half times the total land area of New Jersey.

Seven completely urban New Jerseys! That is crowding—crowding through planned dispersion! Imagine the shopping centers, the freeways, and the Great American Strip! In a moment of uncommitted reflection, *Fortune* put it this way: "'Crowding' means that the citizens have arranged something —usually traffic—stupidly." What the editors of *Fortune* failed to ask was whether auto traffic in cities can be anything but crowded and stupid.

The plain lesson is that compact development is a very different thing than crowding. Properly planned, compact development is the best way—perhaps the only way—of preventing congestion in a large city.

Our proposals for concentration are hardly without precedent. Great minds have reached the same conclusion. It was noted—by Eugene Canty of General Motors, of all people—that Plato's *Republic*, Thomas More's *Utopia*, and Ebenezer Howard's *Garden Cities of Tomorrow* each reveal a "very high population density design." Mr. Canty himself observed "high-density anomalies" of preserving open space through concentrated development, just as we note the low-density anomalies of crowding by dispersion of development.

Therefore we will be honest with ourselves and reverse our gluttonous *individual* grasping for our pastoral past if we are to preserve any pastoral life at all. High-density living will be accepted, even sought, for it will do exactly what the early automobilists thought they were doing in bringing the city and country together.

But, unlike the early autoists, we will assure the results by design. We will take great care to avoid mere concentration, of bringing people together without form, efficiency, spaciousness, or social focus. That alone would be tragic, just as Ford would have certainly failed by merely pushing machines closer. The great benefits will occur only with strategic concepts, long-range plans, meticulous design, and a loving care of both open and built-up spaces of the city.

So we will start with the idea of concentration, knowing that the clustering of development also clusters open spaces. The whole city is one such cluster. But in this age of vast, faceless suburbia the greater need is to cluster development of each part of the city into meaningful communities. Each community requires its own integrity and vigor through developing both openness and urbanity at the smaller human scale.

Time-and-motion studies will be used to improve the efficiency of the city. But rather than helping only the man on the job, our studies will consider the whole man, and help him establish a pattern for the good life. Instead of zoning family activities apart, the time-and-motion studies will help reintegrate work, shopping, school and public life close to home.

This will be done, of course, in the living environment, which calls for a new kind of building: a community space structure. Let us see how such a structure might measure up in a test of urban geometry. The idea is a space frame for living, a megastructure which almost permits men to eat their cake and have it too. The concept is simple: A few feet of wall or floor is a better sight and sound shield than 1,000 feet of zoning. No waste of land. No ugliness. A short commute by elevator.

Consider a community of 7,500 people. To work, live, and play, they require the equivalent indoor space of eighteen acres (about 900 feet square) built ten stories high. If portions of the space structure are actually built to twenty stories, and if thirty acres (about 1,150 feet square) are allocated instead of eighteen, then ample space is allowed for plazas and squares, as well as to maximize all amenities and design possibilities.

Rockefeller Center is as spacious and urbane as corporately developed Manhattan gets. Yet 48,000 people work on its seventeen acres. And it functions efficiently, for, at least underground, it is a unified structure.

However, we will allocate 640 acres to the community, not 30 acres. Let us see what open spaces this permits.

Community Spaces	Acres
Community space structure	30
Transport lines & roads	20
Playfields	40
Parks (landscaped)	75
Golf course (eighteen holes)	150
Forests (play and natural)	100
Lakes	25
"Farms"	200
TOTAL	640

With almost 95 percent of the land guaranteed open, we have a community built within its own Central Park. Most of the land is usable in every way men enjoy their earthly environment. Yet three times as many people would inhabit this square mile as now occupy a typical square mile of recently built suburbia. Whereas 640 acres now suffices for only about twenty miles of freeway and two major interchanges, that same acreage can provide a uniquely spacious *and* urbane life for 7,500 people.

Should we multiply the community population tenfold to 75,000 people per square mile, to the density of Manhattan, and add huge offices, we can still preserve about 450 acres for open space by building the space structure to an average of twenty stories and portions rise to forty stories.

We needn't apologize for that level of open space, nor for that height. "Vertical is to live, horizontal is to die," says Bucky Fuller, referring to the possibilities of urban life.

Urbane living will appear with imaginative design. When architects are liberated from designing on accounting paper squares made of streets and property lines and when they can shape the environment for public as well as private purposes, then we will break into an entirely new realm for man in making his environment.

The provocative possibilities demonstrated by Habitat at Expo 67 in Montreal can be joined with the space and plaza forms of Rockefeller Center. The superb combination of screened and mixed sights and sounds at Disneyland can be fitted into the community space structure design. The youth plaza and central plaza will be joyous and colorful, the squares serene and restful. Externally, the playgrounds, parks, woods, and water can be situated and designed for the full range of roles between active and passive, private, and public behavior.

The meaning of urbane living is free and diverse choices of behavior close at home—immediately available, socially intermingled, and easily interchanged. But urbanity doesn't result merely from pushing restaurants, theaters, clubs, shops, playfields, and work places together. A balance is necessary between separation and intermingling of activities—while keeping everything close and convenient. Casual activities are likely to be quite freely intermixed. Skilled and specialized activities require more complete separation through various kinds of shields. But all functions need to be as closely joined as possible through imaginative design for free and easy choice. That is the role of the community space structure.

Its geometry will work best in keeping the necessary functions integrated—utilities, transport, production, and the like—without permitting them to foul the human environment or interrupt the important affairs of men living together in society. If we clustered urban development to save open space and enlarge urbanity we will put all non-social or anti-social work in the bowels of the community to protect the human environment and to make the functional things function better. By shifting the main force of zoning from horizontal isolation to vertical integration, all visible terrain and structures will be preserved as part of the human environment.

Even the terrain will be improved for man. In flatlands the tall community structure will break the horizontal monotony, like a cathedral. In uplands it can take advantage of every ravine, slope, and precipice. Two knolls can be bridged, the pure work functions set below, the new "ground level" designed for most public events, and the dwellings fit on highly varied settings of the surrounding slopes. Because the structures will adapt to the terrain, and not consume it, as the vast suburbs are designed to do, the entire environment will better serve men.

Being a space frame for urban development, the community structure will be designed to change with society, and in places alter itself almost like a stage setting. The interior will be built to the specifications of the occupant within the frame surrounding it. Ownership will shift from the land and basic structure to the urban space and its interior private development, setting forth a new balance between the public responsibilities for shaping the natural and man-made environment and the resulting immense private opportunities for fulfillment.

Free Mobility

When the Automobile Manufacturers Association reminds us that "mobility is a correlate of progress," we wonder if the transport crisis now gripping America is just more progress than the country can stand. Forced mobility is threatening to grind down to one gigantic binding halt.

During our awakening we will identify a new correlate of progress: free mobility. Men will be freed from forced movement, from congestion, and from danger. They will be freed to choose when and where they want to travel, that is, for pleasure. Their environment will be freed from division, abrasion, corrosion, and sensory harassment. Free mobility will be realized from the application of urban geometry and by carefully defining the realms of each form of transport.

Now it happens that the form of mobility which is the most free—walking—is also the most efficient, the most invigorating and inspiring, the least burdensome or disruptive, and the most social. Human legs also happen to be at the human scale and coincide perfectly with the natural geometry of the living environment. Hence, we will put man on his feet again, permit him to loiter, and present him with real live faces as he goes. The distances he will walk may range up to a mile if he goes roundabout by the lake, or endless if he follows the many miles of urban woods.

A 1958 Detroit parking survey discovered that parkers at a new garage walked more than 1,200 feet to reach their destinations—a figure somewhat more than the average we calculate for the walking distances in the living environment without the automobile. Hence by working with the natural geometry of cities we will eliminate not only the necessity of the automobile but reduce even the need for walking as well, while improving the walk.

A man size community cannot take cars. One parked vehicle requires the area of about twenty walkers; one moving at 30 mph requires the space of more than sixty walkers. That's partly why cars in today's traffic wait mostly for cars, little for pedestrians, while pedestrians do virtually all of their waiting for cars, rarely and but momentarily for each other.

Everyone knows of course that the walker is happier than the driver. There is human experience in walking, and it is mostly happy. There are incidents in driving and they are mostly unhappy. Experience is open in walking. Observations lead to discovery. Faces and street activity are infinitely fascinating, and make the passage worthy in its own right. But the incidents of driving tend to be closed and sullenly limited to discipline, disruptions, delay, citations, accidents, near accidents, and bullish confrontations. That helps explain why drivers compulsively hurry and walkers are so relaxed about the going.

In a good walking environment only the cripple will want to be motorized. His vehicle will be like a golf cart and will travel at a solid infantry pace of 2.5 mph. There will be no need to travel faster. Intense interests along the way would otherwise lose focus and people might fail to make their greetings.

The walking environment is the community, its urbane center, and its open spaces. It is not the metropolis. We won't put that burden on the feet, throwing us back where Neanderthal Man left off. Swift transit, the second realm of transport, will connect each community to all centers of the metropolis.

Taking an elevator to the station means that the immense efficiency of public transport will become operative. The circulatory system of the city then loses the "weight" that Ford said makes transport weak. Every part works; all parts work together. The city is not heavy with its own weight of dispersion.

And with proper development, crowding would be limited to the few minutes after a football game. There would be no need to reintroduce the courtesy of giving one's seat to the elderly.

The third realm will be the automobile. When it is no longer a necessity, driving will become a pleasure again. Lo, the automobile itself may become the symbol of free mobility, as it was in 1910. Cherished again will be the drive in the country, the cross-country tour, the rally. Then the car's chilling depression of congestion, injury, and death will rapidly fade.

The car will be able to go almost anywhere on the map. But its drive-in, drive-away debasement of cities will completely disappear. Where it threatens to intimidate human life the road will abruptly come to a dead end. And the car will pay its own way, all of it, including its contribution to the general welfare.

Although the decades of tyranny will leave deep prejudices in the public mind, one day man will be free to love the car again. Perhaps there will be a reawakening of the feelings expressed in a 1900 *Outing Magazine:* "The spirit in which the automobile has been seized upon . . . is the best possible . . . index to its likely position in the recreative life of the approaching century."

The walker, the rider, and the driver will be renewed. *Free* mobility will be the correlate of progress. Walking, the most humble mode of all, will be protected most. And in the end the most humble form of movement will make the greatest contribution to free mobility.

Submobility

After walking, the most effective form of urban travel will be fully automated. But the present conglomeration of surface transport remains more primitive than Ford's factory before he found a rational relationship between the functions of passage and place in the process of production.

The main reason for the transport lag is that transport *systems* are very different from the technology they use. The automobile is relatively advanced technically but remains as systematic as a bunch of oxcarts on market day. Rail technology was stranded in the 1920's while its system has not progressed substantially beyond the 1840's.

Our transport plan will therefore bring technology and system into balance. The main burden of improvement will be the system, for we can take highly advanced technology off the shelf at IBM, GE, Con Ed, Disneyland, and the Pittston Coal Co. The system we devise will not be a patchwork to be overcome with advanced technology. It will be devised comprehensively to serve all requirements for the mechanical movement of people and goods through maximum use of advanced technology.

Demands put upon the new system will be severe. Costs must be lowered at least 50 percent while service is multiplied. Our use of urban geometry will put us a giant's step ahead. The radically reduced need for formal transport and the clustering of development directly over stations will simultaneously establish the basis for high efficiency between concentrated points while bringing improved transport closer to every part of the city.

Most of all, the system will preserve the environment for man. We will expect it to operate as effectively as the telephone and as unobstrusively as the sewer system. And for the most part it will operate underground with the sewers. If man is to claim the environment for his enjoyment, he must protect the entire surface of the globe from rampant technology.

Conceptually, our system will be a highly differentiated underground monorail, which we will call tuberail. Fully automated and completely containerized, it will achieve for the whole city the same integrated and continuous flow as the assembly line. Yet it will be instantly accessible and should move a person, letter, drug prescription, refrigerator, or bag of garbage between the most distant parts of Chicago or New York in hardly more than an hour, door to door. Most runs would be a quarter of that—while remaining sightless, soundless, and inexpensive. Some explanation is necessary.

We will start with the movement of goods. First, envisage three boxes: Small Box A will carry most items of human consumption (food, clothing, drugs, books, etc.) through a tube to every residence, store, and factory. The second, larger pallet-size Box B, will carry most items of human use (furniture, appliances, etc.) and most manufactured goods in a larger tube to points very near most residences and into most stores and factories. The third and largest Box C, will carry virtually all goods and equipment requiring movement between major centers of human activity.

Next, envision each box with its own pattern and speed of service. Small Box A will move in metropolitan areas at perhaps 25 mph. Larger Box B will carry greater volumes of goods throughout metropolitan regions at 50 to 100 mph. Big Box C will be continental in scope and will travel at speeds in excess of 100 mph. Thus the size of box, the kinds of things it carries, the speed it travels, and the area it serves will all be functionally related to maximize all benefits of transport.

Then envision integrating the three tuberail subsystems to maximize all of their capabilities. Each of the larger boxes would carry twenty to thirty of the next smaller size. Over 600 A Boxes could be carried cross-country in one Box C. At terminals and stations sorting and loading will be handled as automatically as the switching of long-distance calls. Medieval paperwork like labels, shipping orders, bills of lading will pass on like motor trucks, transhipment handling, less-than-car-loads, and massive marshalling yards. Computers responding to "dialed" instructions on the box will guide all the work.

Consider a twenty-minute uninterrupted trip of a new coat

from Macy's or Sears, delivered to the box delivery table at home as reliably as a telephone call is made, guided there by the imprint of a credit card. Consider a dialed grocery order arriving home in five or ten minutes, loaded, shipped, and billed from an automated supermarket. Consider a plastic bag of garbage disposed at will in the same box. No garbage men—or postmen or deliverymen! Is there to be no life about the place? Certainly —on the plaza and in the community center two or three minutes away.

Box B will be equally valuable, for it will go into the mine or factory and become part of the process of production (thereby eliminating trucking even that twenty feet at the door of Ford's factory), nudging up close to the machines or the end of the production line to reduce extra movements. Much costly packaging may be eliminated. The door-to-door speed and push-button reliability of movement will permit the reductions of costly inventories. This system will follow as a logical conclusion to the rational form of the city and region, exactly as the assembly line was the logical result of rationally organizing the process of production.

At first glance there seem to be many hard *if*'s about building underground. But in America hard construction challenges— like continental railroads and moon vehicles—only set off action. The reverse is more serious: America too often builds fantasies without knowing what it builds. What is hardest is the conception of purpose and the control of results. While the future will solve the technical problems, such as underground boring, the costs and debilities of continuing technological plunder over the surface of the earth now threaten to overwhelm us.

Reparations for Cities

The pervasive destruction of cities by the automobile is no less severe than that arising from the 1940 bombing of Rotterdam or the 1970 earthquake in Peru. The main differences are the nature of the destruction (selective and precise) and the source (planned, budgeted, and contracted).

When we look for possible sources of recovery assistance, none is more promising than that of the automotive economy. Recall that the highwaymen have planned $285 billion to cover "needs" for highway expansion from 1975 to 1985. That is enough to carry out an old-fashioned war. But since it is planned only for the capital expansion of automobility on the ground, it is a reasonable figure to begin to plan for our urban reconstruction and to demand as the first reparations installment.

Upon achieving victory we will establish a Renewal Trust Fund with the $285 billion from the auto war chest. Although the job will be immense, it will not be simply to expend that much money without incurring some of the elaborate waste accompanying automobility. We must not forget, of course, that our problem of making proper use of monies from autocracy will be complicated by unknown billions of dollars transferred from the Auto Production Bank. In any case, here is our initial shopping list.

RENEWAL TRUST FUND SHOPPING LIST

(*in billions*)

I. Reconstruct 5,400 communities (about 8,000 people each)	$135
II. Develop automated transport	70
III. Urban parks and open spaces	40
IV. Comprehensive renewal of highways	5
V. Construct 200 experimental renaissance universities	10
VI. Bonus projects	25
TOTAL	$285

The liberated 1975–1985 highway war chest will be centered, of course, upon unified communities, which will simultaneously organize the city for free mobility. The largest allocation for communities thus will begin to set the urban form. The next largest will begin to give it the necessary skeletal structure.

During the difficult first years of transition it will be necessary to promptly but selectively rejuvenate existing systems of public transit, for which $5 billion will be allocated from the transport account. Although large parts of suburbia will be unsalvageable, others can be modified to achieve many of the advantages of community and free mobility. Consequently another $5 billion will be allocated for "resurrection" transit systems, similar to those used at ski areas and world expositions. A similar amount will be applied to the comprehensive renewal of highways: redeveloping the Great American Strip, constructing the freeway safety measures omitted by the highwaymen, building roadside rests and generally converting all freeways to recreation parkways, and constructing freeway decks and shields to reduce traffic noises and restore important vistas at the most critical locations.

The third major allocation of money will guarantee that far more land is preserved for various kinds of open spaces of the city than for buildings. Priority will be given to acquiring land near the new and rejuvenated communities and, secondly, to protecting millions of acres from further urban scattering.

To consolidate and advance the enlightenment accompanying both the struggle and reconstruction, we will take special interest in underwriting the building of 200 small experimental renaissance universities with an allocation of $10 billion. These institutions will seek to expand knowledge about the good life. To insure them against slipping into the old academic ruts of specialism subservient to bureaucracy and technology, these new universities will not initially teach or undertake research directly in the fields of science, technology, or management, not, at least, until new patterns of investigation and truth have gained independent strength.

That leaves $25 billion for corollary programs, a kind of first installment of a bonus that will grow as the fruits of the renaissance increase. Therefore we will establish a second shopping list in support of the main objectives and also to brighten our lives.

Still, $5 billion will remain, and we are forced to prepare a third shopping list. This list will be different, aimed at fulfilling a need that might otherwise bother our conscience, since we will remove men from everyday exposure to a powerful instru-

RENEWAL TRUST FUND
BONUS SHOPPING LIST
(*in billions*)

I.	6,000 community center grants at $1 million	$ 6
II.	400 zoos at $5 million each	2
III.	400 museum-exhibit halls at $5 million each	2
IV.	2,000 amphitheaters at $1 million each	2
V.	2,000 playhouse theaters at $1 million each	2
VI.	2,000 marines at $1 million each	2
VII.	2,000 golf courses at $1 million each	2
VIII.	2,000 athletic and recreation centers at $1 million each	2
IX.	Bonus projects	5
	TOTAL	$25

RENEWAL TRUST FUND
SECOND BONUS SHOPPING LIST
(*in billions*)

I.	500 water sport centers at $2 million each (boat racing, competitive sailing, water skiing)	$ 1
II.	400 air sport centers at $2.5 million each (stunt flying, sky diving, soaring)	1
III.	400 auto sport centers at $2.5 million each (closed track racing, drag-strip racing)	1
IV.	400 winter sport areas at $2.5 million each	1
V.	10,000 miles of hiking and hunting trails at $5,000 per mile	.5
VI.	100 big-game parks at $1 million each	.1
VII.	100 wild river runs	*
	TOTAL	$4.6

* Free for the keeping

ment of daring, danger, and death. Having this extra money we cannot, therefore, avoid funding projects that provide for what William James called the moral equivalent of war.

Well, $285 billion dollars is not easy to spend. We failed, although we have not considered the funds to be derived from the Auto Production Bank. Perhaps we should refund the unspent $400 million to the autocrats and the highwaymen so that they might write their own history of the conquest of man by motorcar.

We have nevertheless been able to allocate over $284 billion. More explanation is in order. In each allocation the first money will flow into research, but research with a difference. Philosophers and generalists will prevail, since human purpose will be the focal point of all investigations. That is, our research will be for society, not scientists. Specialization will be limited to the final steps of an effort that must be far more integrated than putting men on the moon.

Community research will strive to harmonize the various means and ends of life in society, starting where the Athenians stopped their research into the question a little over two thousand years ago. We will break into the subject by experimenting with the dynamics of urban space, since physical reconstruction is our immediate burden. Every community will constitute a separate experiment, and that will also establish the uniqueness of every community, as well as assist in evolving distinct local traditions.

What we don't know about urban space systems and urban building systems matches our ignorance about man's defeat by the automobile. We haven't learned how to build multiple dwellings that serve individual and family needs any better than the Taos or Zuñi Indians, despite our pipes, wires, elevators, lights, and air conditioning. We don't know how to organize varied activities into multiple buildings for multiple advantage. We don't know how to organize the three-dimensional city.

After community, advanced transport will be the principal research endeavor. Of course, we will unite the best of systems with the best of technology. Experiments to radically improve underground construction techniques will be pressed as part of our demand for complete integrity of the man-made and natural environment. Wherever transport enters into man's realm it must contribute to the quality of place, for we intend to amplify the pleasures of transport as much as reduce the necessity for it.

Though we will be spending to our utmost, the 1975–1985 reparations cannot complete the reconstruction. Eventually the sources for reparations will diminish. But as they do, larger financial resources will appear from the enormous savings of the new order of things. Then, as renewal begins to prevail in the city, and contrary to the insatiable demands of the automobile, the requirements for expansion of public transportation will taper off. At that time our energies can turn toward realizing the Greek ideal of a rich interplay between dynamic individuals and their dynamic community.

Rehabilitating the Auto-crazed Economy

The basic adjustment required of economics during reconstruction is a reduction of economic activity to increase real wealth. The challenge for economists will be elementary in theory but severe emotionally.

A pilot demonstration is already before us. For many decades the farmer has been decreasing his contribution to the economy while increasing his contribution to national wealth. In 1940 one farmer fed eleven people, in 1970 over forty. We want the whole economy to do the same: to grow small in our life while contributing more to it.

Though initial burdens of reconstruction will keep economic activity at a high level for a time, the rollback of automobile production will adversely effect the naked figures of gross national product. This raises a problem of national morale. If the reduction is figured by present accounting methods the international status of the United States could be damaged, as well as the self-respect of Americans. However, by employing other legitimate methods of computing national income, the displaced production might well be figured as an addition to output and services. Then a growing national product will be forever assured, and America's status can be maintained.

Our aim is simply an economy of means. The dollar will be dethroned as an end, worked harder in the factories, fields, and offices, and kept out of society's important deliberations about human prosperity.

Man will truly prosper only when the dollar is no longer the fundamental measure of human progress, when we have passed the economic stage of human development. Two chickens in every pot is no longer a viable goal; nonfulfillment these days is only a rude social oversight. Two cars in every garage simply destroys real prosperity. The organized waste now employed by the economy to maintain its phenomenal output—to make the city grossly inefficient and therefore more consumptive—will be cut out like a malignant tumor.

Social wealth will increase when we will bring back nature for human enjoyment, efficiency and pleasure to travel, urbanity to the city, and when we build community for new human challenge and security. What wealth is greater than this? Now, as the economy recedes and becomes more efficient at producing more relevant goods, it will also produce the greatest benefit of all: leisure.

True leisure we hardly know. The meaning given to it by the early Greeks, which coincided closely with that of the good life, has been lost. We will define leisure as freedom to pursue human interests, not as the lassitude of a work break; freedom to develop human association, not a calculated cocktail circuit; freedom to establish one's own bearings as an individual, not the self-discipline of a ladder-climbing technique.

True leisure will enlighten our prison-camp concept of career, renew the nature of work, broaden the foundations for aspiration, go beyond the shallowness built into education. Men will then rediscover the many ways to like each other. No longer will they endlessly perfect their skills of using each other.

Leisure, not the economy, will therefore become the fulcrum for the human career. Man will rise as money is eliminated as the basic lubricant of human relations.

In future deliberations about rehabilitating the economy and curbing its bureaucratic power, we will heed the advice Henry Ford offered in the 1920's, when he said. "A great business

is really too big to be human. It grows so large as to supplant the
personality of the man. In a big business the employer, like the
employee, is lost in the mass."

Reuniting Humanity and Society

When we say *community* we mean the social integrity of
the individual, just as when we said *freeway* we meant the
mobile integrity of the motorcar. Social integrity depends mostly
on the structure of things, very importantly on the structure of
the physical environment.

We have shown how the automobile has pre-empted the
pattern of physical development. And with the auto, the
profiteers of the American dream argue that happiness is a man
with his own acre to manage. Acres are like the dollars of happiness. Yes, but how anarchic the tranquility, how cramped the
spaciousness, how isolated the togetherness, how dependent the
freedom. The result is so cumbersome and confounding that
public action can barely rise to meet the tide of civic problems.
That forcibly reduces civic aspiration to the relief of civic crises.

The question that must quicken our awakening is how humanity can also be restored to the structure of the city. The law
of urban geometry which maximizes both urbanity and spaciousness is hardly enough. Through design we will shape each living
environment into a vigorous community with intense and varied
human interests.

As soon as we are able, therefore, urban development will
be devoted to the building of communities which shift aspirations to a positive foundation. Community is a flexible tool to
respond to the needs of social man, as the corporation is for
economic man. What we seek for everyone are three stimulating
levels of life: the intimate and communal life of the family; the
associative and participative life of community; and the anonymous, professional, and cosmopolitan life of the metropolis.

Today, however, community is the all but nonexistent middle ground of human interaction, lost to endless auto-dominated
urbanism. Thus, we will build community to reflect the funda-

mental humanism of the city, both as an important framework for the well-being of the family and as a sound building block for the city and metropolis.

Each community will be unique. Diversity and choice between and within communities will promote individual styles of life and therefore a depth of individuality. Contrasts will abound: open and closed spaces, active and passive interests, individual and common activities, total involvement and non-involvement, young and old, practical and festive.

Community, like free mobility, is a framework to perceive a specific range of possibilities of life within the urban environment in which one lives.

Repatriating Human Rights

Until the car came along, tyranny was exclusively the province of kings, oligarchs, and dictators. Now it has spread from politics into economics and technology with a virulence yet to be diagnosed. It is backed by the dedicated skills of modern administration, the compliance of science, the repertoire of advanced industrialism, and the softly guiding hands of mass persuasion.

Autocracy's onslaught on freedom raises the specter calling for a new bill of rights. However, autocracy is a new breed of tyranny. Human freedom cannot be defended by statutes that simply rule against clear infringements of law. The infringements are too subtle, profuse, and dynamic for that. Some traits of the new tyranny are old; the "minute, regular, provident and mild" processes described by de Tocqueville. Some are new: the awesome accumulation of "natural" reinforcements of autocracy, such as the transformation of the city, and the self-reinforcing myths of free and flexible movement, or of town and country living.

The auto's infringements on life and liberty are not points of law and cannot be taken to court. Indeed, they become necessities of life that become fixed in the physical arrangements and ways of doing things.

A new set of rights is required—social and environmental. They must be more articulate than political rights, for they must focus on what is customary and basic about the main patterns of human behavior, not merely the sudden aberrations. Social and environmental rights are more complex and can be protected only by more complex responses involving initiative and continuing action.

Ironies abound in the new tyranny. Rights must now be formulated to protect the simplest and most natural features of life from the same automobile that was originally thought to expand human freedom through mobility. At the outset cars were mainly for sport, but today most auto sport is illegal for most cars on most highways. People early discovered a great practical use for the motorcar, but today the automobile has very nearly defeated other realms of mobility while also nearly defeating its own practical utility in an environment designed expressly for it. The main advantage of the automobile was in the rural areas and villages. But most automobiles went into the city, where it was least useful and most destructive.

So now we must establish rights that protect not only man's free agency but also the viability of his legs, lungs, and heart; his life and limbs; his eyes and what is worth seeing; nature and open spaces for his enjoyment; the scale and setting of his life in the city; the efficiency and benefits of his daily rounds; the integrity of his association. New rights are necessary to guarantee that the physical, economic, social, and cultural purposes of society abide with man rather than the artful domains of technical, bureaucratic, and monetary power in modern society.

The environment suffers because we have no basic commitment to protect it for man. We permit exploitation. That exploitation makes the world smaller and less usable for man. Our goals need to make the earth larger, as we will make the city larger by building it man-size.

Our rights to the environment will begin with the proposition that the entire surface of the earth and the air above it is the sacred setting for human life. Land, air, water, and minerals are for man to use and husband, not for exploitation and destruction for profit. Without runaway technology, human consumption of resources is slight, industrial blight of the land is negligible, and transport interference with society is unimportant. With honest science, controlled technology, and subordinated bureaucracy, resource depletion could be reduced. Most remaining industrial blight and transport interference can be eliminated by going underground. Then wounds on the earth's surface can be healed. But whatever the means, men should be guaranteed an environment worthy of walking, seeing, feeling, and smelling.

Man should also be freed from privately assessed taxes resulting from the new necessity put upon him to consume more than he desires. And no longer will product selection—the choice between a Bonneville or a Barracuda—become a ruse to stamp a monolithic pattern of life on people. By human rights, the city will be built to respond to the full spectrum of human interests.

Let no one be fooled. Civil rights no longer secures the defenses against tyranny. Like weaponry, tyranny also advances, and the new tyranny is dynamic, pervasive, compelling, and complex. New rights are necessary to contain the peculiarly restrictive power of modernism. More importantly, the new rights are necessary to release the social opportunities promised by modernism. They are more than a minimum security. They open up an unlimited human potential.

End of Autokind, Era of Mankind

In retrospect one thing is certain. The automobile has given America its clearest goal—uncluttered by the wanton diversities of human values. That goal mobilized science, technology, enterprise, and government to fulfill its destiny. The automobile is the greatest self-generating, self-sustaining development since the living cell first appeared on earth and began to populate it with the species.

The environment was just right, of course, for the auto to prosper, as it was for the cell. In corporate terms, Alfred P. Sloan put it only slightly differently when he said that General

Motors "was to become critically attuned to the course of American history."

Under the modern corporation, Autokind's rise was managed with vigor, if not ruthlessness at times. Sloan himself admitted that "an industrial corporation is not the mildest form of organization in society," stressing also that ". . . there is no resting place for an enterprise in a competitive economy." Thus, to quote Halprin, there is "nowhere to go but forward." Politics accommodated itself almost from the first. Herbert Hoover himself advertised for the industry in his victorious campaign of 1928, calling for "two cars in every garage."

Everyone seemed to have a special interest in the auto boom, and it was for the special interest of automobiling that government struggled with the mud and then the muddle. That is how the auto could become the supreme special interest of the land.

Perhaps it is from this question of special interest that our greatest lesson arises. For when special interests dominate the structure as well as the content of a society the sovereignty of society surely drifts away from men. The special interests centered on the automobile merely highlighted the errant powers of the age of industry.

To illustrate, take a Sunday drive and see the special interests at work in the environment. But look through the eyes of a person, not the eyes of a driver. Examine ten or twenty miles of the Great American Strip: the streetscape as an environment for man (or motor) and the shopping center as the scale for man (or motor). Then examine the urban freeway and consider this movement to organized waste—private time, public space, and everyone's money. Why—but for the special interest of production and consumption—must the American driver spend about 330 hours (or forty working days) behind a wheel each year? Why do we tolerate about 1.6 million man-years of life being snuffed out every year in traffic deaths?

Perhaps we are lucky that elevators can be used only in buildings; otherwise they too might grow as special interests and occupy or deny life while being proclaimed among our national priorities.

That is why, in retaking social sovereignty and building a renaissance, we have begun to turn the method around. We are approaching a special problem of society, the automobile, and using it as a lever to widen many foundations for better living. For example, the transport system which replaces automobility will be founded upon urban geometry; the most appropriate roles for walking, riding, and driving; and the optimum uses of technology. Many special functions fit into a whole without incurring special interests.

For us, putting the car in its place is not enough. Nor is a new system of transportation enough. Only better living will satisfy us. The meaning is that corporate kinds of interests will decline as their functions are coordinated to enlarge the interests and freedom of the individual.

The very plethora of special interests bidding us to strive for a thousand special benefits has distracted us from the general conditions necessary for the good life: a fundamentally efficient urban environment, a rational system of movement, a social structure framed about the requisites of the individual, an urbane setting for the home, and a healthy accommodation between the man-made and natural environments. Therefore, with the passing of the auto necessity, we will not only seek relief from accidents, pollution, and congestion, we will expect to reduce the cost-benefit calculation of emotion, the monetary pollution of behavior, and the technological congestion of culture.

As we look forward, the qualities of life we now claim only fragmentedly or not at all will become the central characteristics of our environment: the excitement of a fair, the discovery of a university, the serenity of a national park.